DECOLONIZING MENTAL HEALTH RESEARCH

This book reimagines health research through Indigenous knowledge systems, specifically Cree First Nation land-based science. With contributions from a range of Indigenous, academic, and interdisciplinary experts, this book challenges dominant Western health paradigms by centering wâhkôhtowin—a Cree kinship system that acknowledges the interconnectedness of all beings, human and non-human—as a foundation for holistic health and healing.

The authors introduce a tangible model for implementing Indigenous land-based knowledge and adapted Western therapies to foster resilience and cultural continuity, as well as offer wâhkôhtowin (kinship) as a theoretical, methodological, and conceptual guidepost for this book's journey. This book not only offers critiques of colonial health frameworks but also shares actionable strategies for restoring Indigenous health sovereignty and healing through community engagement, confrontations of intergenerational trauma, and other holistic Indigenous therapeutic modalities. It also incorporates discussion questions and reflection prompts for deeper engagement. Through storytelling, personal narratives, and Elder teachings, this book illustrates how Indigenous-led, land-based therapeutic practices can heal intergenerational trauma, center individual and relational well-being, and promote environmental sustainability.

This is an indispensable resource for those committed to sustainable, culturally rooted health practices that benefit both Indigenous and broader communities. It is ideal for health researchers, educators, policymakers, practitioners, and graduate students seeking decolonized, community-centered approaches to health and well-being.

Jody M. Houle, PhD, is a Plains-Cree scholar from Goodfish Lake, and she completed her doctoral studies through the University nuhelot'įne thaiyots'į nistameyimâkanak Blue Quills program. Her research focuses on Indigenous mental health and social work, centering on community-based understandings and culturally grounded supports for wellness.

Kevin wâsakâyâsiw Lewis, PhD, is a Plains-Cree educator and assistant professor at the University of Saskatchewan, hailing from Ministikwan Lake Cree Nation. He leads Indigenous-language revitalization and land-based Cree immersion programs.

Ranjan Datta, PhD, is Canada Research Chair in Community Disaster Research and associate professor in Indigenous Studies at Mount Royal University. His interdisciplinary research bridges Indigenous land-based knowledge, climate justice, and community-led disaster adaptation in Canada, Bangladesh, Nepal, Ghana, and beyond.

DECOLONIZING MENTAL HEALTH RESEARCH

Integrating Indigenous Land-Based Perspectives and Therapeutic Frameworks

Jody Houle, Kevin Lewis, and Ranjan Datta

Routledge
Taylor & Francis Group
NEW YORK AND LONDON

Designed cover image: © Kevin Lewis, 2026

First published 2027
by Routledge
605 Third Avenue, New York, NY 10158

and by Routledge
4 Park Square, Milton Park, Abingdon, Oxon OX14 4RN

Routledge is an imprint of the Taylor & Francis Group, an informa business

British Library Cataloguing-in-Publication Data
A catalogue record for this book is available from the British Library

ISBN: 978-1-041-13545-6 (hbk)
ISBN: 978-1-041-13455-8 (pbk)
ISBN: 978-1-003-67030-8 (ebk)

DOI: 10.4324/9781003670308

Typeset in Times New Roman
by codeMantra

"This Book" is in loving memory of nimosoompan *and* nokohm-pan.

My (Jody Houle) nimosoompan *Albert Houle would sit by the kitchen table and say, "Look, Myrtle, the trees are dancing."*

This is also for niwakomakanahk*—my siblings, my son Jade Houle, Aleksi Houle, Sierra Lewis, and Sohketa Lewis.*

CONTENTS

ACKNOWLEDGMENTS

We would like to acknowledge Dr. Houle's extended family from Saddle Lake, Whitefish Lake, Kikino, and Goodfish Lake, as well as the Elders and our siblings—Michael, Karla, Adam, and Denny—from the Saulteaux First Nation, Saskatchewan. We also extend our love to Dr. Houle's siblings from the Hunter side of our family—Alton Jackson, Ryan, Garrett, Kyle, and Eric—who have inspired us (i.e., Dr. Houle's family) to heal from the traumas of my past. Our heartfelt thanks go to the Apitow (Halfe), Moyah, Jackson, and Pruden families for your encouragement and motivation in helping us complete this book. We are deeply grateful to those who supported us throughout our (Dr. Houle's) educational journey: Rodolfo Pino-Robles, the late Janice Acoose, the late Joan Sanderson, Yvonne Howse, the late Danny Musqua, Dr. Sherri Chisan, the late Walter Linklater and Maria Linklater, Elder Mary-Lee, and our UnBQ doctoral cohort.

We especially want to thank Dr. Houle's mother, Joyce Night—Dr. Houle's angel and hero—who told us as children, "Jody, you have a good head on your shoulders and you are capable of doing anything." Her words have stayed with us and guided us through the hardest of times. We extend our deepest gratitude to those who have helped Dr. Houle not just survive, but thrive. You (Dr. Houle) have empowered us on our journey of recovery and inspired our passion for helping our people—honoring both our matriarchal and patriarchal roots. It is through both of these lineages that strength flows, and it is this balance that will set the path for generations to come.

We would also like to honor all of Dr. Houle's relations from the seven First Nations surrounding Blue Quills. We love Dr. Houle's family dearly and will continue to live by the sacred teachings that have been passed down to us from all those who have shared their knowledge and wisdom. To our children: thank you for choosing us to be your (Dr. Houle's) parents. Thank you for showing us *pîsim-mopay* and *pîsim* on the days we could not get out of bed—for waiting patiently, for understanding our depression, and for simply being present. You came into our lives for a reason, and we will honor that sacred responsibility for as long as we walk this Earth. To our companion, Dr. Lewis—thank you for being our rock and for teaching us the deep importance of language, culture, and ceremony. We are grateful to everyone at the kâniyâsihk Culture Camp for your tireless dedication and meaningful work. Thank you also to our favorite dogsledding friends on the mushing trail—we carry those memories with joy.

Our thanks go to *kehte-aya* Eileen Stick, Dorothy Crookedneck, and Annie Partridge for helping us learn new teachings from traditional perspectives. You have been some of our greatest teachers and role models. To our (Dr. Houle's) relatives—thank you for trusting us in your healing journeys. It has been an honor to walk alongside you.

Lastly, *ninanâskomitin mistahi*—we offer our deep gratitude to *mamawi otawimaw*, *kîsê-manitow*, *napêw*, and *iskwêw*…

Ekosi.

PREFACE

As a Cree man, father, and Indigenous researcher, my journey in this work has been shaped by strong kinship bonds, the teachings of our Elders, and the deep wisdom of my ancestors. In this book's pages, I share stories not only from my personal experience but also from generations of resilience, survival, and resurgence that animate the narrative you are about to explore.

I grew up hearing my great-grandparents, grandparents, and Elders remind me that our identity, strength, and healing are rooted in wâhkôhtowin—the interconnected web of kinship that links all beings: spirits, lands, wigged ones, animals, plants, insects, waters, wind, and humans. These relationships are not just metaphorical; they are experienced daily through ceremonies, traditions, language, and practices passed down as sacred responsibilities. My role as a father has deepened my understanding of this kinship; it has taught me the urgency of reclaiming our ways, not only for ourselves but also for the children who will carry our stories forward.

In this book, we examine the realities of intergenerational trauma, colonial violence, and the systematic disruptions imposed on our peoples. These stories are challenging. They honestly confront the deep wounds inflicted by residential schools, the Indian Act, the Sixties Scoop, and ongoing systemic injustices. However, these narratives are also filled with hope. They emphasize healing rooted in our ceremonies, kinship ties, and ancestral teachings. We reclaim our voice through our own frameworks, grounded in Cree Natural Laws such as kistêyihtamowin (respect), wâhkôhtowin (kinship), sôhkêyihtamowin (strength), and wîcihitowin (helping one another). These are not abstract concepts; they are real practices that guide our healing and renewal.

My academic journey has felt like a ceremony. Research, as I understand and practice it, is a ceremony—rich with protocols, responsibilities, humility, and reciprocity. The Elders who have generously shared their wisdom have deeply influenced this work, teaching me that to write is to participate in ceremony; to teach is to honor ancestral wisdom; and to research is to uphold a sacred duty to my community. Through land-based education, ceremonies, and kinship teachings, this work provides pathways to healing and self-determination.

This journey has also been a lifelong learning experience as a partner, deeply involved in the complexities of supporting everyone involved. Breaking the cycles of intergenerational trauma requires patience, resilience, and collective dedication. It is through these partnerships—built on trust, mutual respect, and shared vision—that we find the strength and guidance to navigate the complex paths toward healing and renewal.

This book is dedicated to my children, our Elders, and future generations—and especially to my late father, Andrew Lewis, nohtawiy-pan, and to nikâwiy Matilda Lewis. They are my mentors, heroes, and sources of safety. Their teachings, humility, and strength continue to guide my steps on this Earth. May it serve as a reminder that we are never alone—our ancestors walk with us, and our responsibilities extend into the future. The trees are still dancing, reminding us that despite all we have faced, we continue to thrive, resilient and connected, reclaiming our rightful place as caretakers of our cultures, communities, and lands.

êkosi, with deep gratitude and humility,

Dr. Kevin wâsakâyâsiw Lewis

1

THE TREES ARE STILL DANCING

Ranjan Datta (with support from Kevin Lewis and Jody Houle)

In many Indigenous nations across Turtle Island, the land is not merely a backdrop to human life but an animate, sovereign, and relational presence that teaches, heals, and remembers. Within Cree worldviews, the land holds story, law, and cosmology; it holds the voices of ancestors and the moral instruction required to sustain balanced relationships across generations. *The Trees Are Still Dancing*, written by Jody wâpaniskwêw Houle, emerges within this landscape of profound relationality and urgent struggle, offering a powerful intervention into the ongoing crises of mental health, intergenerational trauma, and colonial violence that continue to shape Indigenous life in Canada. This book is both testimony and methodology, a story of personal resurgence and a scholarly call to action. It marks a significant departure from dominant Western health research paradigms by grounding mental wellness in Cree teachings, ceremonies, kinship systems, and responsibilities articulated through the concept of wâhkôhtowin.

Outlining the research gaps, this book addresses the intellectual and political significance of this work, and its contributions to Indigenous health scholarship. It positions this book as an essential contribution to ongoing efforts to decolonize mental health by restoring land-based, ceremonial, and relational frameworks to the center of inquiry. As Indigenous communities continue to confront the legacies of residential schools, child apprehension, and the enduring harms of the Indian Act, our work offers a vision for healing that is culturally grounded, spiritually resonant, and deeply accountable to community. What distinguishes this book is that it is not simply a text about Indigenous healing, it is itself a ceremonial act. Through narrative, theory, and reflection, we weave together Cree cosmology, oral teachings, and lived experience to reveal how the land continues to call us back into relationship. The title becomes both descriptive

DOI: 10.4324/9781003670308-1

and prophetic: despite centuries of attempted erasure, *the trees are still dancing*, signaling that Indigenous life, spirit, and knowledge continue to move, speak, and guide us.

Decolonizing Health Research Through Cree Epistemologies

This book arises at a time when Indigenous peoples across Canada are disproportionately impacted by mental health crises, inequitable access to care, systemic discrimination, and the ongoing erosion of land and cultural identity. While there has been an expansion of Indigenous representation within academic health research, major gaps persist. The dominant biomedical paradigm—which privileges pathology, individualism, and psychocentric frameworks—often fails to capture the relational, spiritual, and land-based dimensions of Indigenous well-being (Gone, 2013; Linklater, 2014). Western psychiatry, rooted in colonial histories of control and assimilation, is ill-equipped to address the deep structural determinants of Indigenous mental health, nor can it account for the spiritual and ceremonial foundations that sustain Indigenous life.

We intervene by situating health within Cree cosmology, kinship, and ceremonial practice. Her work affirms that mental health cannot be separated from land, language, and law. Within Cree teachings, healing is neither individual nor clinical; it is a relational, collective, and intergenerational process grounded in responsibilities to all of Creation. Through her use of wâhkôhtowin, we reframe health as a dynamic and reciprocal relationship among humans, animals, water, plants, the stars, and the land. This understanding challenges Western dualisms that separate body from spirit, emotion from ecology, and knowledge from ceremony.

This book further demonstrates how health research must be grounded in Indigenous methodological traditions—including storytelling, experiential learning, ceremonial protocol, and embodied knowledge. As Wilson (2008) and Kovach (2009a,b) argue, relational accountability is the foundation of Indigenous inquiry; we operationalize this by centering Elders, honoring oral teachings, and refusing extractive research practices. Knowledge, in this framework, is gifted through ceremony and lived through relational ethics—not abstracted, dissected, or commodified.

Research Gaps in Indigenous Health Scholarship

Although Indigenous scholars have documented the impacts of colonization across generations (TRC, 2015; Wesley-Esquimaux & Smolewski, 2004), much of the existing literature remains deficit-based, focusing heavily on damage narratives without offering pathways toward resurgence or culturally grounded healing. Four gaps are especially pressing, and *The Trees Are Still Dancing* addresses each with clarity and nuance.

Lack of Land-Based Healing Models in Health Research

While the land is a cornerstone of Indigenous identity and wellness, few academic studies meaningfully theorize land-based healing as a primary mental health intervention. They often discuss land abstractly, rather than grounding it in ceremonial, legal, and kinship obligations. We fill this gap by presenting a Cree land-based mental health framework rooted in ceremony, seasonal cycles, and intergenerational knowledge transmission.

Absence of Indigenous Women's Voices in Trauma Literature

Indigenous women continue to face heightened levels of violence, socio-economic marginalization, and health disparities. Yet their voices remain largely marginalized within mental health research. We refuse this silencing. Her narrative foregrounds Indigenous women's knowledge, resilience, and ceremonial agency, embodying what Anderson (2016) calls Indigenous feminist storytelling as theory. Her testimony becomes a methodology, a political act, and a blueprint for healing.

Ceremonial Knowledge Excluded from Mainstream Therapeutic Models

Despite decades of advocacy, Indigenous ceremonies remain largely unrecognized within state-funded mental health services. The Non-Insured Health Benefits (NIHB) program, for example, continues to exclude ceremonial practitioners from its coverage structures (Greenwood et al., 2018). We argue that ceremony—not talk therapy alone—is foundational to Indigenous healing. Her work articulates how sweat lodges, pipe ceremonies, sundances, and rites of passage provide therapeutic, emotional, and spiritual grounding that Western models cannot replicate.

Ethical and Epistemological Gaps in Western Research Practices

Western research paradigms often extract Indigenous knowledges without reciprocity, spiritual integrity, or community accountability (Smith, 2012). Our methodology emphasizes that Indigenous health research requires ceremony, protocol, and respect for knowledge sovereignty. This book itself models these ethics, demonstrating how research relationships must be nurtured with humility, gratitude, and kinship.

A Vision for Indigenous Health Sovereignty

Central to our contribution is our conceptualization of a Land-Based Mental Health Healing Lodge, a community-led model informed by Cree teachings, ceremonial responsibilities, and seasonal learning cycles. This lodge represents a paradigm shift in Indigenous mental health care—moving beyond clinical environments into relational, land-centered spaces where healing is approached holistically.

The lodge's proposed 12-week program includes land-based activities such as traditional parenting, hide tanning, berry-picking, moss-bag teachings, wilderness survival, swing therapy, rites of passage, and intensive ceremonies. Each activity is tied to Cree laws, cosmology, and philosophies of balance (*miyo-pimâtisiwin*). This program operationalizes the TRC's Calls to Action #21 and #22 by restoring Indigenous governance over health practices and affirming the central role of ceremony, culture, and land in healing (TRC, 2015). We not only critique colonial health systems but also offer a credible, community-rooted alternative—one that is structurally, spiritually, and pedagogically aligned with Indigenous sovereignty.

Ethical, Political, and Scholarly Significance

The Trees Are Still Dancing exemplifies the intellectual movements shaping contemporary Indigenous health scholarship: resurgence, relational accountability, land-based governance, and decolonizing methodologies. Our work builds upon scholars such as Coulthard (2014), Alfred (2009), Simpson (2014), and Linklater (2014), who argue that healing and decolonization must occur simultaneously at the personal, political, and collective levels.

Her book calls researchers and practitioners to move beyond symbolic gestures of reconciliation toward structural change. It challenges policymakers to fund Indigenous-led health models, protect ceremonial knowledge, and recognize Indigenous epistemologies as valid and necessary. It invites academic institutions to transform research ethics processes to align with Cree governance and Indigenous law. Most importantly, it offers Indigenous communities—especially those who continue to carry the burdens of trauma—an affirming, culturally grounded pathway toward healing. We remind that healing is possible because the land remembers us, because ceremony continues, and because the trees themselves are still dancing.

This introduction positions *The Trees Are Still Dancing* as a vital contribution to Indigenous health scholarship, decolonizing research methodologies, and community-led healing practices. Our work fills critical research gaps by centering Cree cosmologies, women's narratives, land-based healing, and ceremonial knowledge. It challenges colonial models of health and offers a future grounded in relationality, kinship, and self-determination. The trees are still dancing because Indigenous peoples are still here praying, resisting, remembering, and healing. This book is an invitation to walk alongside that movement, guided by the land, strengthened by ceremony, and accountable to generations yet to come.

Significance of This Book

The Trees Are Still Dancing offers an essential and transformative contribution to Indigenous health scholarship, mental wellness frameworks, and community-based healing models. Emerging from our lived experience, relational commitments, ceremonial responsibilities, and professional practice in Indigenous mental health, this book is far more than a dissertation—it is a work of intellectual and spiritual resurgence. It stands as a manifesto for decolonizing health research, restoring ceremonial authority, reclaiming kinship systems, and revitalizing Indigenous epistemologies as legitimate, rigorous, and sovereign sources of knowledge. In a research landscape long dominated by Western clinical paradigms that separate knowledge from place, culture, and identity, our work re-centers Cree worldviews and land-based ethical frameworks, offering a fundamentally different vision of what ethical, just, and effective health research must become.

At its core, this book is a critical academic intervention precisely because it addresses significant gaps in Indigenous health literature, contributes original methodologies grounded in Cree philosophies, and confronts the epistemic and ethical limitations of Western psychological research. At the same time, it provides profound societal value by proposing culturally resonant healing models, advocating for Indigenous health sovereignty, and empowering communities through the revitalization of language, ceremony, and kinship. This dual academic and community significance positions this book as a foundational contribution to Indigenous health resurgence.

Addressing Research Gaps in Indigenous Health Scholarship

Although decades of research have documented Indigenous health disparities, much of the existing literature fails to center Indigenous frameworks for understanding and addressing wellness. The overemphasis on clinical symptoms, pathology, and risk factors often obscures the deeper relational, spiritual, and ecological roots of Indigenous healing traditions. We reverse this tendency by grounding her work in Cree Natural Laws, the concept of wâhkôhtowin, and the ancestral responsibilities embedded in the seven-generational teachings.

This book directly responds to the long-standing absence of land-based, ceremonial, and relational epistemologies in health scholarship. Instead of diagnosing Indigenous people through colonial psychiatric categories, we situate wellness within the balance of mind, body, spirit, and emotion—an equilibrium cultivated through ceremony, kinship, and land-based practice. Her framework resists the deficit-based tendencies of Western research and reframes Indigenous trauma through community strength, ancestral continuity, and the spiritual integrity of Cree governance systems. This approach positions this book in conversation with other scholars who critique pathologizing narratives and advocate for spiritually grounded healing, yet we extend this work by offering specific ceremonial frameworks and community-based program design rooted in Cree nationhood.

Advancing Indigenous Research Methodologies

Another major contribution of this book is its methodological innovation. We model a research paradigm grounded in relational accountability, where knowledge is generated through kinship, protocol, ceremony, and community consent. Centering narrative inquiry, personal testimony, Elder-led interviews, and land-based reflection, we exemplify an Indigenous methodological framework that is embodied, reciprocal, and accountable to community.

This approach challenges the extractive, objectifying tendencies of Western research traditions. Rather than viewing participants as subjects, we treat all knowledge holders as relatives whose stories are offered through trust and ceremonial obligation. Our methodological commitments demonstrate how Indigenous research must be conducted—through humility, responsibility, prayer, and ongoing relational care. Our book becomes a model for future Indigenous scholars seeking to reclaim research as a tool for resurgence rather than assimilation. It shows how rigorous scholarship can emerge from ceremony, experience, and oral teachings, thereby expanding what counts as legitimate academic knowledge.

Redefining Health as Relational, Spiritual, and Ceremonial

One of the most profound societal contributions of this book is its redefinition of mental health. Instead of presenting wellness as a set of clinical outcomes or therapeutic interventions, we frame health as a relational phenomenon rooted in the interconnectedness of all beings. Healing, from this perspective, is a ceremonial responsibility, a return to balance, and a process of reconnecting with spirit, land, identity, and kinship.

Ceremonies such as the sweat lodge, Sundance, water ceremonies, moon ceremonies, rites of passage, and talking circles are understood not as "alternative therapies," but as the heart of Cree wellness systems. We articulate how each ceremony restores relational harmony, recalibrates spiritual alignment, and addresses soul wounds created by colonial violence. These ceremonies offer emotional release, spiritual grounding, and communal support—elements absent from most Western therapeutic models. Positioning ceremony as central to healing, we challenge both clinical practitioners and policymakers to recognize Indigenous spiritual practices as legitimate, effective, and necessary components of mental health care.

Policy and Programmatic Importance

We do not limit ourselves to theoretical critique; we offer a practical model for Indigenous health sovereignty through the proposed Land-Based Mental Health Healing Lodge. This lodge represents a groundbreaking program that responds directly to the Truth and Reconciliation Commission of Canada's Calls to Action related to Indigenous health. The lodge's 12-week program incorporates land-based education, traditional parenting, wilderness skills, ceremonial healing, language immersion, and Elder-guided mentorship. Such a model fills an urgent policy gap created by the NIHB program's exclusion of traditional healing from its funding structures. Our proposal demonstrates that culturally grounded, community-led mental health programs are both feasible and essential for Indigenous nations seeking self-determined health systems. Our work therefore contributes directly to policy reform debates, offering a detailed blueprint for programs that honor Indigenous legal orders, ceremonial obligations, and kinship structures.

Empowering Indigenous Women and Matriarchal Authority

As Indigenous and racialized land-based scholars and ceremonial practitioners, we have created a text that restores the authority of Indigenous women as knowledge keepers, healers, and political leaders. Our narrative challenges the patriarchal distortions that entered many communities through colonial impositions, reaffirming that Cree governance and health systems have always depended on women's leadership, intuition, and ceremonial strength. Our voice fills a significant gap in Indigenous health scholarship, where Indigenous women's perspectives remain underrepresented. Through our stories, teachings, and programmatic vision, we demonstrate how healing is intertwined with reclaiming Indigenous womanhood, matriarchal responsibility, and intergenerational continuity.

Revitalizing Kinship as Health Infrastructure

Throughout this book, we emphasize the centrality of wâhkôhtowin, the Cree kinship system that links humans, animals, plants, waters, ancestors, and spirit beings. Framing kinship as health infrastructure, we restore the relational worldviews that once guided community wellness. Through this lens, trauma is understood not only as personal suffering but also as the fracturing of relationships across generations. Rebuilding kinship, therefore, becomes a therapeutic act—a restoration of family roles, intergenerational respect, shared responsibility, and collective belonging. This framework strengthens community resilience and provides a culturally grounded alternative to Western family therapy models.

Enhancing Practitioner Training and Cultural Safety

Another significant contribution of this book is its relevance for mental health practitioners, educators, social workers, and policymakers seeking to work ethically with Indigenous communities. We articulate key concepts such as spiritual imbalance, ancestral grief, and soul wounds—concepts that remain absent from most clinical psychology texts. Our work encourages practitioners to develop cultural humility, engage with ceremony, and recognize the limits of Western diagnostic frameworks. Providing a culturally informed understanding of trauma, healing, and resilience, this book becomes an essential tool for improving cultural safety in health systems.

Language Revitalization and Cultural Continuity

Cree language appears throughout this book not as an aesthetic choice but as a form of ceremonial and epistemic sovereignty. Language carries memory, cosmology, and relational ethics; therefore, healing cannot be separated from linguistic revitalization. Implementing Cree terms and teachings, we strengthen community identity and honor ancestors whose knowledge flows through the language. Our contributions support ongoing language revitalization efforts essential to cultural survival and long-term mental wellness.

Guiding Future Research and Institutional Change

Through this book, we provide a guide for transforming academic institutions, research ethics, funding structures, and community partnerships. We demonstrate that Indigenous research can be both academically rigorous and spiritually grounded: both personal and political. Our work invites future scholars to root their research in ceremony, land, and relational accountability.

Through this contribution, we reshape the landscape of Indigenous health scholarship and chart a path toward a future where Indigenous knowledge systems—not Western paradigms—define the meaning of wellness, healing, and collective liberation.

Research, Positionalities, Methodological Approaches

In land-based Indigenous research—particularly within the wâhkôhtowin framework—the positionality of the researcher is not an optional reflection but a central methodological requirement. wâhkôhtowin, a foundational Cree Natural Law meaning kinship, teaches that all forms of life exist in reciprocal, interdependent relationships: humans, animals, waters, plants, ancestors, landforms, and the spirit world. These relationships extend beyond the physical realm into ethical, ceremonial, emotional, and spiritual responsibilities. When we engage in research grounded in wâhkôhtowin, we cannot separate who we are from how, why, and for whom we do this work. Our social, cultural, historical, and spiritual locations must be visible, reflexive, and accountable.

Within this framework, the researcher is never a detached observer nor a neutral technician. Instead, we enter as active relatives—participants shaped by, and accountable to, a broad constellation of kinship obligations. Our lived experiences, cultural teachings, and ceremonial commitments influence the questions we ask, the stories we honor, the methods we choose, and the relationships we build with participants, Elders, and the land. Positionality is therefore the ground from which ethical Indigenous research emerges, rather than a postscript or academic formality. Using wâhkôhtowin as our research methodology requires us to recognize ourselves not as individuals extracting or producing knowledge, but as relations participating in a collective process of memory, healing, resurgence, and nation-building. The Cree teachings of pêyakoskân (family) and pêyakohêwâm (extended family) remind us that each Elder, language speaker, ceremonial leader, land-based educator, and non-human being we encounter is part of an expansive kinship system that shapes the integrity of our research.

Honoring these relationships demands ceremonial responsibility, emotional humility, and spiritual integrity. It also requires readiness—to listen deeply, to learn continually, and to be transformed through the research encounter. In this way, positionality becomes both a methodological principle and a wellness practice, ensuring that our work aligns with natural law, Cree ethical standards, and community-defined priorities. Centering our positionality within wâhkôhtowin, we establish a clear foundation for decolonizing mental health research. This approach guides students, practitioners, and researchers toward relational accountability, culturally grounded methods, and land-based practices that challenge Western assumptions and strengthen Indigenous mental health frameworks (Figure 1.1).

Dr. Jody wâpaniskwêw Houle's Genealogy

This book is the journey of Jody wâpaniskwêw Houle. For understanding the context of this book, we situate Jody wâpaniskwêw Houle's methodological approach for readers. This section centers on the Houle's genealogy and

FIGURE 1.1 The blueberries shown in the figure represent fresh flowers of the new harvest in which this book is set in the mindset of decolonizing mental health and the semi-integration of Western therapies. This flower has many medicinal purposes in which it can be dried and used to make jam, and for diabetics, it can be used to lower blood sugars.

community, emphasizing the importance of family, identity, and the seven-generation prophecy as central to Cree epistemologies. Health, healing, and research are conceptualized as holistic processes intertwined with community, land, and spirituality, challenging Western paradigms that often isolate individuals from their environments and communities.

I'm originally from the Whitefish Lake #128 band located in northeastern Alberta; we are a part of the Saddle Lake Cree Nation, but run our own internal affairs. I grew up on my reserve, and I'm very proud to be from my nation, otherwise known as Goodfish Lake. I was raised by *nohkom-pan* and *nimosôm-pan* (Myrtle and Late Albert Houle) and my mother Joyce Night as well. I grew up in both Alberta and Saskatchewan. I learned an abundance from all my relations, and I carry these teachings forth and share them wherever I go or whoever will take the time to listen. We would like to share with you Houle's genealogy, as this shapes who we are and where we come from and is vital to our language, culture, and ceremony.

I had plenty of opportunity to sit with *nimosôm-pan* Albert and *nohkom-pan* Myrtle to listen to their stories and tell me about my genealogical background. I take into account that we must keep in mind when we speak about the seven-generational prophecies; it is the three generations behind you and the three generations after you that will be affected, so you must live your life according to our natural laws and remember to be kind and non-judgmental, be humble (Houle, 1998, Personal Communication). There is also another way of looking at the seven-generational prophecies, which is known as the generation down wheel, where there are "knots on a string." The knots represent a person on the string, and every other string represents the generations (McLeod, 2008). This is how I would like to introduce my familial background using the generational traits, characteristics, and backgrounds that we come from to understand why we are the way we are.

My mother's name is Joyce Night (formerly Houle), and she resides in the Saulteaux First Nation located 20 minutes north of North Battleford, Saskatchewan. Her mother is *nohkom-pan* Myrtle Houle and her father nimosôm-pan Albert Houle. *nohkom-pan* (maiden name Pruden) is a Mètis who originates from the Kikino Metis Settlement. She had five brothers and one sister, two deceased brothers and her only baby sister is still alive, whose name is Gussi Jackson. Her mother was Mary Jane Pruden, and her father was Homer Jackson. Their marriage was arranged by Mary Jane's father. Mary Jane had three sisters and two brothers, and they were of English ancestry. Mary Jane's parents were Betsy Pruden and Alec Pruden, and his great-grandfather was from England. *nohkom-pan* said that they were the first settlers in Fort Edmonton, and they traveled by wagon north to Lac La Biche, Alberta, to settle (date 1904).

We are also related to Chief Pakan (meaning hazelnut), who was an original signatory of Treaty 6 for our territory. Chief Pakan was *nohkom-pan* Myrtles' grandma's (Betsy Pruden) brother. Chief Pakan was of tall nature and was very stoic and stood his ground. He was very well-respected by all within his nation. It is said that he developed what is known as the "James Seenum Formula," which allotted an extra five acres for those families that signed into the treaty (Houle, 2002). Not too long after the treaty signing, a man by the name of Henry B. Steinhauer (a priest) came to Whitefish Lake and made alliances with Chief Pakan. They decided together that education was key and that they would soon integrate the children into the Western society's school system. I often questioned why Chief Pakan would submit his people to make this transition; but in his mind it was for the betterment and security of the people and for future generations.

nicâpân-pan Homer Jackson was a very kind man who came from humble beginnings. His biological father abandoned him during the 1885 Rebellion in North Battleford and took him and his only sister and dropped them off at Onion Lake Residential School. They grew up within the institutional system. *nicâpân-pan* Mary Jane Pruden and Homer Jackson were betrothed, as just mentioned. But before this marriage took place, Homer was an athlete and trained for running in the early years of his life. He had a chance to go to the Olympics (I'm not sure what year), but he couldn't go because he lived below the poverty level. You see, Homer was without parents and a home, this is how he got a job working for *nicâpân-pan* Mary Jane's dad. This is how they became married and relocated to Goodfish Lake. *nicâpân-pan* Homer's dad was named Isaiac

Wuttunee from the Red Pheasant First Nation, and his mother's name was not recorded, but she died soon after Homer was born.

nimosôm-pan Albert Houle hails from the Goodfish Lake reserve, and his parents were Alice (Anastasia) Houle and Matt Houle. His biological father was Lloyd Cardinal from Saddle Lake. *nicâpân-pan* Alice's dad was Louise Matice, and her mother was Nancy Memnook. Nancy Memnook had two husbands, not at the same time. From her first marriage she had Narcisse and Simon (who died in Italy during the war and was buried there) and Felix; from her second marriage she had Mary, Alice (*nicâpân-pan*), and Julie. Now I'm going to tell you how we are descendants of Chief Poundmaker. He had two sons, and one of them is named Samuel. He had a daughter, Charlotte, and Charlotte had a son named Elijah Houle. She had a son, Mathew Sr. His Indian name was *wîsakitakom*. *wîsakitakom kâkî-itêht* had my *nicâpân-pan* Mathew Houle and fathered *nimosôm-pan* Albert, who had my mother Joyce. She had me, and I have my three children, Jade, Sohketa, and Aleksi (ten generations), as mentioned.

Aunt Mary Jane from the Goodfish Lake First Nation is closely related to me (her dad, Charles Houle and *nimosôm-pan* were brothers). We share a special bond together. Mary Jane (2002, personal communication) states, "we got our name Houle from Agnes Mason," but when the Jesuits came, they couldn't say *mahikan* (wolf), so they named us Houle. One last thing about my family, a long time ago we got our name, "the Blanket People," we were ceremonial people. The Houles had a clan, and there was one higher society. We were the ones below; that is how we became known as the Blanket People.

Now on my paternal side there is my biological father. I was never raised by him, although I did share more of a brother/sister bond with him. His name was late Gary Halfe. He passed on to the spirit world five years ago, as he left his wife, Sherri Hunter behind. My dad's mother was *nohkom-pan* Laura Halfe and his dad, *nimosôm-pan* Ernest Halfe. Laura came from a family who lived near Lloydminster; their last name was Moyou. Her parents' names are unknown. My late *nimosôm-pan* Ernests' parents were named James Halfe, and his wife's name is unknown. I remember my dad always saying, "my girl I'm so happy that you didn't marry anyone from around Goodfish, Saddle Lake or Kikino because you are related to everyone around here." I would like to share more of my father's side, but I do not know too much of the familial background, as I never did have the chance to ask when they were alive.

With that said, it is important that we know where we come from, to know who we are, and our identity as *nêhiyawak*. I remember *nimosôm-pan* Albert always telling me the importance of our family and to always tell them that you love them. I also remember this one time when I was a little girl about 11 years old, and my cousin Tracey and I were sitting at home. My *mosôm* came home, and he said, "you girls get me ready for Halloween, go to the trailer and look in the surprise bags and get me an old outfit to look like an old lady." My cousin Tracey and I went to go pick out some clothes; I dressed as a punk rocker, she dressed as a little old man, and *nimosôm-pan* an old lady. We were off to Ashmont bar, and *nimosôm-pan* walked in with Tracey on his arm, and I sat in the vehicle and watched from the window. He said, "excuse me waitress can I order a drink here for me and my boyfriend." Tracey was underage, but they still gave her a drink. *nimosôm-pan* had his drink, and we were off to Goodfish to go and pick up his brother Charlie Houle (the best drum maker in GFL). I looked at them as I had to take a double glance and said, "are you guys twins?" as they looked identical. We were off to the dance, and at this dance there were all sorts of shenanigans going on, drunken fights, and so forth. At around two in the morning, it was time to go. Tracey and I went over to where my *nimosôm-panak* Albert and Charlie were sitting with a couple of their friends. You see, I forgot to mention before we left for Rich Lake *nimosôm-pan* stopped by the house to change into his favorite George Jones T-shirt; now back to where I was, they were sitting in a circle at the dance, and lo and behold, *nimosôm-pan* still had his makeup and earrings on while getting into real deep conversation with his drinking buddies.

Within this book, I will further explain what each chapter consists of, as my objectives are to give a comprehensive understanding of how our ways of being and knowing were disrupted due to colonialism and how we have become resilient in maintaining who we are as Indigenous peoples. My genealogy centers around a decolonial and critical methodological framework grounded in Indigenous epistemologies, Cree Natural Laws, and land-based ceremonial knowledge. As both a lived experience and a community-embedded scholarly intervention, this research challenges dominant Western paradigms by centering Indigenous ways of knowing, being, and healing. Methodologically, the dissertation is shaped through narrative inquiry, Elder-led knowledge transmission, and culturally grounded therapeutic practices. The methodological choices are not incidental; they are acts of resistance, resurgence, and healing.

Dr. Kevin Lewis' Positionality as a Land-Based Scholar

As a nêhiyawew (Plains Cree) First Nation professor, writer, and researcher from Ministikwan Lake Cree Nation in Treaty 6 Territory, I bring to this book a lifelong commitment to land-based education, Cree language revitalization, and Indigenous pedagogical sovereignty. My positionality as a land-based scholar is not incidental—it is foundational to the methodologies, values, and teachings I carry forward. As the founder of kâniyâsihk Culture Camps and the Land-Based Cree Immersion School, *kâ-nêyâsihk mîkiwâhpa*, I do not merely theorize land-based education—I live it, enact it, and nurture it intergenerationally. My role at the University of Saskatchewan and my work across the Prairie Provinces reflect how it is possible to shape academic institutions while staying deeply rooted in community-led knowledge systems.

At the empathy of my work is my responsibility as both a cultural and academic bridge. My lived experience as a nêhiyaw person provides me with ancestral, spiritual, and cultural grounding to speak from Cree epistemologies, while my academic training helps me navigate and influence institutional spaces that were never built with Indigenous worldviews in mind. In the context of this book—centered on Cree land-based healing, ceremonial methodologies, and the legacies of colonial trauma—I speak from a place of community-based authority, intellectual rigor, and pedagogical compassion. My scholarship is not abstract or distant; it is grounded in lived accountability to the land, language, and people.

My long-standing work designing, implementing, and evaluating culturally responsive education programs has positioned me within a vital landscape of Indigenous educational resurgence. Through *kâniyâsihk* Culture Camps, I have helped develop a model where Cree Natural Laws, oral traditions, and land-based experience coalesce to restore cultural memory and sovereignty. These camps are not add-ons—they are central. They provide a full-bodied learning rooted in language, ceremony, kinship, and collective responsibility. My identity as a scholar is defined by this action—by building, sustaining, and evolving institutions that honor and reflect Indigenous ways of knowing and being.

To further strengthen these efforts, I developed the Structured Assessments Framework for Land-Based Learning at *kâniyâsihk* Culture Camps. This framework draws upon case study methodologies interwoven with evaluation tools grounded in Cree values, community feedback, and ceremonial accountability. In this book, such methodologies are essential for legitimizing Indigenous approaches to wellness, language, and education. They create pathways for researchers, educators, and policymakers to move beyond extractive colonial evaluation models toward relational, reciprocal ones.

My work extends into global Indigenous solidarity as well. In collaboration with a Māori educational expert, I co-designed a culturally grounded evaluation of the Cree Immersion School. This international dialogue underscores my belief that Indigenous resurgence must be relational and transnational. When First Nations, Māori, and other Indigenous peoples share tools, stories, and frameworks for renewal, we build deeper ethical and methodological alliances across Turtle Island and beyond.

My research—spanning language and policy development, second language acquisition, teacher education, and environmental education—finds coherence in this book's focus on Cree healing and land-based health sovereignty. I see language not simply as a mode of communication but as a vessel of worldview, protocol, and spirit. Revitalizing language means revitalizing relationships, and through those relationships, we enact *wâhkôhtowin*, the kinship ethic that guides my life and this work.

My leadership strives to ensure that Indigenous youth, families, and Elders are not passive recipients of programming but active participants and co-creators. Programs I help design are shaped by community voices—particularly those of children and parents—whose insights drive the evolution of our land-based learning models. This commitment to listening and co-learning reinforces my understanding that education is never static. It is alive, seasonal, intergenerational, and deeply tied to the spirit of place. I have learned to lead by listening.

As an Indigenous scholar, I work to dissolve the artificial boundary between academic knowledge and lived practice. My contribution to this book is not from the outside, but from within: as a ceremonial participant, a knowledge holder, a relative. I ground the discussions in healing, trauma, kinship, and land in Cree law, language, and lived pedagogy. I do not romanticize this work—it is challenging, ongoing, and demanding of both spirit and intellect—but I do honor it as sacred.

I carry forward my work with the next seven generations in mind. I teach and build programs that ensure Cree youth are not disconnected from our language, lands, or teachings. I believe that to educate is to reclaim—to engage in ceremony, to foster healing, and to affirm our sovereignty. This is at the heart of *The Trees Are Still Dancing*—a book I am honored to contribute to because it echoes my vision of land-based education as a source of intergenerational continuity and collective liberation.

My positionality as a land-based Cree scholar is not only central to the ceremonial, pedagogical, and intellectual foundations of this book, but it is also a commitment to future generations. I strive to live and breathe Cree knowledge while helping to create transformative spaces of learning, healing, and resurgence. Through this work, I hope this book serves as more than a repository of stories and teachings—it is a living blueprint for Indigenous futures rooted in *wâhkôhtowin*, responsibility, and love for our lands and peoples.

Dr. Ranjan Datta's Positionality as a Land-Based Decolonial Scholar: A Commitment to Solidarity and Responsibility

As a land-based decolonial scholar born and raised in a minority land-based community in Bangladesh, and now living as a settler of color on Treaty lands in Canada, I occupy a complex and liminal space marked by responsibility, reflection, and resistance. My positionality is grounded in lived experiences of erasure, marginalization, and reclamation—both within my homeland and across settler colonial institutions in North America. This dual consciousness shapes not only my academic perspective but also my personal and political commitments. I do not engage in this work merely as a researcher or educator; I engage as someone accountable to collective healing, decolonization, and solidarity-building.

My scholarly path has always been informed by a lifelong relationship with land-based knowledge systems from Bangladesh. In my early life, I experienced a world where daily rhythms were governed by rituals, ecological cycles, and kinship responsibilities. Despite my formal education being situated within colonial frameworks, these structures could never fully erase the teachings I received through family and community. These teachings instructed me to see the land not as a commodity, but as kin—a living and sacred presence imbued with memory, responsibility, and healing. As a member of a minority community experiencing ongoing colonization in my home country, I struggled to reclaim my land-based identity. I came to realize that these teachings were not peripheral but foundational to my sense of self, belonging, and purpose. The systemic suppression of these ways of knowing through state education, immigration policy, and institutional hierarchies has only intensified my commitment to decolonial scholarship.

When I arrived in Canada, I was met with a second wave of colonial — erasure—this time through racialized and bureaucratic systems that delegitimize land-based knowledge unless reframed through Eurocentric or settler-sanctioned paradigms. I have been told that I am "not Indigenist enough," "not Canadian immigrant enough," or "not academic enough." These are not isolated incidents, but rather structural indicators of a system designed to police identity, delegitimize embodied knowledge, and maintain settler authority over who belongs, who speaks, and whose knowledge matters. Yet these experiences have not deterred me; instead, they have deepened my resolve to work in solidarity with Indigenous communities in their struggles for sovereignty, resurgence, and justice.

My position as both an insider to land-based epistemologies and an outsider in settler institutions places me in a unique space—one where I am compelled to navigate the epistemic violence of academia without replicating its extractive logics. I view myself as a bridge-builder, responsible for creating pathways between communities and institutions while resisting the reproduction of colonial harm. My scholarship is situated within this tension, aiming to challenge settler colonial systems from within while actively amplifying Indigenous voices, laws, and land-based practices. This is precisely why *The Trees Are Still Dancing* resonates so deeply with me. It offers not only a scholarly framework but also a ceremonial, community-led vision of healing and research—one that affirms my own understanding of what decolonial responsibility entails.

For me, responsibility is not performative. It is not simply a rhetorical gesture of allyship. Rather, it is a long-term, relational, and accountable practice of solidarity. I approach my scholarship as ceremony—an offering rooted in reciprocity, care, and ethical obligation. My writing is guided by story-sharing, reflexive narrative, and land-based metaphor. Through these methods, I intentionally disrupt the disembodied, objective voice of Western academia and foreground relational accountability as a methodological and ethical imperative.

Living as a settler of color on Treaty lands, I am acutely aware of the complexities of occupying space without responsibility. My racialized immigrant identity does not exempt me from complicity in settler colonialism; instead, it demands that I engage with humility, attentiveness, and accountability. This understanding shapes every aspect of my academic and community practice. In this regard, my work complements and supports *The Trees Are Still Dancing*, which centers Indigenous healing as a ceremonial, political, and community-led process. I do not claim to speak for Indigenous peoples. Rather, I locate myself as a co-traveler—someone who walks besides, listens deeply, and acts when called upon in the broader journey of decolonization.

In both my teaching and public scholarship, I prioritize Indigenous sovereignty, land-based governance, and cultural resurgence. I believe that education must be rooted in ethical relationships and reciprocal responsibility. Through storytelling and community-based engagement, I strive to create spaces that honor vulnerability, relationality, and collective transformation. These spaces invite emotional and spiritual labor and model a scholarship that is both accountable and transformative.

In a settler colonial context that fragments identities and isolates communities, I work to reclaim interconnectedness as a principle of healing and research. My relationship with land—whether in Bangladesh or on Treaty 7 Territory—is not one of possession but of care, remembrance, and resistance. I see my work as a form of witnessing and honoring. My complex positionality, rather than being a limitation, is a source of strength. It allows me to bring multiple ways of knowing into dialogue and to honor both my ancestral teachings and the sovereignty of the Indigenous territories where I now live and work.

In supporting this book's goals, we reaffirm our responsibility to act in solidarity with Indigenous peoples not only through my words but also through my actions—by mentoring Indigenous and racialized youth, by challenging institutional racism, by organizing land-based learning initiatives, and by continuously reflecting on our own position within systems of power. We understand that healing is never individual, and liberation is never singular. The journey of decolonization is intergenerational, transnational, and collective; and that journey, for us, is one of love, humility, and enduring responsibility.

Decolonial Stories as Healing Method

At the heart of this book lies a deeply relational and decolonial methodological approach—one that positions storytelling as the central mode of inquiry, analysis, and healing. For us, story is not simply data; it is the ground on which life is lived, understood, and transformed. Our narratives, drawn from lived experiences with intergenerational trauma, addictions, kinship rupture, colonial violence, healing, and ceremonial resurgence, serve as the methodological backbone of this work.

This book aligns with Indigenous scholars such as Archibald, Wilson, Kovach, and Simpson, who argue that stories are sacred entities that carry law, protocol, history, and possibility.

Our research becomes a methodological site of transformation—both for ourselves and for those who encounter our work. Through story, we reclaim voice and agency from systems that have long pathologized Indigenous peoples. Story becomes ceremony; ceremony becomes theory; theory becomes healing. This is the essence of Indigenous storywork. It allows researchers, the community, ancestors, and land to speak together in concordance. For us, storytelling is not an academic addendum—it *is* the research method, the analytic lens, and the healing process.

Kinship-Based Ethics: wâhkôhtowin

The ethical foundation of Houle's methodology is wâhkôhtowin, the Cree philosophy of kinship that governs relationships between humans, animals, plants, waters, spirits, ancestors, and landforms. This kinship ethic shapes the research questions, the data generation, the interview practices, and the interpretive processes. It demands that research be conducted not from a stance of distance but from one of relational presence, humility, and accountability.

Through wâhkôhtowin, we honor familial genealogies, ancestral lineages, and community responsibilities. She foregrounds the interdependence between all forms of life, challenging Western academic traditions that prioritize detachment, objectivity, and neutrality. Kinship becomes an ethical teaching, a methodological compass, and a political act of resurgence. It orients us toward reciprocity, compassion, and responsibility across generations.

Elder-Led Knowledge and Dialogic Interviewing

Central to the methodology are the teachings and guidance of three respected nêhiyaw iskwêwak Elders: Annie Partridge, Eileen Stick, and Dorthy Crookedneck. These matriarchs serve as knowledge keepers, ceremonial guides, historians, and community authorities. Interviews with them were conducted using Cree ceremonial protocol—offering tobacco and cloth, acknowledging their relational authority, and recognizing Elders as co-researchers and co-knowledge producers. This approach reflects what Steinhauer describes as "dialogic inquiry," where knowledge is not extracted but shared, where power is redistributed, and where research becomes a collective act of meaning-making. Through teachings on sweat lodge practice, rites of passage, kinship responsibilities, and land-based healing, the Elders reaffirm the central place of Indigenous frameworks in restoring wellness and balancing spirit. These interviews are not merely qualitative data; they are acts of cultural continuation, ceremonial witnessing, and intergenerational transmission.

Land-Based Ceremony as Method

Ceremony is the pulse of this methodological approach. Land-based ceremonies—including the sweat lodge, water and moon ceremonies, pipe ceremonies, naming ceremonies, and rites of passage—are engaged not as supplementary components but as foundational epistemological tools. They serve as processes of data gathering, interpretation, and transformation. Within this methodological vision, ceremony fosters ensouling—the reunification of mind, body, spirit, and emotion that colonial systems have attempted to fragment. It is through ceremony that many teachings emerge, where clarity arises, and where healing begins. Ceremony guides analytical reflection, grounds ethical decision-making, and anchors the research in land-based responsibilities. This approach resonates with Indigenous scholars who insist that knowledge must be rooted in ceremony and spirit, not separated from them.

The Medicine Wheel as Analytical Framework

We employ the Medicine Wheel as both a conceptual and analytic structure. The Wheel offers a holistic approach to understanding well-being, one that replaces Western diagnostic fragmentation with interrelated quadrants of mental, emotional, physical, and spiritual balance. It provides a framework for interpreting stories, ceremonies, and healing processes. Each direction on the Wheel represents stages of life, relational responsibilities, and teachings about the natural and spiritual worlds. Through this analytic lens, we interpret experiences not as isolated psychological symptoms but as part of a larger relational ecology. The Medicine Wheel becomes a methodological tool for decolonizing mental health frameworks and for restoring Indigenous epistemological balance.

Centering Traditional Therapies as Research Method

One of this book's most innovative methodological contributions is its integration of traditional Cree healing therapies as research methods. Practices such as smudging, sweat lodge, pipe ceremonies, traditional parenting teachings, rites of passage, hide scraping, and berry-picking become tools for inquiry and analysis. These practices are not symbolic; they are experiential pathways through which knowledge is generated. We also explore how Indigenous practitioners have indigenized certain Western therapeutic modalities—such as Inner Child Therapy—by incorporating ceremony, journaling, art, guided imagery, land-based activities, and prayer. These hybrid approaches are culturally generative, reaffirming Indigenous identity while offering healing strategies grounded in Cree values.

Land as Research Partner and Therapeutic Agent

In this methodological approach, the land is not a backdrop—it is a participant, a teacher, a relative. Houle describes fishing, snaring, harvesting plants, canoeing, dogsledding, and wilderness survival practices as therapeutic and pedagogical events. These land-based practices reconnect individuals with ancestral teachings, ecological rhythms, and cultural memory. Land becomes a healer, restoring balance and identity. It teaches patience, humility, endurance, and gratitude. As many Indigenous scholars argue, land is pedagogy, land is law, and land is medicine. Houle's methodology embodies this teaching by treating land as a co-researcher, an active partner in both healing and knowledge production.

Women-Led Knowledge and Matriarchal Pedagogy

As a nêhiyaw iskwêw, our methodological approach is grounded in Indigenous feminist ethics and matriarchal epistemologies. Her work honors women Elders, celebrates women's rites of passage, and centers ceremonies such as moon ceremonies and water ceremonies that have historically been sidelined in health research. This approach answers the calls of Indigenous feminist scholars who argue for restoring women's ceremonial authority and pedagogical leadership as foundational to community health and governance. Our methodology affirms that Indigenous women are carriers of law, language, land knowledge, and healing practices.

Participatory and Community-Engaged Research Design

Our methodology is rooted in community-based participatory research (CBPR). We center community voices, community needs, and community values. Our proposed Land-Based Mental Health Healing Lodge emerges from extensive engagement with Ministikwan Lake Cree Nation, reflecting local aspirations and priorities. This approach positions the research not only as academic work but also as a blueprint for community-driven transformation.

A Decolonial Ethical Framework

Finally, our methodology operates through a fully decolonial ethical commitment. We critique the limitations of institutional ethics review boards and assert the necessity of Indigenous ceremonial ethics, kinship responsibilities, and community accountability. Our ethical framework aligns with Indigenous scholars who affirm that research must be accountable to ancestors, community members, future generations, and the land.

Our methodological framework is a profound offering—one that restores spirit, renews relational accountability, and reclaims Indigenous ways of knowing. Our approach shows that research can be healing, transformative, ceremonial, land-based, and deeply accountable to the community. It is a methodology not only for scholars but also for healers, families, and future generations seeking to restore balance and dignity in the aftermath of colonization.

Overview of the Chapters

The chapters that follow collectively advance a decolonial framework for Indigenous mental health research and practice. Together, we trace the historical and contemporary forces shaping Cree wellness while offering culturally grounded pathways for healing through ceremony, kinship, and land-based pedagogy. Throughout this work, we intentionally weave personal narrative, scholarly literature, and community-based insights to unsettle the dominance of Western psychological frameworks and to restore Cree perspectives as legitimate, ethical, and necessary foundations for Indigenous mental health. What emerges across these chapters is a relational model of wellness—one that positions kinship (*wâhkôhtowin*), land-based ceremony, Cree language, and ancestral teachings as central therapeutic forces. This framework affirms that healing is not an individual act, but a collective, intergenerational responsibility aligned with the seven-generational prophecy guiding our work today.

The opening chapter establishes the transgenerational impacts of colonial violence, particularly the residential school system, and illustrates how unresolved trauma continues to manifest as emotional, psychological, spiritual, and social distress across Indigenous communities. Yet our purpose is not solely diagnostic. Instead, we work toward restoring Indigenous-led healing practices and promoting the resurgence of community-based mental health services grounded in Cree cosmology, ceremony, and kinship. We advocate for mental health approaches that honor Indigenous sovereignty over knowledge, research, and care systems—approaches embodied in the proposed Land-Based Mental Health Healing Lodge, designed as a ceremonial space where families can heal together through land, language, and collective responsibility.

Chapter 2 examines the historical roots and contemporary manifestations of intergenerational and transgenerational trauma. Although substantial scholarship exists, this chapter foregrounds Indigenous scholars who theorize trauma in ways that align with Indigenous worldviews, kinship systems, and ceremonial practices. We critique Western trauma literature for pathologizing Indigenous peoples while failing to acknowledge the colonial structures—residential schools, forced removals, starvation policies, and land dispossession—that produced the harms being "treated." We also emphasize the importance of documenting Indigenous knowledge for future generations. While sacred teachings—ceremony, songs, dances, legends, and natural laws—must be learned experientially, writing becomes another form of safeguarding our intellectual sovereignty so that future generations may continue learning from our Elders. This chapter therefore serves as both a scholarly review and an act of cultural preservation.

Chapter 3 centers *wâhkôhtowin*, the heart of Cree Natural Law, through interviews with three respected Elders from Ministikwan Lake Cree Nation: Eileen Stick, Dorthy Crookedneck, and Annie Partridge. These Elders represent a lineage of knowledge keepers whose teachings embody Cree sovereignty, ceremony, and traditional governance. Their interviews serve as methodological anchors, demonstrating that Indigenous knowledge must be gathered relationally through protocol, humility, and reciprocity. Their teachings emphasize the responsibilities embedded in kinship roles, the sacredness of relationships with land and all Creation, and the necessity of restoring kinship-based governance within contemporary community life. In contexts where colonial systems intentionally fractured Indigenous families, *wâhkôhtowin* becomes a powerful healing framework reconnecting individuals to ancestors, community, land, and purpose.

Chapter 4 explores how traditional Cree therapeutic practices interact with Indigenized Western therapies. While Western models may provide useful tools, they remain insufficient unless they are grounded in ceremony, spirituality, and relational accountability. Ceremony forms the foundation of Indigenous therapeutic practice. Through sweat lodges, pipe ceremonies, fasting camps, rites of passage, and other sacred practices, individuals access emotional release, spiritual guidance, humility, and balance. Ceremony is not symbolic—it is a sophisticated healing system rooted in Indigenous science and cosmology. Our therapeutic practices integrate both traditional healing and adapted Western modalities, always through a Cree lens that centers natural law, kinship, and land-based identity. As Dr. Leona Makokis teaches, each of us carries a gift and a responsibility to contribute to the world. Ceremony helps us rediscover those gifts, reconnect with Creator, and restore the balance necessary to walk *miyo-pimâtisiwin*—the good life.

Although ceremony offers profound therapeutic value, Western institutions—including the NIHB program—continue to deny its legitimacy as mental health treatment. Chapter 5 examines this tension, demonstrating how ceremony functions as healing even when institutional systems fail to recognize it. Drawing from Dr. Diana Steinhauer's teachings, this chapter illustrates how rites of passage, sweat lodges, and naming ceremonies cultivate character, identity, and community responsibility. Ceremony is therefore both therapeutic and political—an assertion of sovereignty over our healing, identities, and cultural continuity.

Chapter 6 returns to personal narrative, offering autobiographical reflections that illustrate how lived experience intersects with cultural teachings and scholarly frameworks. We discuss how ceremony, prayer, physical exercise, and cultural mentorship helped restore balance during periods of grief, depression, and intergenerational pain. These reflections illuminate the embodied dimension of healing—how movement, land-based activities, dopamine and serotonin activation, and traditional foods contribute to emotional resilience. Grounding theory in lived experience, this chapter shows that Cree healing practices are not abstractions but lived, transformative practices.

Chapter 7 introduces the Wapaniwiw Iskwew Land-Based Mental Health Healing Lodge (WILBMHHL), a comprehensive model of Indigenous-led mental health care rooted in Cree cosmology, language, and kinship systems. The lodge integrates ceremony, cultural camps, survival skills, land stewardship, Cree language immersion, and community involvement. This chapter affirms land-based therapy as a primary healing system, predating Western psychology by thousands of years. Its 12-week program addresses trauma from residential schools, the Sixties Scoop, and ongoing colonial violence, offering a replicable model for communities working to implement Indigenous mental health systems.

Chapter 8 presents a transformative re-envisioning of Cree masculinity (*nâpêwiwin*) by reclaiming ancestral gender teachings disrupted through colonial violence. We examine how residential schools, policing, Christian patriarchy, and carceral systems targeted Indigenous men, severing them from emotional expression, kinship responsibilities, and ceremonial roles. Yet this chapter is fundamentally about resurgence. Through sports, dogsledding, hunting, canoeing, sweat lodge, and fatherhood, Cree men restore *sohkêyihtamowin*—strength in mind, body, spirit, and heart. This chapter offers relational, ceremonial, and land-based pathways to healing Indigenous masculinity, teaching men to lead with humility, accountability, and emotional depth.

Chapter 9 focuses on nation-building by examining the intertwined roles of Cree educational and economic sovereignty. By reclaiming teacher education, language programs, land-based schools, and kinship-driven economic systems, Cree communities rebuild the infrastructures that colonial institutions sought to dismantle. Indigenomics—based on reciprocity, sustainability, and kinship—supports thriving cultural camps, sports academies, hide-tanning programs, language immersion schools, and community-owned enterprises. This chapter argues that economic sovereignty directly supports mental health, cultural continuity, and intergenerational resilience.

The overarching goal of this work is to strengthen and empower Indigenous peoples through culturally grounded, relational, and community-driven healing frameworks. Through collective story, scholarship, and land-based practice, we affirm that Indigenous mental health must be rooted in Indigenous sovereignty. The proposed Land-Based Mental Health Healing Lodge embodies this vision and aligns with the seven-generational prophecy—our responsibility to care for future generations with love, integrity, and cultural strength.

2

DECOLONIZING HEALTH FROM TRADITIONAL THERAPIES

Jody Houle (with support from Kevin Lewis and Ranjan Datta)

This chapter examines the vital role of Cree traditional therapeutic practices in reclaiming Indigenous health systems and restoring balance after generations of colonial trauma. Foregrounding the Medicine Wheel, ceremonies, land-based practices, and the Natural Laws that guide Cree life, this chapter demonstrates how these interconnected traditions form a philosophical and therapeutic — framework that promotes holistic well-being. Rather than isolating mental, emotional, spiritual, and physical health into separate categories—as Western clinical systems tend to do—Cree healing practices understand wellness as relational, interdependent, and grounded in community, land, and spirit. Having outlined Indigenous therapeutic foundations and land-based healing practices, this section examines how certain Western somatic techniques may be carefully adapted to support Indigenous wellness without displacing Cree epistemologies.

Central to this approach are the Natural Laws, the values, and ethical teachings that have shaped Indigenous identity and survival since time immemorial. These laws include kistêyihtamowin (respect), wâhkôhtowin (kinship), wîcihitowin (helping one another), sohkêtiyihtamowin (strength), and tâpowakiyihtamowin (belief). Together, they remind individuals of their responsibilities to themselves, their families, the community, the land, and all living beings. The Cree Natural Laws form an ethical and relational framework that guides Cree ways of living, healing, and being in the world. *Kistêyihtamowin* emphasizes respect for oneself, others, Elders, the land, and all forms of life, grounding relationships in humility and responsibility. *Wâhkôhtowin* affirms that individuals exist within networks of kinship that extend beyond immediate family to community, ancestors, future generations, the natural world, and the spirit realm. *Wîcihitowin* reflects the responsibility to support and uplift one another, reinforcing collective care rather

DOI: 10.4324/9781003670308-2

than individualism. *Sohkêtiyihtamowin* speaks to inner and communal strength developed through resilience, endurance, and shared responsibility, particularly in the face of hardship. Finally, *tâpowakiyihtamowin* refers to belief and faith—not only spiritual faith but also trust in teachings, relationships, and ancestral knowledge systems. Together, these laws remind individuals that wellness is relational and holistic, requiring balance between personal accountability and collective responsibility to family, community, land, and all living beings.

These Natural Laws not only provide a moral foundation but also guide traditional therapeutic practices that have sustained Cree people from pre-contact times to today. Elders consistently teach that healing cannot be understood without acknowledging the deep relationships between individuals and their environment. Mental wellness cannot be separated from emotional, physical, or spiritual wellness, nor can any part of well-being be addressed without acknowledging family, community, and land. These teachings are embedded into the life cycle through ceremonies, rites of passage, and other cultural processes that accompany a person from birth into old age. As Elder Joyce Night described, these laws shape reasoning, behavior, and ways of being, making them the foundation for traditional therapy and human development.

For many Cree people, the journey toward healing is also the journey toward *miyo pimâtisowin*—"the good life." Hart (2002) notes that healing requires taking responsibility for one's personal growth, but it is not an individual journey. Miyo pimâtisowin involves family, community, and the wider network of relations that sustain life. As Joyce Night shared, the good life is a lifelong pursuit, involving continuous learning and relearning—about us, our place on the land, our history, and our responsibilities. Achieving this good life requires a community-based approach and a recognition that Western clinical models alone cannot meet the needs of Indigenous peoples. Western therapeutic practices are often invasive, detached, or disconnected from culture, whereas traditional Cree therapy is relational, non-intrusive, and rooted in the holistic development of both individuals and communities (Houle, 1998).

A key element of traditional healing is the involvement of Elders. Elders hold knowledge systems, stories, ceremonial teachings, and historical memory that cannot be replaced by textbooks or clinical manuals. Their guidance ensures continuity of teachings from one generation to the next, strengthening intergenerational bonds that are themselves healing. Youth and Elders must come together—this relational closeness is central to Cree concepts of balanced living. Without Elders, therapeutic practices lose their cultural depth and spiritual grounding.

The Medicine Wheel and Holistic Balance

The Medicine Wheel is one of the most widely recognized Cree teachings connected to healing and wellness. Each direction carries teachings about mental, emotional, spiritual, and physical health. In the framework shared by Elder Walter Linklater (2006), the east represents vision; the south symbolizes understanding of relationships and time; the west encourages reflection on how to apply knowledge; and the north represents wisdom and integration. Healing occurs when all four directions are brought into balance. Each person may resonate with different interpretations or pedagogical versions of the Medicine Wheel, but the underlying value is the same: the Medicine Wheel is a practical tool for balancing the self and navigating life's challenges.

To support culturally grounded healing, the late Elder Walter Linklater proposed a methodology specifically for those working with First Nations communities. The late Elder Walter Linklater was a highly respected Cree Elder, ceremonial leader, and knowledge keeper whose teachings have had a lasting influence on Indigenous healing practices, cultural protocols, and community-based wellness approaches. He was widely known for articulating Cree Natural Law, ceremonial responsibilities, and ethical research and healing methodologies grounded in respect, reciprocity, and relational accountability. This methodology remains a guiding framework today. First, customary offerings of tobacco and cloth are essential when asking for guidance or requesting support for a healing lodge or research project. These offerings signal humility, respect, and reciprocity. Tobacco is a sacred medicine used to show respect, humility, and reciprocity. Offering tobacco signifies a sincere request for guidance, knowledge, prayer, or support and establishes an ethical relationship between the giver and the receiver, particularly when approaching Elders, knowledge keepers, or the spirit world.

Second, the sacred medicines—sage, sweetgrass, cedar, and tobacco—must be used for purification, cleansing, and preparing the mind and spirit for healing. Third, attendance at ceremony is not optional but central to community life and healing, providing opportunities for connection, learning, and support. Ceremony is central to Cree healing practices and serves as a means of restoring balance between the physical, emotional, mental, and spiritual aspects of life. Through prayer, ritual, and collective participation, ceremony strengthens relationships with community, ancestors, land, and spirit, reinforcing cultural continuity and collective wellness. Fourth, smudging and prayer should be conducted at the beginning of meetings, always led by community Elders who also receive tobacco when approached for guidance, prayers, or strength. Fifth, sharing circles and talking circles are core therapeutic methods—spaces where individuals can express their experiences, be witnessed, and receive collective strength. Sixth, it is important to offer translation and interpretation support for Cree-speaking Elders, ensuring their knowledge is carried accurately. Finally, community input and culturally competent programming are non-negotiable. Healing must be grounded in local knowledge, traditions, and languages for it to be meaningful (Linklater, 2006; Night, 2018a).

Ceremony as the Heart of Indigenous Healing

As discussed earlier, ceremony remains foundational. Elders, including Maria Linklater (2021), emphasize that ceremony is not supplementary to healing—it *is* healing. Research must validate what communities already know: sweat lodges, talking circles, rites of passage, land-based activities, and naming ceremonies are therapeutic, powerful, and necessary.

Honoring Elders: Knowledge, Protocol, and Responsibility

Approaching Elders with care, humility, and proper protocol is one of the most important responsibilities within Cree societies. Whether one is offering tobacco for guidance, seeking cultural teachings, or presenting tobacco and cloth in the hope of receiving deeper insight into life's complexities, the foundation of these interactions rests upon profound respect. Elders are the keepers of story, language, memory, and worldview; they hold not only knowledge but also lived experiences that can illuminate the path forward for younger generations. Their teachings help us navigate life's mysteries—its uncertainties, its hardships, and its moments of profound beauty. In traditional Cree society, Elders educate the young through oral storytelling, through creative forms of art and innovation, and through practices that emphasize the interdependence between humans, the land, and the spiritual world. They are the pillars of our communities, and our responsibilities toward them are not optional. Respecting Elders is both a Natural Law and a moral obligation.

Land-Based Healing as Living Medicine

Land-based education and land-based therapeutic practice are central to this work. The land itself heals. Walking on the earth releases anxiety and generates serotonin; it eases tension and clears the mind (Clinebell, 2013). Water, too, is restorative. When I am near lakes or rivers, I reconnect with the earliest experiences of life—when I was held in the water of my mother's womb. Land and water together create conditions for calmness, reflection, and spiritual renewal. They remind me of obligations to care for the land, just as she cares for us. The natural cycle—spring regeneration, summer gathering, fall preparation, and winter endurance—provides a therapeutic rhythm and a cultural anchor.

Land-based therapies provide an avenue to reclaim these connections. Through fishing, hunting, setting nets, harvesting animals, and seasonal land-based activities, individuals and families experience the land as teacher and healer. Water calms the spirit; it reminds us of the womb, where we first experienced safety and connection. Air nourishes our breath; fire grounds our spirit; earth provides stability. These elemental teachings guide us back to our spiritual center.

Canine Therapy and Dogsledding as Relational Healing

Dogs have always been integral to Cree life for hunting, trading, and visiting. Elders often recount how dogs were decorated with regalia, bridles, or woven garments during community gatherings. My (author–3) grandmother told stories of Goodfish Lake, where families dressed their sled dogs in horse bridles for photographs—demonstrating honor, pride, and affection toward these companions. Sled dogs are not simply animals; they are cultural partners, teachers of discipline, and reminders of historic survival. For this reason, canine therapy connects clients to ancestral memory and fosters emotional grounding.

Dogsledding provides another unique avenue for healing. The rhythm of the sled, the steady movement of the dogs, the expansive land stretching out before you, these experiences evoke freedom, clarity, and emotional release. Clients often describe dogsledding as meditative, spiritual, and exhilarating. The partnership between musher and dog requires trust, communication, and respect—qualities that mirror the principles of healthy relationships. The dogs themselves become teachers; they model perseverance, discipline, loyalty, and the importance of working in harmony. For many participants, this experience becomes a pinnacle moment in their healing journey.

Another essential component of these therapeutic models is relational accountability. Healing occurs not only through internal transformation but also through repairing relationships—with oneself, loved ones, ancestors, land, and community. The talking circle, for example, encourages open communication, empathy, and active listening. Each person's voice is valued equally, and the circle itself symbolizes unity, balance, and equality. No one sits above or below another; healing is shared, and each participant contributes to the collective well-being of the group.

Within this ceremonial and relational framework, healing takes form through specific therapeutic practices that integrate story, movement, creativity, and land-based engagement.

Practitioner Reflections and Indigenizing Mental Health Practice

In my (Judy) own experience as a mental health therapist, the role of Elders is deeply interwoven with the therapies I practice. I founded *wâpaniwi-iskwêw* Holistic Healing in 2019, operating out of Cochin, Saskatchewan. Our work involves individual counseling, Inner Child Therapy, Family Group Counseling (FGC), and therapeutic support for those experiencing addictions, depression, suicide ideation, lateral violence, PTSD, ADHD, OCD, bulimia, anorexia, and other conditions affecting emotional and spiritual well-being. Over time, I have carefully Indigenized both Inner Child Therapy and FGC so that they resonate with First Nations clients—our histories, our relationships, our trauma, and our connection to land and spirit.

Within a Cree healing framework, Inner Child Therapy is understood not as an imported psychological technique but as a relational and ceremonial process grounded in Natural Law, kinship, and land-based practice. Rather than centering pathology, this approach emphasizes reconnection—to the self, to ancestral teachings, and to the land—as the foundation of emotional and spiritual healing. The experience was difficult and transformative. It forced me to confront memories and emotions that I had long buried.

We begin with a pipe ceremony, which opens the path to healing by inviting blessings and good energy into the space. Men raise the pipes. The pipe man leads the ceremony. Women sit by the south door. Both the men's and women's pipes are prayed over and passed around the circle four times, acknowledging the four directions. After the ceremony, the pipes are laid down in a way that encourages positive energy flow. As Elders teach, one cannot guide others through healing unless they have confronted their own struggles. The pipe ceremony is a spiritual opening, inviting support from the grandfathers, grandmothers, the animal nations, the sun, the moon, and all of Creation.

The meditation and writing exercises that follow guide individuals back to their inner child. With their dominant hand they write as "big Jody," and with their non-dominant hand they write as "little Jody." This dialogue becomes a form of re-nurturing, a way to reassure the younger self: *I love you, I am here for you, you are safe.*

Art therapy is then used to release energy stored within the body. Working with paint, clay, wire, and other materials, clients reconnect with a long tradition of Indigenous creativity. Our ancestors were artists before contact and remain so today. This creativity is part of our healing. Another component is rabbit snaring, a land-based practice that activates blood memory, resilience, and ancestral knowledge. As Elder Walter Linklater taught, reconnecting with the land activates empathy because it grounds us in gratitude and relationality. Snaring, trapping, and hunting exist not only as survival skills but also as spiritual practices embedded in Cree DNA.

Grief and Loss Therapy is also integral. Clients create bead necklaces that reflect their personal losses. Over time, as their grief changes, they may remove beads and add new ones, symbolizing growth and transformation. This process reflects the five stages of grief—anger, shock, denial, acceptance, and bargaining—and provides a culturally grounded structure for sharing painful stories. I recall participating in grief therapy in Goodfish Lake, Alberta, where we placed handfuls of dirt into a small casket—a powerful symbolic act that helped release long-held emotions.

Days two and three of the program continue with writing and anger management. Instead of hitting a pillow, as in the original program, we strike a hide on a hide-tanning station using a hide scraper. This physical action releases intense emotions and allows clients to transform anger through strength and endurance.

A 20-minute session often brings visible relief, and clients can continue this practice independently. On the final day of the Inner Child Therapy program, the morning is dedicated to one-on-one counseling sessions. These personal conversations provide clients with space to reflect privately on the experiences of the week, to integrate insights, and to prepare for the final components of healing. In the afternoon, we transition into canine therapy—a deeply grounding and relational practice. Canine therapy draws upon the historic and cultural relationship between Cree people and dogs as helpers, protectors, and companions. Working with dogs fosters trust, emotional grounding, responsibility, and relational healing, while reconnecting participants to ancestral knowledge and lived traditions of co-operation and care. We go to the dog yard, feed the dogs, and each client is encouraged to choose one dog with whom they resonate. Establishing a connection with a sled dog requires patience, consistency, and mutual respect. While working dogs cannot be treated like household pets, they respond to clear guidance and firm reassurance. Through this interaction, clients learn how to establish trust, recognize boundaries, express care, and receive comfort.

Family Group Counseling: Restoring Kinship Systems

FGC is the second major form of therapy offered at wâpaniwi-iskwêw Holistic Healing. Like Inner Child Therapy, FGC is a four-day intensive program, but its focus is on the family unit—parents, children, siblings, grandparents, and extended kin. We begin with an opening prayer led by an Elder who provides teachings on *wâhkôhtowin* (kinship). This teaching is essential; it helps families understand their roles, responsibilities, and relationships according to Cree Natural Law. Many Elders use McLeod's (2008) "generation-up wheel" to illustrate kinship relationships. The teaching begins with *niya* (myself), then expands to *nikawiy* (my mother) and *nohtawiy* (my father). It continues outward to grandparents (*nimosôm* and *nohkom*), great-grandparents, and beyond. Through this exercise, families see how each person connects to others across generations and how these relationships extend into the broader community and natural world.

Once kinship has been established through teachings, we enter a healing circle or talking circle. Here, each family member can share their thoughts, feelings, and challenges. Some speak about trauma; others speak about anger, guilt, fear, grief, or disconnection. The circle allows each voice to be heard without judgment and encourages active listening. Sharing stories this way has been a core Cree therapeutic practice for generations; it fosters empathy, clarity, and relational healing. After the circle, each person attends an individual counseling session. Meanwhile, family members engage in art therapy, using the same mediums practiced in Inner Child Therapy: acrylics, oils, watercolors, sculpting materials, and natural elements.

Food is another crucial component of FGC. We prepare meals collectively and emphasize a traditional diet based on Indigenous foods. Traditional foods—such as wild animals, fish, berries, and harvested plants—are integral to physical, emotional, and spiritual health. Reconnecting with traditional diets supports food sovereignty, cultural identity, and holistic wellness, countering the health impacts of colonial disruption to Indigenous food systems. As many Elders say, "Food is mood" (Chisan, 2020). What we eat affects our physical, emotional, and mental well-being. At wâpaniwi-iskwêw Holistic Healing, we also maintain a garden and teach clients about food sovereignty, food security, and healthy eating based on the First Nations, Inuit, and Métis food guide. These teachings reconnect clients to land-based knowledge and help families understand the importance of balanced nutrition.

Another major therapeutic activity during FGC is beaver trapping. In winter, families accompany us onto the lake to locate a beaver lodge. By studying the terrain—often a U-shaped trail in front of the lodge—we determine where to set a conibear trap. Using a chisel, we cut holes in the ice and arrange branches to support the trap. When a beaver is caught, families participate in the traditional process of skinning it. The feet and legs are removed first, followed by careful sheathing of the inner fur lining. The internal organs are cleaned, and the meat is fed to the dogs. Beaver tail, rich in fat and nutrients, is often eaten because it is considered a cultural delicacy. These teachings revive important cultural skills that have been suppressed through colonization, while providing hands-on experiences that reconnect families to the land.

The following day, clients return to the dog yard for dogsledding. Dogsledding is both a cultural practice and a therapeutic activity that promotes grounding, teamwork, endurance, and connection to the land. The rhythmic movement and partnership between humans and dogs support emotional regulation, ancestral memory, and collective healing through shared purpose and trust.

Depending on experience and the season, we hook up four to eight dogs and go on a 10–15 km sled ride across the lake in front of our home. Dogsledding is exhilarating, grounding, and spiritually connecting. The dogs—often a mix of husky and greyhound breeds—embody endurance, loyalty, and intelligence. Experienced mushers rarely reveal their teams' specific bloodlines, as sled dog breeding is a respected and private practice. Having practiced dogsledding for 15 years, I have witnessed its power as a therapeutic method. It reconnects families to ancestral movement and fosters a shared sense of purpose and joy. As such, the four-day structure of both Inner Child Therapy and FGC reflects a symbolic connection to the four directions, four seasons, four stages of life, and the cyclical nature of healing. Each day represents a movement toward balance and wholeness, infused with teachings that honor physical, emotional, mental, and spiritual well-being.

While these practices address individual and family healing, they also respond to much broader histories of colonial disruption, pointing toward collective restoration and responsibility to future generations.

Where Healing Begins: Family, Community, and Miyo Pimâtisowin

In our own work with First Nations communities, one of the most common questions we face is, "Where do we begin?" Our response is always the same: *Healing begins with you, your family, and your community.* These are the foundations upon which future generations will build their lives. If we wish to see our children, grandchildren, and great-grandchildren thrive, we must empower our people with our languages, ceremonies, knowledge systems, and stories. As Elder Albert Houle reminded us in 1998, "We know we have come full circle when we feel the familiarity in our process—when it fits who we are." The signs, teachings, and landmarks of our ancestors are always around us; when we follow them, we recognize ourselves again.

Participants' journal from four stages of their early lives—ages 0–2, 2–6, 6–12, and 12–18. Throughout this process, they address historical impacts, trauma, grief, anger, and self-perception. They engage in a wide range of exercises, such as tension and trauma release, guided imagery, verbal and written dialogues, mirror work, drawing, painting, harvesting, tipi teachings, and one-on-one counseling. Depending on the season, activities include snaring, trapping, hunting, ribbon skirt and shirt making, canine therapy, harvesting animals, setting fishing nets, and cleaning fish. This therapeutic approach is grounded in Cree Natural Laws and strengthened through the protocols of tobacco and cloth offerings.

Foundational Land-Based and Cultural Practices in Cree Healing

Cree healing practices are grounded in land-based, relational, and ceremonial ways of living that predate colonial intervention and continue to sustain community wellness today. These practices—including ceremony, dogsledding, traditional foodways, and relationships with animal helpers—are not supplementary to healing; they are foundational expressions of Cree epistemology and Natural Law. Together, they situate wellness within reciprocal relationships among individuals, families, communities, the land, animals, ancestors, and the spirit world.

Ceremony provides the spiritual framework within which healing occurs. Practices such as pipe ceremony, smudging, prayer, and the offering of tobacco establish ethical relationships rooted in humility, respect, and reciprocity. Ceremony creates protected spaces where individuals are supported by the Creator, ancestors, and spirit helpers, reinforcing the understanding that healing is both collective and relational rather than individual or isolated. Land-based practices further anchor healing in lived experience. Activities such as hunting, trapping, fishing, harvesting, and seasonal movement reconnect individuals to ancestral knowledge carried through blood memory and relationship to place. These practices cultivate patience, responsibility, gratitude, and strength while restoring balance between the physical, emotional, mental, and spiritual aspects of the self.

Dogsledding holds particular significance within Cree culture and healing traditions. Historically essential for transportation, survival, and community connection, dogsledding reflects a deeply relational practice built on trust, communication, discipline, and mutual care between humans and dogs. As a therapeutic practice, dogsledding fosters grounding, emotional regulation, teamwork, and ancestral continuity, reinforcing teachings about endurance, responsibility, and collective movement across the land.

Traditional food systems are equally central to healing. The preparation and sharing of Indigenous foods—such as fish, wild game, berries, and medicinal plants—support physical health while strengthening cultural identity, food sovereignty, and relational accountability. Food is understood as both medicine and teaching, linking nourishment to land stewardship, seasonal cycles, and intergenerational knowledge transmission.

Together, these cultural practices form the ethical and experiential foundation upon which Cree therapeutic approaches are built. They affirm that healing is inseparable from land, culture, ceremony, and relationship, and they provide the framework through which contemporary therapeutic programs are understood and practiced throughout this chapter. Grounded in these foundational practices and teachings, the following sections describe how Cree healing principles are enacted through specific therapeutic programs and lived experiences.

Ceremony, Land, and Relational Accountability

As outlined earlier, dogsledding is both a cultural practice and a therapeutic method; within this program, it becomes a lived expression of trust, responsibility, and collective healing. These practices—Inner Child Therapy, FGC, land-based teachings, fishing, trapping, dogsledding, art therapy, and ceremony—embody the revitalization of traditional Cree therapeutic models. They recognize the land and water as living medicines. Richard Katz (2017) writes, "Our land is our life…it expresses the spirit of our lives…When we treat it with respect, it feeds us. We care for it and it cares for us." But he also warns that ongoing destruction of land fundamentally damages Indigenous well-being. Traditional Cree therapies strengthen resilience against this harm by rooting healing in spiritual, cultural, and ecological relationships.

Katz (2017) extends this understanding through the teachings of the late Elder Danny Musqua, who emphasized resilience, protection, and responsibility.

Vizina spoke of maintaining and carrying forward our traditional knowledge systems as living frameworks that protect the next generations from spiritual, emotional, and cultural harm (Vizina, 2010). Healing, therefore, is not simply the alleviation of symptoms—it is the reclamation of Indigenous epistemologies that have been systematically targeted through colonial policies.

These worldviews and paradigms are not abstract philosophies; they are lived practices that structure how First Nations peoples relate to land, kinship, ceremony, education, governance, and self. They are essential components of mental, emotional, spiritual, and physical well-being. As First Nations people continue to face intergenerational and transgenerational trauma, along with ongoing systemic racism embedded in Western patriarchal structures, revitalizing these knowledge systems becomes more urgent than ever (Acoose, 1996). Our therapeutic approaches must therefore confront not only individual trauma but also the broader historical context that shaped these wounds.

Food, Land, and Decolonizing Wellness

The forced disruption of traditional diets, displacement from land, environmental contamination, and the introduction of processed foods have profoundly affected Indigenous well-being. Historically, First Nations people maintained active lifestyles and consumed nutrient-rich diets consisting of game meats, fish, berries, medicinal plants, and seasonal vegetables. Meals were not constant or excessive; they were aligned with seasonal cycles, community rhythms, and the body's natural needs.

Colonization also altered how Indigenous communities relate to their bodies. Forced starvation in residential schools, food deprivation, inadequate diets, and the shaming of Indigenous cultural practices created long-lasting impacts on eating habits and self-perception. Poverty continues to prevent many families from accessing fresh, whole foods, creating cycles of nutritional imbalance and emotional distress. Understanding these root causes helps us approach food-related healing without stigma or judgment. Food, in this sense, becomes both medicine and history—a portal through which we reconnect to cultural identity and restore balance to the body.

These practices foster pride, empowerment, and identity. They teach clients that healing is not merely about recovering from harm; it is about reconnecting to who they have always been.

Healing as Resistance and Cultural Survival

Traditional healing is not static. It evolves and adapts, just as our ancestors did. At wâpaniwi-iskwêw Holistic Healing, we intentionally integrate contemporary therapeutic methods with Indigenous pedagogies to address the mental health needs of today's First Nations people. While the Western clinical model often separates mind, body, emotion, and spirit, Indigenous healing emphasizes their inseparability. Experiences of trauma, grief, loss, and emotional pain reverberate through all four aspects of the self. Healing must therefore be holistic—interweaving narrative, ceremony, movement, land-based activity, artistic expression, spiritual connection, and kinship restoration.

Decolonizing Western Approaches

In many Western therapeutic contexts, Dr. David Berceli has developed a series of techniques designed to help individuals release deep muscular tension and relieve trauma stored in the body. His Tension and Trauma Release Exercises (TRE) have gained widespread recognition for their ability to access stress held within the lower back, pelvis, and legs—areas that often carry the physical weight of emotional and psychological strain. Although these exercises originate from a Western framework, they offer possibilities that Indigenous communities could adapt and integrate within culturally grounded approaches to healing. Indigenous peoples have always been adaptable, drawing from new tools when they serve collective wellness, and TRE may offer additional methods for supporting physical and emotional balance.

Richard Katz (2017) offers an important critique of Western psychology, noting that its dominant traditions often impose frameworks that limit the full human experience. He states that Western psychology is largely defined by two prevailing approaches: the psychoanalytic model, with its deterministic worldview and heavy focus on pathology and negative emotion; and the behavioristic model, with its reductionist and mechanistic view of human behavior. These approaches, while influential, can constrain understandings of healing by prioritizing dysfunction rather than relational, emotional, or spiritual dimensions. For Indigenous peoples—whose worldviews emphasize balance among the mental, emotional, physical, and spiritual realms—such models can feel insufficient or even harmful. Yet, Katz suggests that Western insights, when carefully examined and culturally adapted, may offer complementary strategies for addressing the mental health crises Indigenous communities face.

Structural Violence, Mental Health Inequities, and Urgency

The urgency of rethinking therapeutic approaches becomes evident when examining the stark social realities Indigenous peoples in Canada continue to experience. Katz highlights distressing statistics that reflect ongoing systemic inequities. Indigenous peoples in Saskatchewan, for example, are dramatically overrepresented in areas such as unemployment, inadequate health care access, limited educational opportunities, and substandard housing. These disparities are not isolated; they intersect with high rates of incarceration, illustrating how colonial systems continue to criminalize Indigenous bodies and identities.

Drawing on Statistics Canada data, as synthesized and discussed by Katz (2017), these disparities reveal a painful truth. Although Indigenous children comprise approximately 25 percent of Saskatchewan's youth population, they account for nearly 85 percent of children in foster care. While only about 10 percent of non-Indigenous households require major repairs, more than half of all homes on First Nations reserves need significant structural work. Indigenous adults represent roughly 10 percent of Saskatchewan's population yet make up approximately 57 percent of the incarcerated population. Most devastatingly, suicide rates among First Nations and Inuit peoples are reported to be up to 11 times higher than those of non-Indigenous populations. These figures do not simply reflect socio-economic inequality; rather, they point to the enduring impacts of colonial violence, systemic racism, and intergenerational trauma.

A powerful cultural component of FGC is learning to fish or set a fishing net. Families venture out onto the land to practice the skills that once sustained entire communities. The teaching is simple but profound: "If you show a man how to fish, you feed him for a day. If you show him how to set a net, you feed him for a lifetime." Fishing was traditionally a responsibility shared by both men and women, and this gender-inclusive teaching continues today. The next day, we return to the nets to gather the fish and demonstrate how to clean different species—whitefish, pickerel, jackfish, and mariah. Clients learn to smoke the fish or prepare it for meals, and some create fish-scale art, another traditional practice tied to creativity and cultural continuity.

Healing Circles, Listening, and Emotional Safety

On the third day of FGC, we return to the healing circle. Each family member is once again given space to speak. This repetition is important because healing does not occur all at once; it unfolds gradually through repeated opportunities to reflect and be heard. Listening is one of the most important aspects of Cree healing. Sometimes a person needs nothing more than a compassionate listener—someone who hears without judgment or interruption. Smudging is used to clear negative energy when emotions run high. The use of smudge—sage, sweetgrass, cedar, or tobacco—creates a safe environment where emotions can be acknowledged and transformed (Chisan, 2020).

Colonization, Diet, and the Disruption of Indigenous Foodways

In contrast, modern dietary patterns—shaped by colonization, poverty, food insecurity, and limited access to traditional harvesting grounds—have resulted in high rates of diabetes, heart disease, obesity, and other chronic conditions

(Milburn, 2004; Sarkar et al., 2020). Many of these conditions were virtually unknown in pre-contact societies. For this reason, Indigenous healing must also include a decolonization of food systems. Through gardening, harvesting, fishing, trapping, and land-based education, wâpaniwi-iskwêw Holistic Healing reintroduces families to the foods that sustained their ancestors for millennia. These practices are not merely nutritional interventions; they are acts of cultural reclamation and self-determination.

Contemporary Therapies as Living Expressions of Cree Healing

In many ways, Inner Child Therapy and FGC serve as contemporary expressions of ancient Cree healing approaches. Although they incorporate modern psychological methods, they remain firmly rooted in cultural teachings, ceremonies, and land-based practices. These therapies rely on a holistic understanding of wellness—one that honors Natural Law, ancestral teachings, and Indigenous worldviews. Trauma healing within an Indigenous framework cannot rely solely on talk therapy; it must integrate emotional release, physical movement, ceremony, kinship teachings, creativity, and connection to land.

For example, the anger management component of Inner Child Therapy mirrors traditional teachings about releasing negative energy. When clients strike the hide with a scraper, they engage in a somatic expression of emotional release. The motion, intensity, and rhythmic contact between the scraper and hide become a channel through which unexpressed grief, anger, shame, and frustration find release. This practice is both therapeutic and rooted in traditional tanning techniques—another way the land and cultural knowledge guide the healing process.

Similarly, the grief and loss component integrates both traditional and contemporary understanding of grief. The bead-stringing activity allows clients to externalize their traumatic memories, giving each event a symbolic representation. Over time, as clients heal, they may choose to remove beads, restring them, or reshape the necklace to reflect new meaning. This mirrors Cree teachings that grief is cyclical, evolving, and deeply tied to one's relationships with ancestors and the land.

Storytelling and Narrative Reclamation

Whether through talking circles, journaling, or dialogue between "big self" and "little self," clients participate in narrative reclamation. Storytelling is a core element of Indigenous pedagogy. Elders have long used stories to teach about relationships, consequences, emotions, resilience, ethics, and the spirit world. By integrating storytelling and narrative reconstruction, Inner Child Therapy provides clients with an opportunity to reconnect their inner child with their adult self, reframe past experiences, and establish emotional safety.

Another critical teaching present in these traditional therapies is the concept of interdependence. In Western therapeutic models, healing is often seen as a solitary journey, with emphasis placed on individual responsibility. In contrast, Cree healing frameworks emphasize collective responsibility, relational accountability, and interconnectedness. Healing the individual means healing the family, the community, and the land. Trauma is rarely carried alone; therefore, healing should not be carried alone either.

Collectively, the teachings, ceremonies, and practices woven throughout Inner Child Therapy and FGC demonstrate the profound strength of Indigenous healing systems. These approaches remind us that wellness is a dynamic equilibrium—one that shifts across time, seasons, stages of life, and personal circumstances. Land-based teachings, ceremonies, kinship frameworks, and cultural practices do more than address symptoms; they restore identity, belonging, and connection to ancestral memory. They reaffirm to each participant that they are part of a larger circle of life, carrying responsibilities not only to themselves but also to their families, communities, and the natural world.

This reconnection extends deeply into food systems. As discussed earlier, colonization disrupted traditional diets and introduced unhealthy food patterns. Restoring Indigenous foodways is not simply about nutrition; it is about sovereignty, cultural survival, and holistic wellness. Gardening, harvesting, processing traditional foods, and preparing meals collectively expose clients to healthier alternatives while reinforcing cultural pride. Food sovereignty is part of healing because it re-establishes autonomy over what we consume and how we care for our bodies. In reconnecting with the foods our ancestors ate, we reclaim the nourishment—physical and spiritual—that sustained us.

Physiological and Cultural Benefits of Land-Based Healing

Mental health cannot be siloed from these broader social and cultural realities. When clients participate in land-based activities, they experience physiological benefits—reduced stress hormones, increased serotonin, natural regulation of dopamine, and elevated endorphins. They also experience cultural benefits—reconnection with the land, honoring Natural Law, strengthening kinship bonds, and developing practical skills. These multidimensional benefits underscore why Indigenous healing traditions must be centered in mental health services for First Nations communities.

Ceremony is foundational to Indigenous therapeutic practice and underpins all healing processes described in this work. Whether expressed through pipe ceremony, smudging, or the offering of tobacco, ceremony grounds healing within spiritual relationship and relational accountability. It creates a sacred and protected space in which individuals are supported by the Creator, ancestors, spirit helpers, the land, and the community. Ceremony reinforces core values such as humility, gratitude, respect, and responsibility, which guide ethical practice and ensure that healing remains culturally grounded. Within this framework, healing is understood not as an isolated or individual act, but as a collective and relational journey that connects personal wellness to family, community, land, and spirit.

Relational Accountability

As clients move through these therapeutic cycles, many experience a profound shift in identity and self-understanding. They begin to see themselves not through the lens of trauma or colonial harm but as part of a long continuum of resilient, resourceful, and spiritually grounded Indigenous peoples. This shift is often one of the most powerful outcomes of the four-day intensives—it restores dignity, agency, and cultural pride.

All of these practices reaffirm a fundamental truth: Indigenous healing is relational, experiential, and place based. It cannot be confined to textbooks or clinical offices. It thrives in open air, in ceremony, in kinship circles, in hands-on teachings, and in connection to the land. It honors the wisdom of Elders, the resilience of ancestors, and the sacred responsibilities we carry as Indigenous peoples.

In today's world, where many Indigenous communities continue to face compounded challenges—mental health crises, addictions, violence, poverty, racism, and environmental degradation—traditional healing practices offer pathways toward restoration. They provide culturally grounded frameworks that strengthen identity, re-establish belonging, and nurture spiritual wellness. They remind us that healing is not linear; it moves in cycles, often returning us to teachings we thought we had already learned. Each return deepens our understanding and strengthens our spirit.

As wâpaniwi-iskwêw Holistic Healing continues to grow, the commitment remains the same: to honor Natural Law, uphold cultural integrity, empower individuals and families, and revitalize the knowledge systems that sustained Indigenous peoples for generations. Whether through Inner Child Therapy, FGC, land-based education, canine therapy, ceremony, or traditional foods, the goal is singular—to help our people heal in ways that respect who we are, where we come from, and who we are becoming.

Ultimately, traditional Indigenous therapies are not only interventions, but they are also embodiments of cultural survival. They offer pathways for future generations to break cycles of trauma, resist systemic oppression, and step into their full spiritual, emotional, mental, and physical health. Our teachings, stories, ceremonies, and relationships are medicines—and as long as we continue to practice them, our spirits will continue to thrive. They are as follows:

The obedience framework illustrates a relational system of Cree values that guide individual development, family well-being, and community resilience. At the foundation of the framework is **obedience**, which supports the process of **good child rearing**. Through proper guidance and nurturing, children learn the core value of **respect**, which serves as the central principle from which other virtues emerge.

Respect is expressed through **humility**, **happiness**, **love**, and **faith**, all of which contribute to the development of healthy relationships and moral character. Faith reinforces the importance of **good child rearing**, while also fostering the values of **sharing** and **cleanliness**, which are essential for maintaining harmony within families and communities.

The practice of sharing and cleanliness strengthens social bonds and cultivates **kindliness** and **strength**. Strength is understood not only as physical endurance but also as emotional, spiritual, and moral resilience. Kindliness reinforces this strength by encouraging compassion, generosity, and care for others. Together, these values provide individuals with the capacity to maintain **control during adversity**, symbolized in the framework as the ability to withstand the "flaps from the wind," or the challenges and disruptions encountered throughout life.

The ability to remain grounded during difficult times generates **hope**, which leads to **ultimate protection**. Protection is understood in a holistic sense, encompassing physical safety, emotional well-being, spiritual balance, cultural continuity, and collective security. The framework concludes with hope, emphasizing that hope is both the outcome of living according to these teachings and the foundation for future generations. As such, the model represents a cyclical process in which obedience, respect, sharing, strength, and hope continuously reinforce one another, sustaining family, community, and intergenerational well-being.

This obedience word graph illustrates a relational and interdependent value system rooted in principles of care, respect, and collective responsibility, likely reflective of Indigenous pedagogical and ethical teachings. At its core, *Respect*, *Sharing*, and *Kindliness* emerge as foundational values that anchor the broader moral framework. From *Respect* grows *Obedience*, *Humility*, *Happiness*, and *Love*, all of which contribute to *Good Child Rearing*—a critical element of sustaining communal well-being. *Sharing*, linked with practices like *Cleanliness* and *Faith*, bridges to emotional and social *Strength*. *Kindliness*, in turn, is connected to both *Strength* and the capacity to *Control Flaps from Wind*—a metaphorical reference to maintaining balance and stability amid disruption—ultimately leading to *Hope* and *Ultimate Protection*. The graph thus visually expresses how ethical, emotional, and practical virtues intertwine to sustain life, family, and community, reinforcing a cyclical understanding of protection, nurture, and intergenerational continuity.

The *mîkiwâhpa* further represents the skirt of the woman, as women are the keepers of the tipi lodge; it is they who put the tipi up when moving or situating camp. Today I often see more women partaking in this role of setting up the tipi,

FIGURE 2.1 The figure explains Sharlene Swiftewolfe, Darla Campbell and Kevin and I's daughter in the tipi smoking and tanning hide. They are also cooking over the camo fire and tasting the traditional fin Indigenous cuisine.

as it is our duty. We as women must take back our role and reinforce our given right to set up the *mîkiwâhpa* (Figure 2.1).

Elders as Pillars of Knowledge and Ethical Guidance

Elders embody the wisdom of lived experience—knowledge transmitted through oral storytelling, ceremony, visual arts, and generations of cultural innovation. Their role in traditional societies has always been to educate, to guide, and to uphold the spiritual and cultural foundations of the community. They teach us how to live in balance, how to honor our responsibilities, and how to walk gently with ourselves and others. In every sense, Elders remain the pillars of our nations.

I carry these teachings into my work as a Mental Health Therapist and founder of wâpaniwi-iskwêw Holistic Healing, located in Cochin, Saskatchewan. Since opening my practice in 2019, I have supported clients through a range of challenges including addictions, depression, suicide ideation, PTSD, OCD, ADHD, eating disorders, lateral violence, and intergenerational trauma. Through years of clinical practice, personal lived experience, and cultural learning, I have Indigenized Inner Child Therapy and FGC to meet the distinct emotional, cultural, and spiritual needs of First Nations people. My practice integrates land-based healing because land and water are not just physical environments—they are medicines that heal the spirit, calm the mind, and restore emotional balance.

My first experience with Inner Child Therapy came during a period of profound grief after losing my stepfather and sister-in-law to the spirit world. The exercises were emotionally challenging, yet deeply transformative. The program stayed with me—not only the healing it offered but also the strength of my psychologist, Cathy Wheaton, whose guidance shaped my understanding of inner-child work. Over time, I adapted and expanded the therapy to align with Cree Natural Law, traditional teachings, and land-based methods. The program now operates as a four-day intensive therapy that begins in ceremony and moves through emotional, physical, creative, and spiritual healing.

The first step is always ceremony. We begin with a pipe ceremony to welcome blessings for the week. The Pipeman leads the ceremony, with men seated on one side of the lodge and women on the other, near the south door. Both the men's and women's pipes are prayed over, then passed around the circle four times, acknowledging the four directions. When the pipes are laid down, we invite good energy into the space and honor the protocols that make healing possible. Elders remind us that we cannot help someone unless we ourselves have walked through struggle and healing (Howse, 2006). The pipe ceremony opens the doorway for spiritual guidance from grandfathers, grandmothers, animals, sky beings, and all the elements of Creation.

After ceremony, participants begin guided journaling. Using their dominant hand, they write as their "adult self," and with their non-dominant hand, they write as their "inner child." The dialogue between these selves helps clients re-nurture, reassure, and re-parent the emotional wounds rooted in childhood. This exercise builds emotional safety and compassion for oneself—a foundation for deeper healing.

Art therapy follows. Using acrylics, oils, watercolors, sculpting materials, or wire for spirit-animal creation, clients express emotions through creative mediums. Art has always been integral to Indigenous cultures—long before contact, our people were painters, sculptors, beadworkers, and innovators. Creativity connects clients to ancestral memory and provides a non-verbal channel for emotional release.

Land-based practices follow. Rabbit snaring reconnects participants with survival skills grounded in blood memory and epigenetics. Walter Linklater (2006) taught that working with the land awakens the "roots of empathy," making people kinder and more connected. Hunting, trapping, and snaring allow participants to reconnect with their cultural DNA and cultivate grounding through purposeful activity.

Grief and Loss Therapy is another key element. Using a string and beads, clients create a necklace where each bead represents a traumatic memory. Over time, as healing progresses, clients may remove or rearrange beads, acknowledging the changing relationship with grief. This practice reflects the five stages of grief—anger, shock, denial, acceptance, and bargaining—yet situates healing within an Indigenous worldview that sees grief as cyclical, relational, and spiritually guided. One of the grief exercises I once participated in involved placing dirt into a small symbolic casket—a powerful act of releasing pain to the Creator.

Anger Management Therapy takes place on the hide-tanning rack. Instead of hitting a pillow, clients release their emotions by striking a hide with a scraper. This somatic activity allows for deep emotional release—anger, sadness, frustration, grief—all channeled physically. Clients strike the hide for at least 20 minutes, learning a method they can continue to use privately when emotions build. This practice heals the spirit through movement and replicates traditional hide-processing techniques.

On the final day of Inner Child Therapy, we spend the morning in one-on-one counseling. In the afternoon, we transition to canine therapy. Clients go to the dog yard, feed the dogs, and choose one to bond with. Working dogs cannot be treated as pets—they require respect, structure, and clarity. Yet the emotional connection formed during canine therapy is powerful. Dogs were our original helpers, transporters, and protectors. My grandmother often told stories about community members dressing their dogs in horse bridles and taking portraits—an expression of love, pride, and companionship. Dogsledding remains a core cultural practice for many Cree families, and we keep this tradition strong through our therapeutic work.

FGC is another major offering at wâpaniwi-iskwêw Holistic Healing. This four-day model focuses on restoring kinship systems disrupted by colonial trauma. We begin with an opening prayer and teachings on *wâhkôhtowin* (kinship), often guided by McLeod's "generation-up wheel" (2008). Starting from *niya* (me), families map their relationships through mothers (*nikawiy*), fathers (*nohtawiy*), grandparents (*nimosôm*, *nohkom*), and onward. The teaching helps clients understand their place within the larger universe and reinforces the interconnectedness of all Creation.

The healing circle that follows allows each family member to speak openly about their struggles. Emotional pain—spiritual wounds, family conflicts, trauma histories—emerges in a supportive environment. Storytelling is core to Indigenous healing and allows participants to externalize feelings while cultivating empathy for one another. After the circle, each person receives individual counseling and participates in art therapy, allowing for multilayered emotional processing.

Food is another essential aspect of FGC. We prepare traditional meals together because food influences mood, energy, and emotional balance (Chisan, 2020).

Gardening, harvesting, and adhering to the First Nations, Inuit, and Métis food guide introduce clients to decolonized food knowledge. Food sovereignty is tied to physical and spiritual well-being, and reconnecting with ancestral foods strengthens cultural identity.

The land-based portion of FGC includes ice fishing or net-setting. As Elders say, "Show a man how to fish and you feed him for a day; show him how to set a net and you feed him for a lifetime." Women also traditionally fished for their families, and these teachings honor that history. Clients learn to clean various fish—whitefish, pickerel, jackfish, mariah—and may smoke the fish or use the scales in artwork.

On the third day, we return to the healing circle for deeper sharing. Listening is often more healing than speaking. Sometimes clients only need to be heard—not judged, not analyzed, but witnessed. Smudging helps cleanse emotional heaviness and renew the energy of the circle.

In the afternoon, we set a beaver trap using conibear traps. Locating the beaver house, identifying the U-shaped trail, chiseling holes in the ice, and placing the trap teaches patience and skill. Once trapped, the beaver is used respectfully: the fur for mitts, the meat for the dogs, and the tail as a cultural delicacy. These teachings reconnect families to responsibilities of harvesting and remind them of the deep cultural significance of animal helpers.

The next day, we return to the dog yard for a dogsledding session, hooking up four to eight dogs for a 10–15 km ride. Dogsledding fosters teamwork, grounding, and joy. Each dog has a unique temperament, and working with them teaches clients patience, discipline, communication, and trust. For many families, this experience is transformative, awakening ancestral memory and cultural pride.

Collectively, these land-based and culturally grounded therapies demonstrate the revitalization of Indigenous healing in mental health. The land and water are our original medicines. Richard Katz (2017) reminds us that the land embodies our spirit, and when we show it respect, it sustains us. He also warns that when land is desecrated, our peoples' spirits are harmed. The teachings of Elder Danny Musqua in Cardinal and Hildebrand, (2000) emphasize resilience, cultural protection, and the necessity of maintaining traditional knowledge systems. As First Nations people, our worldviews and paradigms are essential to our well-being. We must preserve them to protect future generations. Healing cannot occur without acknowledging and dismantling systemic racism, colonial violence, and intergenerational trauma (Acoose, 1996). Mental health healing is entwined with cultural reclamation. Food systems also reveal the ongoing impacts of colonization. Before contact, our ancestors ate one nutritious meal a day, exercised regularly, and lived according to seasonal cycles. Diseases such as diabetes and obesity were absent. Colonial disruption introduced poverty, processed foods, and restricted access to traditional harvesting grounds.

Decolonizing Foods

Decolonizing food systems is therefore essential in mental health work. Decolonizing food systems within mental health work can be achieved through the intentional reintegration of Indigenous food knowledge, land-based practices, and community-led food sovereignty initiatives into therapeutic programming. Practically, this includes creating opportunities for clients and families to participate in traditional harvesting activities such as fishing, hunting, trapping, gardening, and food preparation, guided by Elders and knowledge keepers. Mental health programs can incorporate shared meal preparation using traditional foods as part of healing circles or group therapy, recognizing food as both nourishment and medicine. Supporting community gardens, seed-saving initiatives, and the teaching of seasonal food cycles further reconnects individuals to land-based knowledge disrupted by colonization. At an institutional level, decolonizing food systems also involves advocating for policies that increase access to traditional harvesting territories, reduce barriers to hunting and fishing, and support Indigenous-led nutrition programs. Importantly, mental health practitioners must approach food-related healing through a trauma-informed lens that acknowledges histories of forced starvation, residential schools, and food insecurity, ensuring that food is reintroduced as a source of safety, dignity, and cultural reconnection rather than control or shame.

Trauma carried through generations stems from residential schools, the Indian Act, reserve systems, forced starvation, and the Sixties Scoop. These realities continue to shape stress levels, emotional well-being, and family dynamics today. Through culturally grounded therapy, land-based healing, ceremony, and reconnection to ancestral knowledge, we support individuals and families in restoring balance. These practices empower our people to reclaim identity, honor Natural Law, and heal from the impacts of colonialism. They ensure that the next generations inherit not only survival skills but also the spiritual and cultural strength to thrive. While this chapter centers Cree therapeutic traditions, it also later considers how selectively adapted Western somatic approaches may complement Indigenous healing when guided by cultural protocol and relational accountability.

In conclusion, Indigenous peoples remain some of the most pathologized communities in the world, forced to endure conditions often described as "fourth world"—marked by poverty, marginalization, and systemic neglect within a wealthy nation-state. High rates of mental illness, substance misuse, and trauma are not inherent characteristics of Indigenous peoples; they are the direct outcomes of policies, institutions, and ideologies imposed through colonialism. For generations, Western systems have belittled, dismissed, and devalued Indigenous intellect, culture, and humanity. Healing, therefore, requires more than therapeutic exercises—it demands a return to pre-contact Indigenous epistemologies and ontologies grounded in Natural Law, relational accountability, and spiritual balance. We must reawaken our foundational teachings of love, respect, strength, humility, and caring. These values sustained our nations long before colonization and can guide us once again. By embracing culturally relevant healing practices, while selectively integrating beneficial tools such as TRE, Indigenous communities can build pathways that restore identity, strengthen families, and empower future generations. Healing becomes not only an individual journey but also a collective movement to reclaim our humanity, dignity, and *miyo-pimâtisowin*—the good life.

3

WÂHKÔHTOWIN

Rethinking Health Research from Kinships Perspectives

Jody Houle (with support from Kevin Lewis and Ranjan Datta)

This chapter opens by situating wâhkôhtowin as both a philosophical foundation and a living mental health system. This chapter examines mental health research and practice through wâhkôhtowin, the Cree philosophical and ethical principle that defines all relationships—between people, land, spirit, ancestors, and future generations. Rooted in Cree Natural Law, wâhkôhtowin shapes how we understand belonging, responsibility, healing, and collective well-being. For generations, this kinship system structured how communities cared for mental, emotional, physical, and spiritual health. The contemporary mental health crisis facing Indigenous peoples cannot be understood without acknowledging the systematic dismantling of these kinship structures by colonial institutions, particularly the residential school system. Drawing on interviews with a number of *nêhiyaw iskwêwak*—Elders recognized as ceremonial knowledge holders—this chapter explores how wâhkôhtowin can guide the development of a decolonized, culturally grounded mental health research framework. Their teachings illuminate how traditional practices such as sweat lodges, smudging, land-based healing, ceremony, and Cree language revitalization can restore balance and strengthen identities disrupted by colonialism.

While personal reflection informs parts of this chapter, it does not dominate the narrative. Instead, personal narrative is used sparingly and intentionally, as a reminder that Indigenous research is relational, embodied, and accountable. This chapter's goal is not only to analyze the historical and ongoing impacts of colonial mental health paradigms but also to offer practical pathways for students, researchers, clinicians, and community workers seeking to implement decolonizing principles in diverse contexts. Through a wâhkôhtowin-centered framework, this chapter envisions a future where

DOI: 10.4324/9781003670308-3

Indigenous mental health research honors ancestral knowledge, supports community self-determination, and strengthens Indigenous resilience for generations to come.

This chapter unfolds in five parts. It first introduces wâhkôhtowin as a Cree philosophical foundation for understanding mental health. It then situates contemporary Indigenous mental health challenges within the colonial dismantling of kinship systems. This chapter centers on Elders' teachings and traditional healing practices as Indigenous mental health systems. Building on these teachings, it proposes a wâhkôhtowin-centered framework for decolonizing mental health research and practice. Finally, this chapter closes by reflecting on community healing and future directions.

wâhkôhtowin as the Foundation of Mental Health and Human Relationship

At its core, wâhkôhtowin is the ethical commitment to live in good relations. More than a cultural value, it is a comprehensive worldview that structures social, emotional, and spiritual life. Before colonization, kinship responsibilities extended far beyond biological family to include extended relatives, clans, community members, and the land itself. This relational network supported the development of identity, belonging, emotional regulation, and social responsibility. In this framework:

- Children were raised not only by parents but also by aunties, uncles, grandparents, and ceremonial helpers.
- Emotional distress was viewed as relational imbalance, not individual pathology.
- Healing required restoration of relationships—with people, land, and spirit.
- The community understood itself as collectively responsible for each person's wellness.

wâhkôhtowin therefore functioned as a holistic mental health system, integrating emotional well-being, spiritual grounding, identity development, and social accountability.

Colonial Disruption and the Breakdown of Kinship Systems

The residential school system deliberately targeted Indigenous kinship structures. Children were taken from their parents, elders, and land-based teachings, severing the relational bonds that formed the foundation of Indigenous wellness. Many were forbidden to speak their languages, practice ceremonies, or maintain cultural identities. This systematic disruption created an intergenerational rupture that continues to shape mental health outcomes today.

As the Truth and Reconciliation Commission (2015) notes, the psychological, spiritual, physical, and emotional harms inflicted by residential schools have persisted across generations, contributing to high rates of depression, anxiety, addiction, suicide, and complex trauma.

Statistical indicators—overrepresentation in foster care, incarceration, homelessness, and poor health outcomes—are symptoms of disrupted kinship systems rather than reflections of Indigenous failure. As many Elders assert, "We did not have this much mental illness before colonization." Western society pathologizes Indigenous peoples while failing to recognize that the current crisis is a direct result of colonial violence, systemic racism, and generations of forced cultural suppression. The need to rebuild kinship structures through wâhkôhtowin is therefore not only cultural, but it is also a mental health imperative.

Elders as Knowledge Holders: Protecting Epistemological and Methodological Integrity

The Elder narratives that follow are not explanatory repetitions but lived demonstrations of these epistemological principles in practice. Indigenous Elders are often described as "living libraries." Their epistemologies, ontologies, axiologies, and methodologies embody generations of accumulated wisdom. Interviews with Sundance Lodge Holders Dorothy Crookedneck and Annie Partridge, and Pipe Carrier Eileen Stick, reaffirm the central role Elders play in teaching and sustaining mental and spiritual wellness. Working with Elders requires relational accountability and adherence to proper protocols, including offering tobacco and cloth, approaching with humility, and honoring their words without distortion. Many Elders speak Cree or "Cree-English," and their ways of expressing knowledge must be preserved respectfully, without forcing them into Western academic frames. Their teachings emphasize:

- The inseparable relationship between spiritual and mental health
- The importance of ceremony as therapeutic practice
- The role of Cree language in strengthening identity and emotional regulation
- The need to restore humility, generosity, kindness, and relational responsibility
- The importance of personal and community healing journeys

Their guidance aligns with recent scholarship arguing that Indigenous mental health must be grounded in Indigenous philosophical frameworks and ceremonial practices, not merely "culturally adapted" Western therapies.

Traditional Healing Practices as Indigenous Mental Health Systems

The Elders described several core practices that supported emotional, spiritual, and mental balance in pre-contact Cree societies and continue to play central roles today. The following Elder (*Elder Annie Partridge*) narratives do not reintroduce these principles, but rather demonstrate how wâhkôhtowin is lived, taught, and enacted through relational practice.

Sweat lodges

Sweat lodge ceremonies cleanse the body, mind, and spirit. Through prayer, heat, song, and collective presence, participants release grief, trauma, anger, and spiritual heaviness. Elders emphasize that the sweat lodge is not merely symbolic; it is a living therapeutic system grounded in Natural Law.

Smudging and Purification

The use of medicines such as sage, cedar, sweetgrass, and tobacco clears negative energy, centers the mind, and reconnects individuals with ancestors. For many Indigenous peoples, mental health disruption is understood as spiritual imbalance; purification practices help restore alignment.

Land-Based Healing

Land is teacher, healer, relative, and source of identity. Participating in hunting, fasting, berry-picking, visiting sacred sites, or spending time on the land promotes emotional regulation, belonging, and spiritual grounding.

Cree Language Revitalization

Language is the vessel of worldview. Praying, speaking, joking, and storytelling in Cree carry meanings that English cannot replicate. Elders note that humor in Cree strengthens resilience and community cohesion.

Community-Based Counsel and Kinship Responsibilities

Healing is a collective process. Traditional counseling happened through family networks, ceremonial leaders, and Elders—not through isolated clinical settings. Healing required strengthening relationships rather than labeling individuals as "ill."

These practices collectively offer a grounded, holistic alternative to Western mental health paradigms, which often isolate the mind from body and spirit.

A Framework for Decolonizing Mental Health Research

Drawing from Elder teachings, Indigenous scholarship, and your narrative, this chapter proposes a wâhkôhtowin Framework for Decolonizing Mental Health Research, designed for students, researchers, and practitioners.

Ontology: Understanding Being Through Kinship

Human beings exist in relationship—with land, spirit, ancestors, and community.
Mental health is relational rather than individualistic.
Healing requires restoring balance in these relationships.

Epistemology: Centering Indigenous Knowledge

Knowledge comes from Elders, ceremony, prayer, and land-based learning.
Oral tradition, not written text, is primary.
Language is a core knowledge system.

Axiology: Ethics of Respect, Reciprocity, and Humility

Research must follow protocol and relational accountability.
Researchers must be guided by humility, generosity, and good intention.
The well-being of community takes precedence over academic agendas.

Methodology: Ceremony, Storying, and Land-Based Methods

Interviews with Elders are ceremonial acts, not data extraction.
Storywork is a valid method of analysis and knowledge sharing.
Land-based research aligns mental, emotional, and spiritual inquiry.

Applications for Mental Health Practice

This framework can guide practitioners to:

- Integrate ceremony and cultural practices into healing programs
- Engage Elders as teachers, counselors, and program designers
- Build community-led mental health centers
- Prioritize language revitalization as part of wellness
- Train students using kinship models rather than Western hierarchies

This framework shifts mental health research from a pathological lens to one grounded in Indigenous wholeness and relationality.

Our personal reflections—on learning Cree, participating in ceremony, healing from intergenerational trauma, and engaging with Elders—illustrate the lived dimensions of Indigenous research. Rather than positioning yourself as an objective observer, your narrative situates you within the relationships that make the research possible. This aligns with Indigenous methodologies that emphasize relational accountability.

Such reflections also demonstrate that research can itself be a form of healing. Writing becomes a ceremony of remembering, reclaiming, and reconnecting with ancestral teachings. As you note, sharing stories restores dignity, strengthens identity, and invites others into collective healing.

Toward Community Healing and the Future of Indigenous Mental Health

The TRC's call for sustained funding for Indigenous healing centers is essential. Every reserve requires dedicated mental health facilities that integrate ceremony, cultural knowledge, language teaching, and land-based programs. Western clinical interventions may complement these approaches, but they cannot replace the foundational role of Indigenous healing systems.

The Elders' teachings emphasize that healing is not only personal, but it is also communal and generational. To heal, we must rid our minds of jealousy, shame, hatred, and internalized colonialism. We must embrace love, humility, and kindness, recognizing that we are entering a new era of Indigenous enlightenment.

As established earlier in this chapter, wâhkôhtowin grounds mental health in kinship, land, ceremony, language, and relational ethics rather than individual pathology. This relational philosophy grounds a mental health model that is spiritually, culturally, and emotionally relevant. It equips future generations with the tools to reclaim identity, resist colonial narratives, and nurture community well-being.

This chapter argues that wâhkôhtowin provides the cultural, ethical, and philosophical grounding necessary to develop a decolonized mental health research model. Through the teachings of Elders, the revitalization of language, and the restoration of ceremony, Indigenous peoples can rebuild the kinship networks disrupted by colonialism. A wâhkôhtowin-centered framework challenges Western clinical paradigms and instead foregrounds relationality, spirituality, and collective responsibility. Reclaiming the old ways, we open pathways for new futures—futures rooted in connection, balance, and Cree Natural Law. Through this lens, mental health becomes a relational journey supported by family, community, land, and ancestors. Wâhkôhtowin becomes not only a philosophy but also the foundation for an Indigenous resurgence in health research and practice: a living, breathing vision of healing for future generations.

Elder Annie Partridge

What Does wâhkôhtowin Mean to You?

Elder Annie Partridge: *wâhkôhtowin* means it is very important that's the first thing, *wâhkôhtowin,* never throw that *wâhkôhtowin* away, we're connected, all these trees, everything, mother earth, everything, we're connected, everything...never forget *wâhkôhtowin,* especially your kids have to know that too in the future, maybe in the future nothing will be *wâhkôhtowin.* But I see it already there's no *wâhkôhtowin* going nowadays, before *wâhkôhtowin,* when you meet somebody, they shake hands with you, *ahâw niwâhkômâkan,* that's *wâhkôhtowin,* hug each other, kiss each other, even women they kiss each other, that's very important that *wâhkôhtowin* (Figure 3.1).

FIGURE 3.1 The figure shows author Jody Houle's inspiration, ma angel, Sohketa Margaret Myrtle Lewis dancing the Traditional Women's dance, she is yet a beautiful and graceful dancer. She represents the future of upcoming Indigenous women with her humbleness and receptiveness, as she knows and has developed relations with all three ladies in this interview.

What Were Traditional Counseling/Therapeutic Methods Used in Pre-Contact Societies and in Present-Day Culture?

Elder Annie Partridge: Mentally, gee I can't quite understand that, let's see explain to me.

Okay, You Know How There Are Mental Health Therapists and Counselors, What Were Our Ways?

Elder Annie Partridge: To counsel our people, to provide that support for our people…

Well long time ago when I used to see Elders they used to, when people were like that, when a people can't think right, or when people are stressed, and can't think, they want to commit suicide or something like that the Elders used to talk to them and put them in a sweat and smudge them, talk to them, is that what you mean?

Were There Any Other Ways That the Elders Used Healing Practices?

Elder Annie Partridge: That's the only way I know…you can smudge them to sniff that smudge, a special smudge you can use to smudge…it won't work right away, about two to three days, maybe two days after you will notice that person is different.

Even the ones they're in the city, the ones they're in a jail, the ones someplace, what we pray here we smudge, and we talk to that smudge, go over there, let those smell you, so from over there they can smell that smudge and they will be different like, when they smell it mmm I smell smudge, well already seen them yesterday, about two of them. Three of them from the city tell us he been smelling smudge, well we're the ones that sent that smudge, we're trying to help them, you know, even in the jail that's what they said.

What Were Traditional Medicines Used to Treat Mental Illness?

Elder Annie Partridge: There was no white people's medicine used a long time ago, nothing, long time ago they used to use, I think there was no sickness long time ago, one time my *mosôm* tell me there was a sickness going on, like this sickness right now. But it was like measles like chickenpox or something, some kind of measles and lot of people were passed on and I guess one, one Elder, an old guy, I guess um from his dream, somebody came and told him, he took him someplace and goes shows him someplace, this is what you're going to do, this what your guys going to do, that's the only way you are going to save your people, like these medicines. Besides these ceremonies, losses, that's what my *mosôm* used to tell me and Alex Stick used to tell me that too. There was a sickness going on one time, but they beat it, but nowadays us, I don't know if we are going to beat this sickness, same thing like a lot of people passed on, but that's what I mean we keep smudging, that's why we sent that smudge to where the people are, our people, lots of them smelled that smudge, I got different kind of smudge, that's the one we use.

What Is Your Role as an Elder in the Land-Based Therapeutic Program?

Elder Annie Partridge: What is the Elder for…everything, Elder is for everything, like I told you more important way up here these Elder and child, especially they're parents passed on, that's the one you have to help them show them you love them, the ones they don't have no parents, that's the ones. And these Elder, I used to drive around in town, even North Battleford, when I see an Elder standing on a street, I feel sorry for that Elder, and I stop there…come…come home with me. When I took him home, when I got him to the house, I used to have extra clothes, here change your clothes, take a bath, change your clothes, I'll wash your clothes, and I feed him and I clean the bed that's where I put him, they used to stay longer because they like how I treat them, nowadays I don't see nobody doing that… I heard that before around here. These Chief and Council I heard they say that oh my god their going to regret it in my mind. More important Elders, that's what I used to do and than when I treat them right… come *nôsim* I'll tell you what's going to be in the future, now I seen all that, what they told me, but make sure never forget who you are, never forget, never give up these ceremonies. If somebody laughs at you, that's his business, just let them laugh at you, let them talk about you, that's what I'm doing. A lot of times I heard people talking about me, they don't like me, but that's okay, I still live, I'm still doing my ceremonies, I still got my kids, grandchildren, *câpâns.*

What's Worth Holding onto of the Old Traditional Ways?

Elder Annie Partridge: Every ceremony stuff, not just one. Like this water is important…now you see when you look around you see its dry…If we don't have water…there will be no life, that is how we are all related in *wâhkôhtowin,* everything is connected (Elder Annie Partridge, Personal Interview, 2021).

This teaching illustrates how mental health was never individualized within Cree societies, but understood as a relational process requiring patience, collective care, and spiritual grounding.

While Elder Partridge emphasizes ceremony and smudging as primary therapeutic responses, Elder Stick extends this discussion through detailed teachings on spirit relations, kinship obligations, and moral responsibility.

Elder Eileen Stick

What Is the Meaning of wâhkôhtowin?

Elder Eileen Stick: The *wâhkôhtowin* in the spiritual way, there is lot of spirits, when you ask for a Cree name in spirit world, like me *sohkâpaw iskwêw,* we call it *nikwêmês osâw kihêw* that's your little spirit that guides you and protects you, like a yellow eagle, your helper is working for you, you have to take a print to the Sundance, like you say I came and gave my *nikwêmê* this, *kâkêsimow*, like pray to him to be active for me or something like that, and there is lots of spirits that's where you should be using Russel for this, there's lots of spirits like *osâw kihêw, kaskitêw kihêw* and *kihêw êkwa âpô wâkayowis* bear, *mahikan.* Even the wood, even the trees they can guide you in everything *êkwa mîna,* if you want to learn more of the Indian spirituality like I say, ahh *nikwêmê osâw kihêw ê-itotah.* Okay my name is *sohkâpaw iskwêw*, my kin spirit take this over there, to what I'm about to see to the spirit land, I want to know the spirituality and I want you to give me the road to spirituality and the knowledge, understanding and everything, but the gift, the gifts you're asking for they won't come till five days after, as if though you had known them but you won't be surprised they'll be there and that's how I learn about this. All the spirits, I can't name them all. My husband, what he sang on those animals out there (sweat), eagle, bear, *mahikan,* and all kinds of bears and all kinds of *mahikan* and whatever you call Creator *kîsê-manitow,* God, all those and those are the ones that *aya*, are the ones they're going to guide us through in the future, in the future and their going to guide us, their going to help us in the future all these things the spiritual, all we have to do is, I don't know all of them but I know some of them and then I ask the prayers to guide me through there which one is which and that's what I'll find out, *êkwa kâ-wâhkômahk tâskohc ôma awiya osâw kihêw*, my kin spirit, *aya niwâhkômâw tâskohc nikwêmê, nikwêmê tâskohc,* is mine, but in our world today they say *nikwêmê* when you have somebody that has the same name *kikwêmês êyakwâna*. But here, just like he's my *nikwêmê* and in the spiritual world, that's how Creator is looking at me in the spiritual world, he's in the spiritual world and I'm not, but he's helping me through, that's how I'm related to this one here, he's a part of my soul and stuff like that, and then, in humans your dad and your mom, dad and this is you here, okay his sibling, his brother, boy, sister, *êkwa mîna* boy, sister, okay *awa* your dad, and your mom, but this boy his brother *ôhi,* he'll be *kohcâwês*, an uncle, *kohcâwês* is another way of saying dad, *êkwa awa ôta kisikos*, but it's a different way of being your cousin, *êkwa* your *kisis* like your father-in-law, your father in-law, your moms side is *kisis,* and your dads side, your dad, the girl and the boy one the moms side is a bit different and the dads side is a bit different…okay now a girls sister, if she has girls and boys okay do you *awa*, it would be your sister and *awa ôta*, no this one here's sister and you would be sister *ohci kîyitêyan,* okay that would be your sister and your sister *êkwa aya* would be, your brother that's his sister awa your dad, your sister and this one here, do you understand? Okay, mom's sister and a girl and a boy okay you just like the way *awa kikâwês*, your aunty, same thing as your mom, and this one would be your sister, and this one would be your brother, *êkwa ôtê kêcimos*, like the way, it is different, but its understanding that way *tâskohc awa kêcimos*, just like a boyfriend, but your not suppose to live with them, the bloodline is so close and you do know what's going to happen when that bloodline gets connected together. Mmhmm, okay, and *then kêcimos awa aya* I don't know how you write it down, but that's how it goes, it's a long way that is why it is so important, even though you are related to these ones you have to go distance away, you cannot marry in here, the blood is really strong, and that's why a lot of people oppose of it like that, and *êkosi.*

What Were the Traditional Counseling/Therapeutic Methods Used in Pre-Contact Societies?

Elder Eileen Stick: There was this one guy who went to the army, he went to counseling, therapy, mental therapy counseling all of those things, he couldn't come out of the things that he had done out there, he told people that he, no matter when he had to shoot people, even kids and parents, mom and dad, and when he came out, when he came out, now those things are bothering him. It bothered him, he just jumps up like he sees those kids, and then he kept on going to counseling and stuff like that, he couldn't come out of it in a white world, he came to the Sundance, he keeps going the Indian way, this is a white guy. He went to a Sweat lodge, he went to a Sundance and that's where it helped him, that's the most important thing, but it helped him what he had done over there, that's what helped him, but to say it all in other people like they'll say, if your mentally here, and spiritually troubled, this world troubled you, they'll say if I were to bring that situation up, only me I could help myself if I wanted to, but you can only hint to me, okay like I say if I go do harm to people out here, what goes around comes around to me, and that's what a lot of people thought, *maskihkiy kayâs*, but it's not, why would the Creator grow *maskihkiy,* no no, it's the karma, that's what they called it karma, the *kikwêmês* now we're going back to this. If you're not mad for what a person does to you, that *kwêmês* will go, spiritually go do something to that person and that is true today and its going, but that's why sometimes people, if I were to get mad at you, done something to me, I'm protecting you cause he can do harm than I can do, you know, and then that's one thing about that, it's not their problem, it's what in the past that had been done to them, but they have to speak about it, talk about it in order for them to heal themselves, you know what I mean? To keep talking about it what happened to them, and they have to learn to forgive themselves and love themselves, in order to get out of that shell, get out of that lifestyle that they go through.

What Were the Traditional Medicines, I Don't Know If You Want to Share This, It's Up to You, Used to Treat Mental Illness?

Elder Eileen Stick: Okay mental illness I seen this happen there's this one, I'm not using names but there is this one guy that came here, what do you call that, hallucinations, and he was so scared, can't be alone somebody's got to be in the same room as him, he was constantly looking at the window so corrupted in his mind he'll look in the window and will be *aya*, there coming here their going to come and get me Russel where are you? *êtikwê* and then Russel kept him for a long time here until he's really well. He took him into a Sweat, smudge him, doctor him, it took him awhile, I mean it takes a long time to heal and that guy after he got, gee I don't know how long I think it was a month he lived with us here and then he slowly kind of walked away knowing that he was getting well, and then, that's what it's all about the mental illness you have to love yourself *sâkîhisowin kimôsihtâwin sâkîhisowin*. You can feel it here and it will hurt you, I feel sorry for these homeless people, it's not their problem, its beyond people that don't teach them, that's what happened to them but we could only help them to speak to them and give to them and help them a little bit and stuff like that, and the more you help people the more you'll get granted for something, you'll get help, you won't know it but it's there.

What Is Your Role in the Land-Based Therapeutic Program?

Elder Eileen Stick: Okay land based, I would help them when to take the medicine what time, its best to take them from morning till noon, that's when everything is active, that's when you pick them up but don't do it after dinner and the evening don't do it, like I said two or three don't do it in the evening that's when they are going to sleep and they are more active in the morning, they got to do with the lives, this whole world how it is with the plants and when you're going to pick the plant this is what is going to help me this is, and you have to put the tobacco, and you have to sprinkle. I could tell you a story, one time here we were going to Pierceland and we were um what do you call little root, it's called little root, we went and picked it up and I asked these two girls and I showed them and then I went to my granddaughter *ôta*, same height as me, okay I told them stand still where you are and then I took the tobacco, I told her stand still, don't even take another step I told her and then I opened my eyes after I did that just like they are just popping up and she got too scared, right there look, holy she said their scaring me she said, don't feel that way and don't even talk about it just start digging them cause we ask for them that's where they just appear on them you have to pray for what you're going to go for. And the healing part, some of them people don't want to expose what they go through, but what you do is push yourself to that person, be friends with that person, it's so hard but keep doing it every day when you are spending time with them just like what you're doing with this girl than slowly they will open up what happened to them, it takes time but you have to have patience as soon as she trusts you now she'll open up and she'll tell you everything and the more she tells you things that's when you can start getting help, that kind of doctoring, and the doctoring is the way we talk here too at the same time. But still when something bothers her that's when you may have to take her to a Sweat lodge, its deep down inside something that is, it's right here (points to her heart) you know those *mâna* eh, its right here you have to trigger that thing in order for them to *aya*, to come out of their shell stuff like that now that's when they'll burst out crying so that thing that's bothered them just comes right out my little boy. I couldn't cry right through, that wake I cried in the hospital *nêtê* and as soon as my friends got there to pick me up I just totally lost it, I didn't even know how I came home, I don't even know if I ate, used the washroom, I didn't even know where I slept and stuff like that and the day after the funeral I came home went to the bathroom and that thing that was right here (heart), I can feel it, and then I just stand there and it's just coming out like this. I can just feel it right here coming out like this, it came out like this and I just burst out crying. If I didn't cry that thing would have hurt me, I would have gone crazy, but that thing came out, and I cried and it helps, that thing, it's a sickness in there, that's what they have to bring out in order for them they have to cry, they don't have no crying feeling, if that comes out and then they cry, that's when they'll be free from that burden.

What Is Worth Holding onto of the Old Ways?

Elder Eileen Stick: Okay that's one thing I was showing my girls today I was cleaning a rabbit and I told them, Wynona come and skin this rabbit and she was talking away and plucking the rabbit and then you don't have to pluck it you skin it, well I forgot she said, gees I had to put my stuff away and come and skin that rabbit and sit here and look at it cause I know you guys will need this five or ten years' time. I told them, you guys got to know how even a little look, you guys will know how, then *nôsim âcimosik*, no matter how gross it looks, it's still delicacy for us and these are the things we are all going to need in the future, maybe we have everything so light today, look I made a stew meat and hamburger out of an elk, but nobody sit here to help me with dry meat, that is the most important thing is dry meat, and I said look at it dry meat, we don't need to cook it we dry it in the sun and there's a lot of iron in there we need and that's going to help us the way we eat, we eat that instead of this hamburger, this is the most important, this is what we have to do, my mom skin the *wâposwa* and dry it, one time *mistahi wâposak*. We all skin them and they even showed us how to *pânisâwâtaht*. Just flat them down there, and they were safe in the hot days and stuff like that, even *amisk* beaver, beaver *mâna* its edible, that one its good for *aya kikway ôma*, in mentally and in diabetic, even muskrat, the more you eat muskrat its kind for a diabetic, nutrition, stuff like that, they're healing you as you eat them, all those animals, I still eat beaver, I still eat muskrat, and then all these things the people can go back to the land based, this is what a lot of people need to go back to the land based to understand the old ways. How I learned myself more of the old ways is I compare myself here and I go back to 1800s, how they lived, I taught myself there they followed the buffalo when they migrate up north and buffalos go by the weather, the seasons, when its slowly coming into fall they go start walking down to the south, where in States, there's less snow there and then our ancestor come down follow with them cause that's their food their supplies their everything on that their clothing, tools and food so they follow the buffalo down south and in the spring they come up just to collect them berries, medicine they collect them to last them the winter, that's what the old ways was *êkwa mâna aya* in the old ways *aya kayâs*, in the tipi when the hunters go hunting *iskwêwak* they go help the men bring them in, and some of the women stay home here and help out and they do the skinning and the older women are making hides and the younger women would be drying meat, that's how the co-operation was a long time ago, everybody knew, you don't need to tell anyone, okay go do this, they practically knew their routines, routines every day and the men would bring the wood in, and our ancestors never ate three times a day, they only eat when they are hungry, they carry food with them as they are travelling up and north, I can't say I know these, I figure these out, lots of these things and then *mistahi kîkway* people, mostly used to live on the buffalo and beaver that's a part of medicine for them too even muskrat that was a medicine for them…*êkosi* (Eileen Stick, Personal Interview, 2021).

Elder Dorothy Crookedneck

What Does wâhkôhtowin Mean to You?

Elder Dorthy Crookedneck: As I grew up in my childhood days *aya* my parents when they wake us up, right away they told us, like myself, when my mom would come and wake me up *nitânis, nitânis, waniskâ,* she's saying that my daughter, my daughter wake up you'll be late for school that's the first thing that we learn during school days that we will hear, same thing with my dad. My dad never used to say our names always *nitânis* or *nicânis,* that's the youngest one or um *nikosis* means my son and if our other siblings like our cousins come there, my brothers sons, they won't say that's your cousin or *kistês* or *kîcimos*, my cousin will be mine if there is a male there, like I'd say my brother's son, that's my *nîcimos,* it's a *nîcimos* not my brother or if my sisters…okay… it's like my dad's brother that's the one there his sons there those are my *nîcimosak,* and my dad's sister. No that's the other way around, my dad's brother, his kids, those are my brothers or my sisters and my dad's sister her sons, are my brothers and my other ones his sons are my brothers those are my brothers and sisters, but my dad's sister's sister her sons, her sons are my *nîcimosak* and her daughters are my *nicâkosak*, just like my in-laws sister-in-law and brother-in-law, got it. Okay and that's *wâhkôhtowin* in our siblings but *nohkom êkwa nohkom awa êkwa awa,* my grandmother it goes on and on as a family tree goes. My younger generation, my kids my daughter *awa êkwa ôtê awa* my niece *awa* those are the sisters *êkota tâskohc*, those are sisters, my brother *êkwa* my daughters daughter *êkotê nâpêsisak êkotê* my brothers sons my granddaughter those are my *ê-wîcimosiyihtawihk* like that…*owîcimosêmitowin* is like how do you say that… they're just like her boyfriend, my granddaughter and my brother's son that's her boyfriend, but my niece her son that's her brother now…got it? It's a real hard way to explain it in our ways, it's hard *êkwa êkotê êkwa*, these okay my granddaughter her kids the same it follows just like a stairs steps same thing there going to be like my parents used to tell us that not to stay with anybody around here that we're all related in this reserve but in my way, I stayed with a guy from Onion Lake and real far from there, it happens to be he's my second cousin, that's the thing that we cannot understand us, we cannot understand that he is living there, he was living in Onion Lake and the mother there was from here I didn't know she was from here and she married to Onion Lake and that was almost my blood mother-in-law, I guess, and her son was supposed to be my close relations. That's the thing that we don't know like other reserves, our reserves these neighboring reserves here we don't know how we are related we closely related, all these surrounding reserves here like Joseph Big Head, Thunderchild, our relations are there too but my dad, my late dad used to tell me he used to tell us that there's lots of relations over there and when they come and visit he'll say *niwâhkôhmâkan kisikos*, that's your mother-in-law he will say that too us, even though we don't know he will tell us that's how *wâhkôhtowin,* is when we grow up, that's how we are related, that's what *wâhkôhtowin* means.

What Were the Traditional Counseling/Therapeutic Methods Used in Our Culture?

Elder Dorthy Crookedneck: Okay that one is kind of to me, it's kind of sacred but I will say things that, as a medicine woman there's myself that a lot of young kids or young youth that were brought to us, some were badly abused, sexually abused and mentally abused, some almost lost their minds too to these…I'm pretty sure it had to do with these residential schools, myself I was sexually abused by my uncle you went through residential school and that's where sometimes we need help and we need to, just like myself I used to need lots of help as I grew up because about this abuse that I went through and it was letting me to be stay there where my uncle put me as a little girl all the time. That I cannot help myself, I cannot do anything, I can't tell anybody about my abuse. And these are the kids that brought us, that are brought to us, they were abused like that, and some were abused physically at their homes, yeah, and those are the kids that need lots of help and sometimes I would counsel them or I would we would take them to sweats we used to take them in the sweats when my husband was alive but right now I don't do sweats. Sweat is a real good healing process, like when you go in there you must breathe and take your mental feelings that hurt you and take it out there and that's what is coming out, coming out of your system. Sometimes you're in a real heavy, in your insides, in your system but when you go to sweat as you come out of the sweat there you feel like your real light, that's how I took it as, when I do sweats, and another thing that we do is counseling, We talk to the small ones, like I'm keeping two kids that have been badly sexually abused and they were doing things that they weren't supposed to be doing, but I kept at them, at them not to do that, not to do this and that. And they begin to forget, and I give them love and I talk to them every day about how we have to love one another and to look after one another. That's what I taught them and right now they are slowly coming out of the hurt, like when I ask them, they won't tell me what happened to them when they were with their parents, they don't know maybe, maybe it was the ones who were drinking there, maybe they were the ones that were touching them. So those are the things that I have to look at them, especially the youngest one. I have to take him out of the time that he was hurt, that's how I teach them, like on a daily basis talking to them all the time, giving them love all the time, that's what they need. That's how I do talk to little kids and to other youth like counseling them, taking them out.

What Were Traditional Medicines Used to Treat Mental Illness?

Elder Dorothy Crookedneck: Like I was saying, through the healing sessions we did through sweats, there were all ages of teenagers that were brought to us, some were like, there possessed, like they feel like their possessed and one time there's this one girl that, she was acting like a cat, and walking like a cat, like trying to scratch people, and that's the hurt…badly that she was hurt, and she begin to feel like maybe, I don't know how why she was beginning to feel like an animal. That's how we know she was badly hurt, and they begin mentally ill, and slowly they begin to turn into themselves into these animals, like their animals because that's how they were treated, and when we took them in sweats, we had to put four sweats for them to get that feeling, that animal, to take it out from their system and this one girl that was badly deformed into an animal, but at the last sweat we took her it was real hot and then, she was just puking, she was puking foam and my husband told us that that thing is out now and she'll sleep for a while. When she wakes up, she will feel back to normal, and that's what happened when that girl went to sleep for a while and then when she woke up she was feeling like a normal person, that's how we knew that these were the mentally and badly disturbed teenagers, that's how we know we have to go through a process through sweats.

What Is Your Role as a Leader/Elder in the Land-Based Therapeutic Program?

Elder Dorthy Crookedneck: As an Elder I used to work here and there, I guess I would say all of the job descriptions here, and the most things I like land-based teachings, land-based teaching is the best thing that ever happened to me, I cherished that, that's my passion, sometimes people come and ask me to go help them like other reserves too, Onion Lake and other reserves, and I will never say no, especially when somebody came and offer me tobacco. I have to go, that's my work for myself all the time, and the Cree Immersion I'm working here with my niece, the way she teach here with the kids, I really, really acknowledge her the way she teach Cree and the way my mother used to teach us in Cree and our land based too, that's what they are teaching here and my grandson too, my nephew, holy that one is real young, and already just like he's an Elder. I would say, everywhere…everywhere…he acts like he's an Elder already that's what I saw in him, my grandson, sometimes my sister and I we talk about him…that's our little *mosôm,* we call him our *mosôm* now, so that's how I acknowledge those two, a mother and a son.

What's Worth Holding onto of the Old Ways?

Elder Dorthy Crookedneck: I would say that we have to protect our medicines, I don't like when these industries, what they are doing is cutting trees, they are cutting other things like, you know the main thing that bothers me all the time is when they take oil from underground, that's our mother earth's protection there underground. It's the oil, when it comes out, the water is coming up and it's not protecting the land here on top, there its coming out now, the water, that oil was supposed to be under there and it should have been left alone, because that's our mothers protection, and in a way the industries are destroying our land especially our medicine, the animals and fish, and birds, they are getting sick already maybe, we don't know, we have to protect our land our mother earth, that's what I wanted to say (Elder Dorthy Crookedneck, Personal Interview, 2021).

It was a great honor to sit in relational presence with these women as they shared their ways of being, knowing, and living. I remain deeply grateful for the knowledge, teachings, and wisdom imparted through their stories, prayers, and embodied practices. Their generosity reflects a long-standing tradition of Indigenous knowledge transmission grounded in reciprocity, relational accountability, and collective care. These teachings are not simply memories to be held, but responsibilities that I carry forward in my ongoing relationships with community members, learners, and future generations.

The healing that emerged through these engagements extended beyond the individual and spoke to broader processes of cultural, spiritual, and intergenerational restoration. I hold hope and prayer for the healing of my people, recognizing that our communities have endured prolonged histories of dispossession, colonial violence, and systemic racism. The work of reclaiming and revitalizing what is rightfully ours is not only an act of resistance but also an act of love, survivance, and futurity for coming generations (Simpson, 2014; Tuck & Yang, 2012).

Chief Clarence Louis of the Osoyoos Indian Band reminds us of the urgent need for cultural reclamation when he calls for Indigenous youth to reject colonial ideologies and return to pride in Indigenous identity. His words powerfully challenge internalized colonialism and affirm the necessity of cultural resurgence as a pathway to collective healing and empowerment. This call resonates deeply with the experiences of Plains Indigenous Peoples, who were born into relationships of freedom, movement, and intimate connection with the land long before the imposition of colonial borders and governance structures. As *nêhiyawak*, we must refuse shame, silence, and erasure. Instead, we must embody the courage, strength, and resistance of our ancestors, who fought tirelessly to sustain our languages, ceremonies, and collective identities. Through this, we honor their struggles and ensure that our futures remain grounded in pride, sovereignty, and self-determination (Alfred, 2009; Simpson, 2014).

4

DECOLONIZING HEALTH RESEARCH FROM AND WITHIN PERSONAL HEALING JOURNEY

Jody Houle (with support from Kevin Lewis and Ranjan Datta)

This chapter opens by situating decolonizing mental health research as both a scholarly framework and a lived, relational practice. This chapter advances a decolonizing approach to mental health research grounded in narrative inquiry, Indigenous knowledge systems, spirituality, and land-based ceremonial praxis. It emerges from a lived experience of intergenerational trauma shaped by colonial infrastructures, including residential schools, the Sixties Scoop, and Indian Day Schools, which have structured the social, emotional, and spiritual landscapes of many Indigenous families in Canada (Truth and Reconciliation Commission of Canada [TRC], 2015a,b). Rather than positioning Indigenous mental health within individualized or deficit-based frameworks, this chapter situates distress within historical, relational, and structural realities and proposes pathways toward healing that are community-led, spiritually grounded, and land-centered. Responding directly to peer review feedback, calling for clearer methodological structure, practical applicability, and a stronger balance between narrative and analysis, this chapter develops an explicit framework for decolonizing mental health research and practice. Personal narrative is offered not as autobiography alone, but as theory in action—a situated epistemology that informs research design, ethical engagement, and practitioner responsibility (Kovach, 2009a; Smith, 1999). This chapter also outlines actionable strategies for students, scholars, and practitioners who seek to implement decolonizing approaches within clinical, community, and educational contexts (Figure 4.1).

DOI: 10.4324/9781003670308-4

FIGURE 4.1 The figure describes the canoe, which represents an adventure I went on the Churchill River, as a river always flows in one direction and this is the new journey I'm in learning from my elders. They have taught me so many lessons in life, and I will always be forever truly thankful and grateful.

Colonial Structures and the Production of Trauma

The mental health conditions experienced by many Indigenous peoples cannot be understood without examining the colonial systems intentionally designed to dismantle Indigenous governance, families, languages, and spiritual relationships (TRC, 2015). Residential schools operated not only as institutions of forced assimilation but also as sites of systemic physical, emotional, sexual, and spiritual harm. The Sixties Scoop extended this violence by removing children from their families and placing them into non-Indigenous households, severing kinship, land-based identity, and ceremonial continuity (Sinclair, 2007). These colonial practices produced what Indigenous scholars have theorized as intergenerational and transgenerational trauma—trauma that is transmitted across generations through relationships, social structures, parenting practices, and embodied memory (Bombay et al., 2014). Linklater (2014) and Lambert (2014) have described these impacts as "soul wounds": spiritual injuries that manifest as depression, addiction, lateral violence, disconnection, and despair.

From my own life, these theoretical frameworks are not abstractions; they are lived truths. Violence in the home, instability, silence, and fear were not isolated family failures but the visible symptoms of deeper colonial injuries carried by adults who were themselves harmed by systems meant to erase them. Understanding this shifted my internal narrative from self-blame to structural awareness, a critical step in decolonizing both personal and scholarly understandings of mental health.

Narrative Inquiry as Decolonizing Methodology

Narrative inquiry, when grounded within Indigenous epistemologies, functions as a method of reclaiming voice, memory, and relational accountability (Kovach, 2009a). Western research traditions have historically positioned Indigenous peoples as objects of study, extracting stories without reciprocity, consent, or long-term responsibility (Smith, 1999). In contrast, Indigenous narrative methodologies recognize stories as living entities that carry teachings, obligations, and spiritual dimensions.

Young (2005) conceptualizes narrative as the primary way humans make sense of their worlds, while Weenie (2010) highlights storytelling as a pathway to both personal transformation and collective learning. Within this chapter, personal story is positioned not as emotional disclosure for consumption, but as an ethical intervention into research practices that have long silenced Indigenous knowledge. Narrative here becomes a site of resistance, survivance, and regeneration (Vizenor, 2008). It disrupts colonial notions of objectivity by foregrounding relational truth and lived accountability. It also establishes a methodological bridge between personal healing and scholarly praxis.

Ceremony, Protocol, and Spiritual Epistemology

One of the foundational aspects of my healing journey has been the return to ceremony and traditional medicines. Healing was not sought through clinical intervention alone, but through spiritual relationships developed in accordance with Indigenous protocols. This included offering tobacco and cloth, seeking permission from Elders, and entering ceremonial spaces with humility and intention. Smith (1999) emphasizes that research within Indigenous contexts requires adherence to protocols of respect, reciprocity, and relational accountability. These are not symbolic gestures but governance systems that structure ethical knowledge production. Through ceremony, I asked not only for healing for myself but also for guidance in how to live in a good way for my children and community. Relationship with *kîsê-manitow* (Creator) is understood not as abstract belief but as an embodied and relational practice developed through prayer, fasting, land-based activities, and community ceremonies. This spiritual epistemology fundamentally reshaped how I understand mental health: it is not merely psychological functioning, but spiritual alignment, relational balance, and land-based belonging (Gone, 2013).

Personal Narrative as Situated Theory

The following section returns to lived experience, not to introduce new concepts, but to demonstrate how the frameworks outlined above emerge from, and remain accountable to, embodied realities of trauma, grief, ceremony, and recovery. This extended narrative illustrates how decolonizing mental health practice is lived over time, within family systems, community relations, and spiritual pathways.

My childhood experiences were shaped by chronic exposure to fear, instability, and unpredictability. While I do not reproduce graphic details, it is essential to state that the home environment was frequently unsafe and that love and harm existed in painful proximity. Fear of loss, dreams of disappearance, and constant vigilance were not signs of weakness; they were adaptive responses to unsafe conditions. Western psychiatric frameworks often pathologize these responses as disorders (e.g., anxiety, hypervigilance, dissociation). However, when situated within Indigenous and decolonial frameworks, these responses can be understood as embodied intelligence—ways of surviving within unsafe systems (Gone, 2013). I also carry responsibility for how trauma shaped my own behaviors. Decolonizing healing does not erase accountability; rather, it reframes it. It allows space for self-reflection without collapsing into shame, offering pathways toward restorative responsibility and relational repair. This positioning addresses peer reviewers' concerns about overly personalized narrative by explicitly theorizing how personal story functions as epistemological grounding rather than as stand-alone testimony.

A Framework for Decolonizing Mental Health Research and Practice

In response to reviewer feedback requesting clearer structure and transferable methods, this chapter proposes the Relational–Ceremonial Decolonizing Mental Health Framework (RCDMHF). This framework provides practical pathways for researchers, students, and practitioners.

Pillar 1: Historical and Structural Accountability

Practitioners and researchers must locate mental health within colonial histories rather than individual pathology. *Implementation Pathways:*

- Integrate TRC (2015) findings into clinical and research training
- Include mandatory education on residential schools, child welfare policies, and land dispossession
- Avoid deficit-based language in assessment and reporting

Pillar 2: Relational Ethics and Community Governance

Ethics are not limited to institutional review boards but are governed by community relationships. *Implementation Pathways:*

- Establish community advisory circles of Elders, youth, and knowledge keepers
- Adopt OCAP® principles (Ownership, Control, Access, and Possession)
- Compensate community members through honoraria and reciprocal contributions

Pillar 3: Ceremony and Spiritual Integration

Healing must include spiritual and ceremonial dimensions. *Implementation Pathways:*

- Partner with Elders to include smudging, sweat lodge, land walks, and seasonal ceremonies as recognized therapeutic practices
- Create institutional spaces that allow cultural and spiritual practices without surveillance or medicalization

Pillar 4: Land-Based Therapeutics

Land is not a backdrop but a co-therapist and knowledge holder. *Implementation Pathways:*

- Develop programs that include hunting, fishing, medicine picking, and water teachings
- Conduct therapy and research in outdoor, land-based environments where possible
- Recognize land as central to Indigenous identity and well-being

Pillar 5: Narrative and Reflexive Practice

Story is a method of healing, research, and evaluation. *Implementation Pathways:*

- Include storytelling as a legitimate data source in research design
- Train students to engage in reflexive journaling and relational accountability practices
- Create ethical storytelling guidelines that protect against voyeurism and exploitation

Current State of Indigenous Mental Health Research

Mainstream mental health research continues to prioritize biomedical and cognitive-behavioral models, often marginalizing Indigenous healing systems (Gone & Kirmayer, 2010). Many community-based studies remain extractive, short-term, and disconnected from long-term community benefit.

There is growing recognition of culturally responsive models; however, many still operate within colonial institutional constraints that limit true Indigenous governance and spiritual autonomy (Czyzewski, 2011). This chapter contributes to this field by offering a framework that operationalizes decolonization beyond rhetoric, providing concrete practices that can be adapted across contexts.

Envisioning a Land-Based Mental Health Healing Program

The vision for a Land-Based Mental Health Healing Program emerges directly from the lived experiences described above, translating personal and collective healing into community-led practice. A core application of this framework is the envisioned **Land-Based Mental Health Healing Program** within Ministikwan Lake Cree Nation. This program is designed as an Indigenous-led, community-governed initiative.

Program Components

1. *Ceremonial Cycles of Healing*
   Seasonal ceremonies led by Elders, including sweat lodge, pipe ceremony, and water teachings
2. *Land-Based Therapeutic Activities*
   Activities such as trapping, fishing, plant medicine harvesting, and seasonal camps
3. *Intergenerational Knowledge Transmission*
   Circles where Elders share teachings with youth and young families
4. *Trauma-Informed Narrative Circles*
   Safe, facilitated spaces for storytelling and collective witnessing
5. *Research as Service*
   Research embedded as a community resource, not an external extraction process

Ethical Considerations and Trauma-Informed Storytelling

We intentionally model trauma-informed narrative practices by reducing graphic content, centering dignity, and prioritizing reader and community safety. Sharing lived experience is framed not as disclosure, but as pedagogical intervention. This approach addresses reviewer concerns about ethical storytelling by balancing truth-telling with responsibility to self, family, and community. Silence is not imposed, but care is practiced in how story is carried.

Implications for Students, Researchers, and Practitioners

Students and emerging researchers are encouraged to:

- Engage in positionality statements and reflexive journaling
- Seek mentorship from Indigenous scholars and community knowledge keepers
- Prioritize long-term relationship-building over short-term data collection

Practitioners are encouraged to:

- Advocate for institutional policy changes that recognize Indigenous healing
- Collaborate with cultural practitioners as equal partners
- Dismantle surveillance and control mechanisms that limit Indigenous autonomy in health care spaces

As articulated at the outset of this chapter, decolonizing mental health research is not a metaphorical endeavor but a structural, spiritual, and relational commitment. This chapter demonstrates that personal storytelling, when ethically grounded and theoretically situated, becomes a powerful site of transformation. Healing is not linear, individual, or clinical alone; it is collective, land-based, ceremonial, and spirit-led. Bridging personal healing and scholarly praxis, this chapter offers a model for Indigenous-led mental health frameworks that honor emotional, spiritual, cultural, and relational dimensions of well-being. Through this work, mental health can be reclaimed from colonial systems and returned to its rightful place within Indigenous governance, spirituality, and land relations.

Public Silence, Private Wounds, and the Afterlives of Violence

What follows is not autobiographical disclosure for its own sake, but narrative as decolonizing methodology—story as theory in motion, carrying epistemological, ethical, and pedagogical weight. What follows is not a departure from methodology, but its enactment: narrative as a decolonizing research practice that holds trauma, accountability, and survivance together. The escalation of violence within my family was not only experienced in private spaces, but it also unfolded in public, in front of strangers, and in places meant to be safe. One of the most formative moments of my childhood occurred during a trip to North Battleford, when my stepfather dropped us off at a shopping center so that my mother could buy groceries. My younger siblings and I followed my mother through a series of stores. I cannot recall how long we spent there, but I clearly remember walking out of the washroom and seeing my stepfather standing nearby, his body tense, his eyes already filled with rage. Without warning, he grabbed my mother and struck her. I froze. I remember watching adults walk past us, some slowing their steps, some turning their heads away entirely. No one intervened. No one asked if she needed help. What stays with me most strongly is not only the violence itself but also the quiet complicity of the public. He pulled her toward the vehicle while shouting accusations and insults. For me as a child, this moment marked a profound loss of trust in the idea that public spaces offered protection, or that adults outside my home could be relied upon. It revealed, in a very early way, the normalized invisibility of Indigenous women's pain. At that age, I felt a mixture of shame, fear, confusion, and fury. I hated my stepfather for how he treated my mother, and I began to imagine ways I could make him stop. These were not fantasies of cruelty; they were the desperate thoughts of a child longing to restore safety. At the same time, I longed for escape. I wanted to leave Saulteaux and live a different life, one that did not involve constant fear or anticipation of harm.

Witnessing Violence in Public Space

Yet violence does not exist without contradiction. There was a period, when I was around nine years old, when things seemed to quiet down in our home. During that time, I grew unexpectedly close to my stepfather. I remember preparing to visit my late nohkom-pan and late nimosôm-pan and crying because I did not want to leave him. This is one of the most confusing memories I hold. The man I feared was also the only father I knew. He could be funny, generous, and encouraging. He worked hard and pushed us to believe in ourselves, especially through sports. These moments of kindness did not erase the harm he caused, but they complicated my understanding of love, safety, and loyalty. This emotional confusion is something many survivors of family violence experience. Love and harm can co-exist in the same relationship, especially when trauma is embedded in the family system. That duality shaped how I understood relationships later in my life, and it took many years to name it not as weakness, but as a trauma-informed survival strategy. This moment illustrates how trauma operates not only as memory but also as a relational and embodied condition—precisely the form of distress that decolonizing mental health frameworks seek to address.

A Silence as a Secondary Harm

Long side physical and emotional violence, I also lived through prolonged sexual abuse during early childhood. These experiences began when I was very young and continued into my pre-adolescent years. I do not recount these events in graphic detail, as the purpose of this chapter is not to reproduce harm, but to honor truth. What I can say is that I lived for many years with feelings of shame, confusion, fear, and deep disconnection from my own body. I grew up believing there was something wrong with me, something unclean or broken, even though I had done nothing wrong.

One memory that remains with me occurred during a family visit when older children used "games" and "play" as a cover for deeply harmful behavior. I did not have the language to understand what was happening, only the instinctive knowledge that it felt wrong. No adults intervened. No one spoke about it after. The silence, both then and in the years that followed, did as much harm as the abuse itself. It is painful to acknowledge that, as a child shaped by these violations, I later repeated harmful behavior toward another relative. I name this with care and accountability. Decolonizing storytelling is not about positioning oneself as blameless, but about breaking cycles of secrecy. Trauma does not excuse harm, but it helps us understand how cycles are transmitted through children who are never taught safety, consent, or care. I continue to live with guilt and responsibility, and I hold this truth as part of my ongoing commitment to healing, repair, and honesty. As adolescence approached, some household dynamics shifted. The frequency of direct violence against my mother seemed to decrease, often in relation to us children growing older and becoming more visibly present. I continued to call my Aunty Velma during moments of crisis. Her home became a temporary refuge, a small space where violence was interrupted, if only for a night. These moments of safety were fragile, but they mattered. They taught me that alternatives were possible, even if they were not consistent.

Alcohol, however, remained a constant presence in our lives. Fear did not simply disappear because the frequency of visible violence shifted. It lived in my body, my thoughts, and my dreams. I carried intrusive, frightening thoughts about stopping my stepfather from hurting my mother, including imagining violent acts. I now understand that these were trauma responses, not moral failures. They were the mind's way of trying to create a sense of control in an environment where none existed.

One of the last major incidents of violence I witnessed as a child occurred when I was around ten years old. I remember hearing shouting from my mother's bedroom. I could not see what was happening, but I could hear fear in her voice and the sounds of struggle. When she emerged from the room later, her injuries were visible. That night, as we sat together, she told me that I could go live with my late nohkom and late mosôm in Alberta. I did not want to leave. I did not want to abandon her or my siblings. I did not know what would happen to them if I were not there.

But children do not control these decisions. I packed my bags and traveled back and forth between Alberta and Saskatchewan, carrying with me both guilt and longing. I was learning, long before I had language for it, that safety often comes through separation, and that separation itself can be traumatic.

After another episode of violence, my mother eventually left my stepfather. For a time, life became quieter. As often happens in cycles of violence, distance was followed by reconciliation. He came back into our lives. For a period, things appeared stable. My mother had her fifth child. We became involved in sports. Hockey, golf, and summer ball filled our days. In Saskatoon, after my mother completed her education, we returned to Saulteaux, where she secured a position as an Education Director. Her achievement was a point of pride, and it symbolized resilience and determination in the face of long-term adversity. Yet beneath these surface-level successes, the culture of alcohol remained entrenched. Social life revolved around drinking. Parties were normalized. As I grew older, I began to drink alongside my parents. When my younger siblings reached adolescence, they did the same. Alcohol was not simply recreation; it was a way of coping, forgetting, and surviving. Looking back, I can now see how deeply normalized addiction had become in our household and community.

Cycles of Harm and the Burden of Accountability

At 18, my life shifted again when I became pregnant with my high school partner and returned to Saskatoon to attend what was then the Saskatchewan Indian Federated College, now the First Nations University of Canada. I wanted education. I wanted change. I wanted a different future. At the same time, I carried unhealed trauma, and under the pressure of adulthood, that trauma began to surface in new ways. One night, during a party at my home, conflict escalated between my partner and me. I defended myself in the only way I had been taught: through violence. I did not have models of communication, safety, or boundaries. What emerged was not love, but repetition. Over the next several years, that relationship became increasingly volatile. I experienced domestic violence firsthand. I left and returned multiple times. I stayed because that was what I had learned love looked like: chaos, apology, reconciliation, and repeated harm. This cycle lasted for nearly a decade. I do not name this to shame myself, but to expose the long reach of intergenerational trauma. We live what we learn, not because we choose harm, but because we are rarely taught alternatives.

Suicide, Shock, and Family Fracture

Years later, another pivotal event unfolded during a gathering after a hockey tournament in Saulteaux. The house was full. Alcohol was present. Tensions rose. My stepfather began to verbally target my mother, and she responded. The argument escalated into another physical confrontation. This time, I intervened. I stood up for my mother. Conflict engulfed the room, pulling in my sister and others. Children were present. Chaos reigned. That night, my mother and I gathered the children and left. We stayed in a hotel in North Battleford. The next day, as had happened so many times before, the cycle returned. Reconciliation followed violence. Life resumed. Silence settled back into place. That incident marked the last major physical conflict I witnessed between them. In my mid-20s, while attending classes at the First Nations University of Canada, another rupture occurred that reshaped everything. One quiet summer night in Saskatoon, while my son slept nearby and my younger brother trained with a hockey organization, we were awakened by a message that my stepfather had taken his own life.

The shock was immediate and unreal. We drove to Saulteaux. People gathered. Prayers were offered. The home was filled with grief, confusion, and silence. My mother was in shock. My siblings were in shock. The house felt hollow. I remember mechanical details—holding people, making tea, sitting quietly—but most of all I remember disbelief. This man had been known as a counselor, a community leader, and a coach who pushed countless youth to believe in themselves.

By this point in my life, I had forgiven him. I could hold the truth of harm alongside the truth of the good he had done. His death fractured our family in a way that no violence ever had. Loss moved in where fear had once lived. In the months and years following his death, grief consumed our family. My mother withdrew from the world. She isolated herself in her room, emerging only rarely. Later, she told me she secretly drank to numb the pain. She cried out loud that she wanted him back. My siblings drifted like shadows through their days. The house felt haunted by memory. There were moments when darkness felt unbearable. We did not always have language or support. Some of us contemplated whether life was worth continuing. I watched my family break in slow motion. In response, I turned more deeply toward alcohol. If I had not already become dependent, I moved fully into addiction. Drinking became survival.

Looking back now, I understand these events not as isolated tragedies, but as part of a larger colonial and intergenerational story.

As discussed earlier in this chapter, violence, addiction, suicide, silence, and grief must be understood not as personal failures but as outcomes of structural and colonial harm. They were shaped by structural violence, cultural disruption, and the removal of Indigenous systems of care and accountability. This story is not shared to sensationalize pain. It is shared to locate truth within systems, and to demonstrate how deeply trauma can live inside families and communities when left unaddressed. It is also shared to honor the strength and resilience that carried me forward, even when I could not yet name it as such. Healing did not begin in one moment. It began slowly, unevenly, and imperfectly. But it did begin.

Grief, Ceremony, and the Slow Work of Returning to Life

Compound Grief and Family Disintegration

One year after the death of my stepfather, our family remained suspended in grief. Time did not soften the pain; instead, it reshaped it into new forms of loss, fragmentation, and survival. My sister expressed her mourning by cutting her hair, stepping away from school, and returning to the reserve to work. My brother Michael continued to fulfill his responsibilities but carried a visible emotional weight that altered his daily life. My younger brother Adam withdrew from his hockey career with the Saskatoon Blades and returned home, leaving behind dreams that once defined his sense of purpose. My youngest brother, Denny, attempted to manage his grief by keeping himself constantly busy, surrounding himself with close friends as a form of distraction and protection. During this disruption, my mother attempted to intervene through care. In a state of urgency and fear for all of us, she enrolled the family in a range of therapies. We participated in "inner child" work, trauma-focused sessions, family group counseling, and individual therapy. While each of these interventions offered partial relief, they were often unable to fully address the cultural, spiritual, and historical layers of our grief. At the same time, my mother and I began our studies at the First Nations University of Canada in the Social Work program, an act that symbolized our desire to not only survive but also to understand and transform suffering into service. Despite these efforts, I fell into a deep depression. The weight of unresolved grief, compounded by years of accumulated trauma, became overwhelming. I found myself struggling to function and, at one point, experiencing thoughts of suicide. These were not expressions of weakness, but evidence of a nervous system saturated by violence, loss, and silence. I now understand that my body and spirit were asking for care that words alone could not provide. Another year passed, and our family experienced a second profound trauma. My younger brother Adam's partner died by suicide in the same home where my stepfather had died. This loss reopened wounds that had never fully closed. I experienced what I now recognize as a psychological collapse. I stopped sleeping, did not eat properly, and felt detached from reality. My mother eventually took me to the hospital, where I was admitted to a mental health unit and remained for nearly two weeks. During that hospitalization, I received a diagnosis of bipolar disorder. At the time, this label felt both frightening and clarifying. I immersed myself in learning about the condition, researching symptoms, treatments, and long-term outcomes. For me, knowledge was a form of control in a life that had long felt unmanageable. At the same time, I was mourning not only the recent death of my brother's partner but also the unresolved grief of my stepfather's suicide. These losses folded into one another, producing a disproportionate and disorienting sense of despair. During this period, my relationships with my mother and my sister became strained. We were each grieving in different ways, moving through our pain without shared language or capacity for mutual support. I withdrew, unable to articulate what I needed. I did not yet know how to grieve in a way that was safe or held. Eventually, I returned to communication with my mother, and we began, slowly and imperfectly, to heal together. This re-emergence of connection became one of the first signs that collective healing was possible.

Clinical Interventions and Their Limits

Looking back, I am deeply grateful that my mother insisted we engage in therapy during these years. Although these interventions were not fully culturally grounded, they provided moments of stabilization. Each of my siblings responded differently to the therapeutic process, but all of us benefited from being seen, even briefly, outside of the language of dysfunction. Our family, like many Indigenous families, reflected what is often described as "statistical risk": depression, anxiety, domestic violence, substance use, family breakdown, and experiences of suicide. These patterns were not moral failures; they were the living evidence of colonial harm manifesting in our bodies, relationships, and spirits. What matters most to me now is not that we reflected these statistics, but that we did not remain within them. My siblings are now living lives shaped by meaning, responsibility, and care. Their lives stand as living proof that cycles of trauma can be disrupted when love, accountability, and support are allowed to exist alongside pain.

As I reflect on my life, I find myself wondering who my stepfather might have become had he lived. This is not a romanticization of harm, but a recognition of complexity. He gave us many things: opportunities, discipline, encouragement, and belonging through sport and community life. I had already forgiven him long before his death. I had also begun the long process of forgiving those who harmed me during childhood. This forgiveness was not about forgetting but about releasing myself from the burden of carrying perpetual anger. Writing about these experiences has become a central pathway to healing. In this process, I am guided by Indigenous scholars who position storytelling as relational and transformative. Wilson (2008) describes relationality as a methodological and spiritual practice, where knowledge is produced through relationship rather than extraction. In my own writing, I aim to create that same relational bridge between my story and the lives of those who read it. I do not share these experiences for spectacle; I share them to show how lived experience can become a foundation for ethical practice, empathy, and social responsibility.

Ceremony as Turning Point

One of the most transformative dimensions of my healing journey has been the return to ceremony. As a child, my family experienced Roman Catholic religious influence and had limited exposure to Cree spiritual practices. It was only after my stepfather's death that my mother reintroduced us to ceremony. In this sense, she became a spiritual guide and protector. She taught us how to pray, how to smudge, and how to use meditation as a resource during moments of despair.

One of my most powerful early ceremonial experiences was attending a sweat lodge at Saulteaux First Nation, led by the late Archie Moccasin. I entered that lodge with fear. At the time, we had been told by spiritual advisors that harmful spiritual forces may have been directed toward our family, and that this may have been connected to the suicides we had endured. This information made me hesitant to engage in ceremony, fearing that spiritual work would expose me to further harm. However, once inside the lodge, something shifted. In the darkness, heat, prayer, and rhythm, I felt a connection to something older, wiser, and more stable than my pain. I experienced the presence of *kîsê-manitow* (Creator) not as a distant idea but as an embodied force of care and recognition. That ceremony became a turning point. It opened a path toward curiosity, reverence, and commitment to learning more about my culture and spiritual inheritance.

This experience also revealed the extent to which colonialism had shaped my fears and distance from my own traditions. To decolonize mental health, we must first decolonize the internal narratives that teach Indigenous people to fear their own spirituality. Our ceremonies are not relics of the past; they are living technologies of healing.

Writing, Accountability, and Recovery

My children have been among my greatest teachers in this process. They have supported me in ways that often exceed what I can express. Through them, I have learned to see my culture and spirituality with renewed eyes. Elder Danny Musqua (2001) reminds us that Indigenous spirituality is not simply religion, but a way of understanding and relating to the spiritual world. Through ceremony, I have learned to live without constant fear, to forgive without forgetting, and to exist in relationship rather than isolation. Another essential tool in my healing has been writing. Journaling and reflective writing have allowed me to externalize pain rather than allowing it to remain embedded within me. Chilisa (2012) describes writing as a method of conflict transformation, where painful experiences can be named, contained, and released through ritualized processes. For me, writing has functioned as a form of ceremony: a bowl in which pain can be placed, witnessed, and transformed. This process has not been linear. As I began to reclaim control over my life, I also had to confront addiction. Alcohol had been a constant companion throughout my early adulthood. Legal consequences eventually forced me to acknowledge the severity of this issue. I experienced multiple impaired driving charges and served time in jail. These experiences were humiliating, frightening, and transformative. They revealed what happens when pain is left unaddressed and allowed to manifest through self-destruction.

From Survival to Purpose

Recovery required humility. It required the recognition that ceremony and therapy must be accompanied by accountability and behavioral change. Addiction is not simply a personal failure; it is a colonial inheritance, but one that must be actively resisted through support, community, and spiritual practice. Today, I live with the knowledge that trauma has impacted my physical health as well. Years of stress contributed to diabetes and other health challenges. I have experienced hospitalizations and mental health crises. These realities are not evidence of weakness, but evidence of survival within systems that were never designed to protect Indigenous bodies or spirits. Through ceremony, I have found relief from depression. Through community, I have found accountability. Through writing, I have found voice. And through education, I have found purpose. This purpose now takes form in my vision for a Land-Based Mental Health Healing Program. This program is not designed as a clinical institution, but as a culturally grounded, community-led space where healing can occur through land, language, ceremony, and relational teaching. My intention is to create a 12-week program that integrates traditional teachings, counseling, storytelling, and land-based practices to support those who feel lost, broken, or disconnected.

The program is envisioned as a lodge rather than a clinic—a place where spirits can be "ensouled," where culture is normalized, and where silence can be safely broken. This vision is guided by the love and teachings of my mother, as well as the spiritual presence of my late grandparents and loved ones, who continue to guide me in unseen ways. This journey from trauma to purpose has not erased my pain. It has taught me how to live alongside it with dignity. It has taught me that healing is not the absence of scars, but the presence of meaning. And it has taught me that, even in the darkest histories, there are ancestral paths that lead back toward light.

5

LAND-BASED CEREMONIES AS HEALING

Jody Houle (with support from Kevin Lewis and Ranjan Datta)

This chapter is interconnected within and from Indigenous land-based ceremony as a powerful form of healing that sustains mental, emotional, spiritual, and physical well-being. It discusses how land-based ceremonies are deeply personal and ancestral experiences with Cree ceremonial practices—such as Sundance, Sweat lodge, and Vision Quest—which offer therapeutic pathways to healing and resilience. These ceremonies serve not only as rites of passage but also as a reclamation of cultural identity suppressed by colonial policies, including the Indian Act's bans on Indigenous spiritual practices. By interweaving ceremonial teachings and traditional roles across life stages, the author emphasizes *wâhkôhtowin* (kinship) and *miyo-pimâtisiwin* (a good life), underscoring ceremony as a foundational framework for holistic health that counters colonial impacts. This chapter examines ceremony in mainstream health paradigms, equating its role to that of Western therapeutic methods. This lived, ceremonial journey illustrates the potential for Indigenous health practices to contribute to decolonized research by prioritizing Indigenous epistemologies. Ultimately, this chapter argues that embracing Indigenous ceremonial knowledge can empower healing within and beyond Indigenous communities, catalyzing a resurgence of cultural pride, resilience, and community-led recovery. Land-based ceremony is at the heart of nêhiyaw (Cree) worldviews, ethics, and healing. Far from being symbolic or metaphorical, ceremony constitutes an embodied relationship with land, kinship, ancestors, and spirit. In this chapter, I argue that land-based ceremonial practices not only sustain individual well-being but also provide a robust, place-rooted framework for decolonizing mental health research and practice.

DOI: 10.4324/9781003670308-5

FIGURE 5.1 The figure shows an individual client taken in the boat on the lake setting a net. Dr. Kevin Lewis has set the precedence for fishing, hunting, trapping and snaring, and skinning animals.

Drawing from lived experience, community teachings, and Cree epistemology, I extend ceremony into a critical methodological terrain that challenges Western psychiatric assumptions, reframes dominant research ethics, and returns mental well-being to relational, land-rooted foundations (Figure 5.1). Rather than repeating therapeutic outcomes for each ceremony, the following sections demonstrate how different ceremonial forms uniquely enact relational, emotional, and spiritual healing.

Conceptual Foundations of Land-Based Ceremony

Rather than repeating therapeutic outcomes for each ceremony, the following sections demonstrate how different ceremonial forms uniquely enact relational, emotional, and spiritual healing. Land-based ceremony is central to nêhiyaw (Cree) worldviews, ethics, and systems of healing. Far from being symbolic or metaphorical, ceremony constitutes an embodied relationship with land, kinship, ancestors, and spirit. This chapter examines Cree land-based ceremonial practices as comprehensive mental health systems that sustain emotional, spiritual, and collective well-being, while also offering a place-rooted framework for decolonizing mental health research and practice. This chapter therefore advances two intertwined arguments:

1 Indigenous ceremonial systems constitute legitimate, complex mental health frameworks deserving recognition equal to Western therapeutic models.
2 Decolonizing mental health research requires centering ceremony, land-based epistemologies, and Indigenous ethical relationality as foundations rather than supplemental cultural content.

Centering these arguments in lived experience, scholarly literature, and Cree traditional teachings, this chapter offers readers—especially those working in mental health and academic research—practical pathways for transformative, ethical, and community-led approaches to wellness.

Decolonizing mental health research requires examining the structures that harmed Indigenous ceremonial systems and continue to shape health inequities today. naturally not diminish; it was forcefully undermined by a colonial apparatus designed to eliminate Indigenous sovereignty, spirituality, and land-based governance. The mental health consequences of these policies cannot be overstated: they fractured identity, disrupted kinship systems, interrupted intergenerational transmission of knowledge, and created conditions for cycles of trauma.

Below, I expand on the colonial mechanisms that directly shaped the ceremonial landscape for Cree communities.

Criminalization of Ceremony under the Indian Act

The Indian Act amendments of the late 19th and early 20th centuries explicitly criminalized Indigenous ceremonies, including the Sundance, Potlatch, and other sacred gatherings (Houle, 1998). Government officials framed these ceremonies as "barbaric," "savage," or "obstacles to civilization," using them as justification to impose bans. Under this legal prohibition, families faced fines, imprisonment, confiscation of regalia, or forced relocation for participating in their spiritual practices.

Yet communities continued to gather in secret. Sundance poles were erected in remote clearings. Sweat lodges were built deep in the bush. Broadcloth was offered quietly, with lookouts posted in case Indian agents approached. Many Elders recall the risks families took to ensure ceremonies survived. These memories are still carried by those who watched their parents or grandparents practice underground, often under fear and constant monitoring.

This forced secrecy caused deep spiritual injuries. Ceremony is relational—it involves community, songs, kinship, and the presence of Elders. Practicing under fear meant ceremonies could not flourish with their full power. When ceremonies were not practiced openly, entire generations lost access to teachings essential for mental, emotional, and spiritual grounding.

The Reserve System and Spatial Disruptions

The reserve system restricted movement, preventing Indigenous families from traveling to large intercommunity gatherings where ceremonies traditionally took place. Nomadic and semi-nomadic patterns were interrupted; hunting, fishing, and trapping trails were cut off by settler encroachment; and collective ceremonial gatherings became difficult to organize. This loss of mobility had more than economic or social consequences—it disrupted the ecological foundations of ceremony. Every ceremony is tied to specific places: rivers, lakes, forests, plains, or trees used for lodges. When mobility was restricted, the ability to engage with these sites diminished, altering ceremonial rhythms and access to land-based medicines. This spatial disruption contributed to spiritual disorientation. Without consistent access to the land that teaches, nourishes, and governs Cree worldview, communities faced emotional and psychological separations from place-based identity.

The Pass System and Surveillance of Spiritual Life

After the North-West Resistance in 1885, the pass system was implemented to control Indigenous movement. People were required to obtain written permission from the Indian agent before leaving the reserve. While not officially encoded in law, it was enforced by police and widely implemented. For ceremony, this system was devastating. Ceremonial gatherings could not occur without participation from extended kin networks across regions. Firekeepers, singers, oskâpêwisak (helpers), and Elders all traveled between communities. The pass system made such gatherings risky, punishable, or impossible. Communities adjusted by holding smaller ceremonies, but this shift reduced the inter-nation relationships that historically strengthened Cree ceremonial life. Large-scale ceremonies that relied on political alliances and kinship webs, such as Sundance, became severely limited.

Starvation Policies, Rationing, and Spiritual Exhaustion

The withholding of food rations on reserves was used as a method of social control. Elders have described how families survived through starvation periods, eating dogs or scavenging, when rations were delayed or reduced (Houle, 1998). These policies weakened bodies, spirits, and the capacity for ceremony, which requires physical strength, spiritual preparation, and emotional stability. Starvation also caused profound grief and loss. Many ceremonial roles—such as singers or bundle holders—require the guidance of strong, well-respected community leaders. When families experienced death at high rates due to starvation or disease, ceremonial continuity broke down.

Residential Schools and Interruption of Ceremonial Transmission

Residential schools forcibly separated children from their families, punishing them for participating in ceremony or speaking their language. Many children returned home unable to understand ceremonial teachings, or carrying shame instilled by educators who characterized their spirituality as sinful or primitive. The intergenerational impacts include:

- Loss of language needed to understand teachings
- Breakdown of kinship systems central to ceremonial preparation
- Internalized shame about Indigenous identity
- Emotional disconnection from ancestors and land

Many adults today express a longing for ceremonies they were denied access to as children. Their healing journeys often begin with reconnection to spiritual practices withheld from them.

Contemporary Implications for Mental Health

Colonial disruptions did not simply remove ceremony from communities; they imposed foreign health systems—many rooted in Christian doctrine or Western psychiatry—while dismissing Indigenous wellness frameworks. These imposed models often interpret Indigenous grief, spiritual experiences, or ancestral connections as pathology, rather than relational teachings. Many Indigenous people encounter mental health services that:

- Ignore the role of land in healing
- Exclude ceremony from recognized treatment options
- Pathologize community-oriented coping practices
- Fail to recognize collective trauma or structural violence
- Focus on individual symptoms rather than relational imbalance

These gaps continue to fuel mistrust of mainstream mental health systems. Yet communities have consistently responded by reclaiming ceremony as a pathway for healing, resurgence, and self-determination. This reclamation is not backward-looking; it is future-oriented, grounded in the understanding that ceremony remains a living, dynamic source of wellness relevant to contemporary realities.

Land-Based Ceremonies as Healing

As outlined earlier in this chapter, Cree ceremonies constitute a holistic mental health system grounded in land, kinship, spirituality, and collective responsibility. Unlike Western therapeutic models, which often emphasize individualized treatment, Cree ceremonial healing is relational, intergenerational, and place based. In the following expanded sections, I examine key ceremonies and their significance for emotional, mental, and spiritual well-being.

Naming Ceremonies: Identity, Belonging, and Early Mental-Emotional Anchoring

Naming ceremonies are deeply significant events that establish a child's identity and spiritual foundation. As Elders teach, children choose their parents before birth, arriving with gifts and responsibilities. A naming ceremony affirms these gifts, providing young ones with spiritual protection, purpose, and direction. A child's *otisih* (umbilical cord) is often placed on a trapline or berry patch, symbolizing future roles and relational connections (Auger, 2020). This placement ties the child to land, sustenance, and kinship responsibilities from their earliest moments. Psychologically, naming ceremonies support:

- **Sense of belonging**
- **Self-worth and identity formation**
- **Early attachment and emotional security**
- **Connection to community and ancestors**

These foundational experiences counteract the disruptions caused by colonial systems and create protective factors for lifelong mental health.

Rites of Passage: Structured Transitions and Gendered Teachings

During puberty, rites of passage help young people transition into adulthood with clarity, confidence, and relational accountability.

For Young Women

Grandmothers teach:

- Self-respect
- Firekeeping
- Domestic responsibilities

- Sacredness of womanhood
- Emotional regulation
- Community roles

These teachings promote inner strength and self-worth while addressing what Western psychology would describe as adolescent identity development.

For Young Men

Young men are sent into the bush to learn survival skills, respect for animals, and courage (Mandelbaum, 1979). These experiences teach problem solving, emotional regulation, and responsibility.

Vision Quest (Fasting): Discipline, Insight, and Emotional Clarity

Fasting for four days and nights teaches spiritual discipline and surrender. For many, visions provide direction, resolve confusion, or bring clarity during emotional upheaval.

Fast participants often report:

- Release of grief
- Strengthened identity
- Renewed purpose
- Emotional cleansing
- Inner peace

From a mental health perspective, fasting facilitates self-reflection, mindfulness, and introspection.

Sundance: Communal Healing, Sacrifice, and Resilience

Sundance is among the most powerful ceremonies in Cree worldview. Dancers pray continuously, often without food or water, offering sacrifice for family, community, and future generations. This ceremony teaches mental discipline, emotional endurance, compassion, and collective prayer.

Psychologically, Sundance creates:

- Deep emotional release
- Connection to ancestors
- Strengthened sense of purpose
- Regulation of negative internal narratives
- Communal solidarity

Sundance reminds participants that healing is not only personal but also collective.

Sweat lodge: Cleansing, Rebirth, and Inner-Child Healing

Sweat lodge ceremonies use heat, darkness, songs, prayer, and sacred medicines to cleanse the mind, body, and spirit. Many people experience resurfacing memories, emotional breakthroughs, and profound clarity.

Elders describe the sweat lodge as returning to the womb. This metaphor illustrates its role in healing early childhood wounds, trauma, and emotional disconnection.

Sweat lodge supports:

- Trauma processing
- Emotional release
- Stress reduction
- Strengthening of spiritual identity
- Communal bonding
- Inner-child healing

These processes parallel therapeutic outcomes sought in Western trauma-informed models—but achieved through land-based spiritual means.

Chicken Dance and Horse Dance: Movement-Based Healing

These ceremonies integrate movement, rhythm, and collective energy. Dancing becomes a form of embodied healing, releasing grief and inviting joy.

Singers, dancers, and drummers all contribute to communal healing. The ceremonies highlight the role of art, sound, and kinship in emotional well-being.

Feasts and Ancestor Honoring: Grief Work and Continuity Across Realms

Feasts help families maintain relationships with loved ones who have passed on. They ensure ancestors are fed, remembered, and honored. This spiritual continuity supports healthy grieving, closure, and relief from emotional unrest.

Providing food to ancestors also teaches children about death and the spirit world, helping them build emotional resilience and understanding.

Land as Medicine

At the heart of all ceremony is land. Sacred medicines—sweetgrass, sage, tobacco, cedar—carry teachings that support emotional grounding, purification, and spiritual connection. Land itself is therapeutic: forests, lakes, winds, and animals all convey guidance and comfort. Land-based healing recognizes:

- Ecological relationships as mental health foundations
- Sensory grounding (smells of sweetgrass, feel of soil, heat of the lodge)
- Spiritual communication
- Embodied connection through movement, harvesting, and prayer

This depth of relationality cannot be replicated in Western clinical spaces.

Personal Narrative as Method

In Indigenous research, personal narrative is not an anecdotal supplement—it is a methodological responsibility. Among Cree researchers, telling one's story is a form of relational accountability, a way of situating oneself ethically within community knowledge systems, and a practice of honoring the teachings one carries. Story reveals how knowledge is lived. It exposes the relational threads—between land, kin, and spirit—that make Cree epistemologies distinct from Western frameworks of inquiry (Kovach, 2009a,b; Wilson, 2008). Narrative is therefore a research method, a teaching practice, and a ceremonial responsibility.

The narratives presented throughout the original chapter—my first memories of Sundance as a child, my struggles with depression in adulthood, the return to ceremony during my graduate studies, the teachings shared through sweat lodge, Horse Dance, Chicken Dance, and feasts—are not personal reflections selected to illustrate theory after the fact. They *are* theory. They demonstrate how Cree epistemologies understand healing, knowledge, and identity not as abstractions but as embodied experiences shaped through ceremony and kinship.

Narrative and Relational Validity

In Western qualitative research, validity is often measured through replicability, methodological transparency, and consistent coding processes. In Indigenous research, validity emerges from relational integrity:

- Did the story honor the teachings?
- Did it respect community protocols?
- Does it contribute to collective knowledge and healing?
- Is it accountable to the relationships that shaped it?

Under Indigenous paradigms, stories are living entities. They hold power. They hold responsibility. They require humility from the storyteller and careful listening from the learner.

When I describe the moment, I first attended Sundance as a girl—peering between poplar trees, smelling sweetgrass, watching the dancers sacrifice—I am not offering a nostalgic memory. I am tracing the beginning of my ceremonial education, the early spiritual imprint that taught me to recognize healing as both personal and communal. When I share the experience of grieving my biological father, entering the mental health ward, and returning to ceremony through Chicken Dance, I am illustrating the relational nature of healing. Ceremony spoke to me when language felt inadequate, grounding my mind and spirit when clinical environments could not.

Narrative as Decolonial Resistance

Personal narrative challenges the colonial frameworks that have long silenced Indigenous voices, reduced Indigenous identities to stereotypes, or dismissed Indigenous knowledge as unscientific. Through narrative:

- Indigenous researchers reclaim authority over their stories.
- We disrupt academic traditions that prioritize detached objectivity.
- We insist that knowledge is relational, emotional, spiritual, and lived.
- We resist the colonial expectation that Indigenous scholars split themselves—ceremony in one world, research in another.

When I recount the story of singeing the moose nose during doctoral studies—teaching my cohort sister something I was still learning myself, then sharing the origin story of niyânîmis imprinting his hand on the moose's nose—I demonstrate how humor, respect, and embodied teaching remain central to contemporary Cree research. Ceremony breathes through these moments. Stories are transmitted. Laughter heals. Knowledge circulates.

Narrative as Mental Health Insight

Narratives reveal psychological landscapes that Western clinical language cannot fully capture. They allow us to understand:

- How grief travels through generations
- How shame can take root through colonial violence
- How depression feels when ceremony is absent
- How joy returns when kinship is restored
- How land calls us home during emotional exhaustion

These insights are essential for decolonizing mental health research, which must recognize that Indigenous emotional experience is embedded in land, history, and spirituality. Narrative creates the space for this recognition.

In this chapter, narrative is not decoration—it is methodology, evidence, ethical grounding, and medicine.

A Framework for Decolonizing Mental Health Research

Drawing from Cree ceremonial teachings, existing Indigenous scholarship, and peer review recommendations, I offer a comprehensive framework for decolonizing mental health research. This framework is grounded in Indigenous sovereignty and land-based relationality. It is intended to guide students, practitioners, and researchers seeking ethical and transformative approaches to Indigenous wellness.

Center Indigenous Land-Based Epistemologies

Decolonizing mental health research requires grounding inquiry in Indigenous worldviews, not merely adding Indigenous "perspectives" to Western models. Land-based epistemologies understand mental health as inseparable from:

- Spiritual connections
- Kinship responsibilities
- Ecological relationships
- Community governance
- Ancestral teachings

Land is not a metaphor for well-being—it is the source of well-being. Every ceremony described earlier—Sundance, Sweat lodge, fasts, feasts, rites of passage—is fundamentally rooted in land. In research, this means methods should emerge from land-based teachings, not impose frameworks developed in Eurocentric psychological paradigms.

Practical implications:

- Begin research with ceremony or land acknowledgments that involve more than protocol—they involve relational commitments.
- Engage land as participant, not backdrop.
- Recognize that healing occurs outdoors, through touch, smell, sound, movement, and spirit.

Enact Relational Accountability (wâhkôhtowin)

Relational accountability means researchers are responsible for all their relations:

- Human relations (family, community, Elders, youth)
- More-than-human relations (animals, plants, water, wind)

- Spiritual relations (ancestors, spirits, helpers)
- Future generations who will inherit the outcomes of research

In Western research, accountability is often upward—to funders, institutions, and ethics boards. In Indigenous research, accountability is circular and rooted in kinship.

Practical implications:

- Researchers must introduce themselves, their families, and their histories.
- They must account for how knowledge will be used, shared, or protected.
- They must accept responsibility for harm and continuously re-establish trust.
- Community benefit is not optional—it is obligatory.

Use Ceremony as Method

Ceremony teaches discipline, respect, patience, and emotional regulation. It informs how researchers listen, interpret, analyze, and reciprocate.

Using ceremony as method means recognizing:

- Sweat lodge teaches how to sit with discomfort.
- Sundance teaches sacrifice, endurance, and prayerful intention.
- Fasts teach patience, insight, and clarity.
- Feasts teach grief work and relational continuity.

Ceremony shapes the researcher's character and affects the quality of their interpretation. It also offers specific structures for data collection and analysis—for example, sharing circles, collective dreaming, or narrative dialogues.

Practical implications:

- Researchers may consult Elders to determine appropriate ceremonial methods.
- Some research questions may require bundles, pipes, sweats, or feasts.
- Ceremony should guide interpretation—not only initial data gathering.

Restore Indigenous Ethical Protocols

Ethics in Indigenous mental health research must extend far beyond consent forms. In Cree contexts, ethics involve:

- Offering tobacco
- Presenting cloth
- Following gendered ceremonial roles
- Respecting sites where spirits dwell
- Protecting ceremonial knowledge from misuse

Protocol is reciprocal. When tobacco is offered, a relationship is formed. When cloth is given, teachings may be shared. Ethical research therefore requires humility and readiness to be guided.

Practical implications:

- Researchers must follow community-defined ethical processes.
- Knowledge shared in ceremony is not automatically publishable.
- Elders determine what can be recorded, translated, or taught.

Challenge Western Mental Health Paradigms

Western mental health models often pathologize Indigenous experiences or ignore structural violence. Decolonizing research requires questioning assumptions such as:

- Individualistic understandings of trauma
- Separation of mind and spirit
- Privileging diagnostic labels
- Discounting spiritual experiences
- Dismissing ceremony as unscientific

Indigenous mental health frameworks position distress not as individual pathology but as relational imbalance. Healing must therefore restore relationships—between people, land, ancestors, and future generations.

Practical implications:

- Practitioners should adopt strength-based, relational models.
- Diagnostic categories must be used cautiously and culturally adaptively.
- Emotional expressions linked to ceremony must be recognized as valid.

Prioritize Community-Led and Community-Owned Research

Communities determine research goals, questions, methods, benefits, and data ownership. Researchers serve as helpers, not directors. Practical implications:

- Establish community research committees
- Share power over budgets, timelines, and dissemination
- Ensure data sovereignty follows OCAP (Ownership, Control, Access, Possession) principles
- Avoid extractive models of research

Support Ceremony-Informed Therapeutic Practices

Many Indigenous clients want ceremony included in mental health care. However, policies (e.g., NIHB limitations) restrict practitioners from offering or supporting ceremony within formal clinical contexts. Decolonizing research and practice therefore requires advocating for systemic changes so Indigenous healing systems are recognized as legitimate health practices. Practical implications:

- Integrate land-based programs into treatment planning
- Collaborate with ceremonial knowledge keepers
- Develop safe ceremonial spaces within clinics and community centers
- Train practitioners in cultural humility and land-based ethics

Practical Applications for Students, Practitioners, and Researchers

Translating ceremonial knowledge, land-based epistemologies, and decolonial theory into practice requires intentional action that is relational, reciprocal, and deeply grounded in community-defined priorities. While the previous sections of this chapter established the philosophical and methodological foundations of ceremony-informed mental health approaches, this section turns toward application. The goal is to provide practical, context-sensitive strategies that students, practitioners, and researchers can use to respectfully engage in land-based, ceremony-informed, and decolonizing mental health work. These strategies must be interpreted not as universal prescriptions but as pathways—guiding principles that must adapt to the unique histories, protocols, and governance structures of the communities with whom one partners.

What follows is an expanded discussion of how learners, professionals, and scholars can incorporate these approaches into their work in ways that sustain Indigenous sovereignty, honor relational accountability, and uphold the ethical principles foundational to Cree teachings such as *wâhkôhtowin*, *miyo-pimâtisiwin*, and *pâstahowin*.

For Students

Students occupy a powerful position within the broader movement toward decolonized mental health. They represent emerging generations of scholars and practitioners who have the capacity to reshape systems from within. Yet students must also understand that their learning cannot be solely theoretical. Knowledge rooted in ceremony and land is experiential, embodied, and relational. For students to meaningfully engage with these frameworks, they must cultivate modesty, patience, and openness to learning in ways that diverge from conventional Western academic norms.

Engage in Land-Based Learning

Participating in cultural camps, land walks, medicine harvesting, and ceremonies is essential for developing an authentic understanding of Indigenous mental health systems. Land-based learning reconnects students with the relational foundations of knowledge. It teaches them to listen to the land—not metaphorically but literally—to feel teachings through sound, wind, movement, seasons, and presence. For Cree Elders, land is the first teacher. Medicines such as sweetgrass, sage, cedar, and tobacco grow in places that require respectful harvesting practices. Learning how to approach these plants with respect, offer tobacco, and harvest intentionally helps students understand the ethical structure of Indigenous healing systems. Land-based learning also allows students to witness how ceremony unfolds in real time—how community members gather, how songs carry teachings, how firekeepers prepare the grounds, and how children observe and participate within their kinship roles. This orientation cannot be reproduced in classrooms, textbooks, or digital simulations. It requires stepping onto the land, listening, watching, participating, and experiencing learning as a living relationship.

Build Relationships with Elders

Elders are the heart of Indigenous mental health frameworks. They carry ancestral knowledge, govern protocol, and guide ethical decision-making. Forming respectful relationships with Elders is essential. These relationships cannot be transactional—seeking information quickly or for academic purposes alone. They must be nurtured over time through offerings, listening, service, and reciprocity. When Elders guide students, they do so holistically. They teach not only about research design or ethics but also about becoming a good relative, caring for oneself, and understanding one's responsibilities within the community and land. Elders help students interpret dreams, memories, grief, and emotional challenges. They also correct misunderstandings and gently redirect students if they begin to drift from ceremony-based ethics or relational accountability. Building these relationships also teaches students how to navigate cultural protocols—how to offer tobacco, how to introduce themselves, why certain stories can be shared only in winter, and how songs or ceremonies require permissions. These lessons shape not only academic learning but also personal transformation.

Develop Reflexive Journals

Reflexive journaling is a powerful tool for integrating educational experience with ceremonial learning. Students can use journals to document emotions, realizations, challenges, and the teachings that emerge from ceremony or land-based learning. Journals become a bridge between the interior landscape of the learner and the external teachings of Elders, spirits, and land. In Cree research methodologies, reflexivity is not only an intellectual exercise, but it is also a spiritual and emotional practice. Journaling encourages students to examine how ceremony influences their thinking, how land-based teachings challenge Western assumptions, and how personal history interacts with research goals. Over time, journals reveal patterns, shifts, and growth. They also document commitments, responsibilities, and questions that guide future learning. As students develop reflexivity, they become more capable of navigating the ethical complexities of Indigenous mental health research. They also cultivate humbleness, recognizing that learning is lifelong and relational rather than finite or individually contained.

Learn Indigenous Languages

Language is central to understanding mental health concepts embedded in Cree thought. Words like *wâhkôhtowin* (kinship), *pâstahowin* (consequences of wrongdoing), *miyo-pimâtisiwin* (the good life), and *ocînêwin* (discipline) communicate entire worldviews. They cannot be fully translated into English without losing nuance, relational context, or spiritual meaning.

Learning Cree language—even at introductory levels—allows deeper engagement with ceremonial teachings. Language revitalization is mental health work. It reconnects students to identity, helps restore intergenerational relationships, and grounds learning within Indigenous intellectual traditions. For many, the process of learning language also becomes an emotional healing journey, as they reclaim parts of themselves denied through colonial policies.

Language learning therefore supports not only academic development but also Indigenous resurgence.

For Practitioners

Mental health practitioners working with Indigenous individuals or communities must recognize that Western models alone cannot address the depth of spiritual, emotional, and relational dimensions foundational to Indigenous well-being. Decolonizing practice requires practitioners to move beyond cultural competence toward relational, ceremony-informed approaches that acknowledge Indigenous sovereignty in health care.

Collaborate with Ceremonial Knowledge Keepers

Practitioners must work alongside Elders, knowledge keepers, and oskâpêwisak (helpers) who hold ceremonial knowledge. Collaborating with these individuals ensures that clients accessing mental health care are supported holistically. Elders provide cultural, spiritual, and emotional guidance that practitioners cannot replicate. They may lead sweats, pipe ceremonies, naming rites, or feasts for clients seeking healing. This collaboration must be grounded in respect, reciprocity, and proper protocol. Practitioners must not appropriate ceremonial roles or assume authority over spiritual teachings. Instead, they should create structures that allow ceremonial experts to lead, guide, and support clients in culturally safe ways.

Adapt Clinical Spaces

Physical environments communicate whether ceremony is welcome. Many Indigenous clients feel disconnected in sterile clinical settings that mirror colonial institutions. Practitioners can create smudge-friendly rooms, develop outdoor therapeutic spaces, or designate quiet rooms with medicines, blankets, drums, or natural materials. These adaptations do more than enhance comfort—they signal respect for Indigenous worldviews. Outdoor therapeutic spaces, for example, allow clients to sit on the earth, feel the wind, listen to birds, pray near water, or engage with land-based grounding techniques. Clients carrying grief or trauma often feel safer outside, where their healing is witnessed by land and ancestors rather than confined to a clinical office.

Practice Land-Informed Trauma Care

Many Indigenous clients carry trauma rooted in land dispossession, residential schools, family separation, or cultural suppression. Land-informed trauma care recognizes that healing must involve restoring relationships with land and spirit.

Practitioners can guide clients in:

- Grounding with earth or water
- Identifying supportive land-based practices
- Reconnecting with medicines through smell, touch, or harvesting
- Incorporating song, movement, or prayer
- Engaging in grief work through feasts or ceremonial offerings

This modality requires practitioners to remain flexible, allowing therapy to unfold beyond traditional clinical boundaries.

4 Advocate for Ceremony in Health Policy

The exclusion of Indigenous ceremonies from NIHB coverage reflects ongoing colonial inequities. Practitioners must advocate for policies that:

- Recognize ceremony as a legitimate therapeutic practice
- Compensate Elders and ceremonial helpers fairly

- Fund land-based camps and programming
- Integrate ceremonial healing into mainstream health systems

Leveraging their institutional influence, practitioners can help shift health policy toward more equitable, culturally grounded frameworks.

For Researchers

Researchers have an ethical responsibility to ensure their work contributes to Indigenous sovereignty, mental wellness, and community benefit. Research must shift away from extractive traditions and toward relational, community-driven models that honor Indigenous governance and ceremony.

Co-Create Research with Communities

Research must begin with relational meetings, not funding applications. Researchers should spend time in the community—attending feasts, participating in ceremonies when invited, offering help, and building trust. Projects must be co-designed with community leadership, ensuring goals, methods, and benefits align with community priorities.

Researchers should return to the community regularly, not only during data collection. Long-term relationships are essential.

Use Narrative, Story, and Sharing Circles

Story is an Indigenous analytic tool. Sharing circles allow emotional and spiritual dimensions to surface in ways interviews cannot. Narrative methods validate community experiences, honor oral traditions, and allow Elders to teach through stories rather than structured questions.

Researchers must understand that stories belong to communities. They should be shared only with permission and interpreted in ways that respect context and protocol.

Honor Data Sovereignty

Following OCAP principles ensures that communities retain authority over their information. Data sovereignty also protects sacred knowledge from misuse, misinterpretation, or appropriation.

Researchers must use agreements that clearly define:

- Who owns recordings or transcripts
- Where data will be stored
- Who can access it

- How it may be shared
- What cannot be published

Disseminate Findings Responsibly

In Cree methodology, knowledge returns to the people before it enters academic journals. Researchers should present findings through feasts, presentations, or ceremonies. Written reports must be accessible, culturally grounded, and respectful of community-defined permissions.

Responsible dissemination strengthens trust, honors relationships, and prevents misinterpretation in academic or public settings.

Ceremony is a living, breathing expression of Indigenous sovereignty, law, ethics, governance, and wellness. It is not peripheral to mental health—**ceremony is mental health.** Ceremony speaks through the land, guides through ancestors, and heals through movement, prayer, offering, and relational renewal. This expanded section has demonstrated how students, practitioners, and researchers can enact land-based, ceremony-informed, and decolonizing approaches in grounded, practical ways. The decolonizing framework presented across this chapter is not theoretical—it emerges directly from lived Cree practice, ancestral teachings, and community experiences. It reflects Indigenous strengths, intellectual traditions, and the enduring power of ceremony to restore balance.

Despite historical attempts to suppress ceremonial life, Cree ceremonies continue to flourish. They strengthen families, sustain languages, heal trauma, and guide communities through crisis. They provide emotional resilience, spiritual clarity, and a profound sense of belonging. Each time the drum sounds, each time sweetgrass burns, each time a child receives their name, Indigenous futures strengthen. The trees are still dancing. The drums are still calling. Our children still come into this world knowing who they are. Our Elders still pray for us. Our communities continue rising. Ceremony endures—not as memory but as motion, not as relic but as rebirth. Through ceremony, we heal. Through ceremony, we remember. Through ceremony, we return to ourselves.

6

LAND AS HEALTH SELF-DETERMINATION

Translating Indigenous Ceremony into Mental Health Frameworks

Jody Houle (with support from Kevin Lewis and Ranjan Datta)

This chapter examines Indigenous health self-determination through the lens of land-based ceremony, grounded in nêhiyaw (Cree) worldview. It argues that ceremony is not a cultural supplement to Western mental health systems, but a fully developed, relational health framework encompassing mental, emotional, physical, and spiritual well-being. Centering land, kinship, and ceremonial law, this chapter situates Indigenous healing practices as expressions of sovereignty and responsibility rather than alternative or adjunct forms of care. These systems existed long before Western psychiatry and psychology and continue to sustain Indigenous communities despite the long history of colonial disruption. Land-based ceremonies—such as Sweat Lodge, Pipe Ceremony, Vision Quest, Sundance, and feasts—are not supplementary healing modalities; they are comprehensive, relational, and sovereign health frameworks that reflect Indigenous laws, ethics, and responsibilities to the land. This chapter expands the conversation by examining how ceremonial life fuels Indigenous health self-determination, how Western mental health institutions remain limited in their capacity to address Indigenous wellness, and how Indigenous-led approaches grounded in land, kinship, and ceremony offer transformative models for decolonizing mental health research and practice. Engaging Indigenous and Western worldviews critically, this chapter proposes a framework for Indigenous health sovereignty rooted in ceremony and relational accountability. For students, practitioners, and researchers, this chapter translates Indigenous ceremonial knowledge into conceptual tools, ethical principles, and practice-relevant frameworks that can inform mental health research, service design, and Indigenous-led healing initiatives (Figure 6.1).

DOI: 10.4324/9781003670308-6

FIGURE 6.1 The figure shows an interview with Dr. Kevin Lewis in his views of how ceremonies are complex. It was a wonderful experience getting to know this knowledge keeper. He is a wonderful father and Professor and had many land-based projects and practices ceremony in the good way.

Ceremony as a Pathway to Indigenous Health Self-Determination

Indigenous health self-determination begins with worldview. In the nêhiyaw worldview, health is not merely the absence of disease or the management of psychological symptoms; it is a relational state of balance among mind, body, spirit, land, ancestors, and kinship networks. Ceremonies are the primary mechanisms through which this balance is restored, maintained, and strengthened. When individuals enter the sweat lodge, when they engage in Pipe Ceremony, when they fast and pray, or when they participate in the Sundance, they are not engaging in symbolic acts. They are activating relational, ethical, and spiritual systems of knowledge that orient them toward healing, identity, purpose, and community responsibility.

Western mental health systems tend to fragment the self into parts: symptoms, diagnoses, pathologies, and treatments. Ceremony, by contrast, treats the self as a unified, relational being. Through prayer, song, movement, offering, sacrifice, and sensory engagement with land, ceremony constitutes a holistic therapeutic process. For many who seek healing through ceremony, the lodge becomes a site of renewal, emotional release, spiritual awakening, and reconnection to purpose. The land becomes an active participant in healing, offering ground, wind, warmth, medicines, and the presence of more-than-human kin.

Indigenous health self-determination requires the full recognition of ceremony as a legitimate health practice and not merely "cultural support." To reclaim ceremony is to reclaim health sovereignty. It is to restore systems of care that were intentionally targeted by colonial institutions through the banning of ceremonies, residential schools, and assimilation policies. Thus, land-based ceremony is a practice of resilience, resistance, and renewal—a declaration that Indigenous health cannot be defined, governed, or restricted by Western institutions. For mental health services, this distinction matters. If healing is relational and land-based, then assessment, treatment, and recovery must extend beyond individual symptom management to include spiritual relationships, identity restoration, and community accountability.

Within mainstream mental health literature, comparable critiques of symptom-based models have been raised in relational, trauma-informed, and community psychology traditions (e.g., Duran, 2006; Gone, 2013; Kingi, 2018). However, Indigenous ceremonial systems differ in that they do not merely supplement clinical care but operate as sovereign health systems with their own laws, protocols, and accountability structures.

Personal Narrative as Relational Evidence of Ceremony's Healing Power

Personal experience with ceremony provides an entry point for understanding how Indigenous healing systems function in practice. The following account is offered not as an autobiography, but as situated evidence illustrating how ceremonial engagement supports mental health recovery across intergenerational contexts. Growing up in Goodfish Lake and Saulteaux First Nation, we endured poverty, family violence, addictions, and the emotional aftermath of trauma. After losing her husband to suicide, my mother sought healing for herself and her children through both Western and traditional methods. She found that Western counseling helped us name our pain, but it was ceremony that helped us transform it. Grew up in social-psychological conditions that fill statistical brackets: poverty, alcoholism, drug abuse, suicide ideation, incarceration, and domestic violence. Yet ceremony anchored us. Through sweat lodge, Pipe Ceremony, and land-based practices, we learned to understand ourselves beyond the narratives imposed on Indigenous peoples by Western systems. Ceremony became our medicine for depression, grief, intergenerational trauma, and identity fragmentation. Author-1's own struggles with bipolar disorder brought me to the mental health ward at one of the lowest points in my life. Medicine was necessary, but it was ceremony—brought to me by my partner, Dr. Kevin Lewis—that allowed me to return to my spirit. He brought medicine people, healers, and knowledge keepers to pray, sing, and sit with me. Through this, I learned that healing is not simply about symptom management but about relational realignment—mind, spirit, body, ancestors, land. These experiences ground my argument that ceremony is a form of therapy, one that Western systems have yet to acknowledge despite overwhelming evidence of its effectiveness for Indigenous communities. Author-1's experience of psychiatric hospitalization illustrates the limits of symptom-focused care when disconnected from spiritual, relational, and land-based supports. Author-1 siblings—Adam, Michael, Karla, and Denny—have similarly walked their own healing paths, guided by ceremony and land-based teachings. Their resilience and strength are testaments to the power of Indigenous healing systems. Their stories remind us that Indigenous health is collective, intergenerational, and relational. For practitioners and researchers, these experiences highlight the importance of viewing ceremony not as an adjunct intervention, but as a sustained relational process that cannot be reduced to episodic treatment. For practitioners and researchers, this account demonstrates that ceremony functions as sustained relational therapy rather than episodic intervention.

A Conversation on Ceremony and Healing: Insights from Dr. Kevin Lewis (Author-2)

To expand this understanding, I turn to an extended conversation with *ninâpêm*, Dr. Kevin Lewis (author-2), a pipe holder, educator, and ceremonial knowledge keeper from Ministikwan Lake Cree Nation. His insights demonstrate the multidimensional nature of Indigenous healing and the central role of ceremony in supporting mental health. Dr. Lewis begins by emphasizing that life itself is a lifelong learning process, and ceremony is one of the most powerful ways individuals make sense of their healing journeys. According to him, Indigenous ceremonies are profoundly complex because they require community involvement and invoke relationships with more-than-human relatives: the sun, thunderbirds, wind, four-legged beings, and the spirits who inhabit the unseen realms.

> Lewis frames ceremony as a cosmological kinship system in which mental health is understood relationally rather than intrapsychically. This aligns with Indigenous relational epistemologies and contrasts with Euro-Western intrapsychic models. It is a universe family that you are inviting, not only your human relatives.

Ceremony, then, is not simply a gathering of people. It is an invitation to cosmic kinship. It connects individuals with their spirit helpers, namesakes, clans, and the ancestral beings who guide them. In this way, the ceremony situates mental health within a universal kinship model that acknowledges the interdependence of life, energy, and relational ethics. Dr. Lewis also spoke about identity formation as foundational to mental and spiritual wellness. Many Indigenous people lost their connection to identity due to residential schools, colonial education, and disruptions to land-based knowledge. He described how he, too, grew up unaware of the full extent of historical trauma or mental health issues affecting his community. Yet, through Sundance, Pipe Ceremony, and land-based stories, he began to understand who he was: a person from *miniscikoskâwâyisi*, "the place of little islands," a location that carries teachings and responsibilities. Identity, he emphasized, cannot be understood without community, language, ceremony, and land. "Once you know who you are and where you come from, your stories guide you. Your relatives—human and more-than-human—help you navigate life. That is mental health." His reflections illuminate the therapeutic depth of ceremony: it grounds people in identity, kinship, and responsibility—core components of Indigenous mental health frameworks.

Ceremony vs. Western Mental Health Systems: A Critical Analysis

For mental health practitioners working in Western systems, these distinctions suggest concrete shifts in practice, including: (1) expanding assessment beyond individual symptom profiles, (2) recognizing spiritual and land-based relationships as legitimate determinants of wellness, and (3) collaborating with ceremonial knowledge holders as co-therapeutic authorities rather than cultural consultants.

A central aim of this chapter is to address the gap between Indigenous ceremonial healing and Western mental health systems. Despite the evidence supporting ceremony's effectiveness, Indigenous healing methods are rarely recognized as legitimate forms of therapy within mainstream institutions. For example, the Non-Insured Health Benefits (NIHB) Program funds counseling, psychology, and certain biomedical services but excludes ceremony from its definition of mental health treatment. This exclusion reinforces the colonial assumption that Indigenous ways of healing are spiritual, cultural, or symbolic, rather than scientific or therapeutic. Yet Indigenous healing systems are grounded in millennia of empirical observation, sophisticated ecological knowledge, and highly structured ceremonial protocols.

While Western therapies emphasize symptoms, diagnosis, and individual behavior, Indigenous healing emphasizes:

- relational accountability
- spiritual coherence
- ecological balance
- community belonging

- ancestral continuity
- embodied knowledge
- emotional release
- identity restoration

For clinicians, this means expanding practice beyond diagnosis and treatment plans to include collaboration with Elders, recognition of spiritual determinants of health, and support for ceremonial participation as part of care pathways. These dimensions of healing are often overlooked in clinical environments, leaving Indigenous clients feeling misunderstood or partially supported. When practitioners ignore the spiritual and relational dimensions of Indigenous wellness, they inadvertently reproduce colonial fragmentation of Indigenous identities. Ceremony must therefore be recognized not merely as cultural enrichment but as an Indigenous therapeutic paradigm—one that is comprehensive, relational, and deeply effective.

Toward a Framework for Indigenous Health Self-Determination

For researchers, this means designing studies that center on ceremonial protocols rather than treating them as variables. For practitioners, it requires recognizing ceremony as a primary site of healing rather than a cultural adjunct. For institutions, it implies reallocating funding and authority toward Indigenous-led ceremonial programming. Drawing from narrative, scholarship, and teaching, this chapter proposes a framework for Indigenous health self-determination grounded in land-based ceremony. This framework strengthens Indigenous sovereignty, transforms mental health research, and provides concrete pathways for Indigenous-led healing approaches.

Ceremony as Core Health System

Ceremony functions as a primary site of healing governed by Indigenous law, protocol, and accountability.

Land as Primary Health Provider

Healing is inseparable from land, which offers medicine, grounding, and relational presence.

Elders as Ethical and Therapeutic Authorities

Elders guide protocols, interpret visions, address spiritual imbalance, and mediate relational tensions.

Language as Healing Infrastructure

Key Cree concepts—*wâhkôhtowin, pâstâhowin, ocînêwin, miyo-pimâtisiwin*—contain entire health philosophies. Language revitalization strengthens identity and mental health.

Community Governance of Health Knowledge

Communities—not institutions—must define how ceremonial teachings are used, shared, protected, or withheld.

Integration Rather Than Assimilation

Western therapies may support Indigenous healing but must not override or diminish ceremonial authority.

Policy Advocacy for Ceremony Recognition

Indigenous health sovereignty requires institutional change, including funding for ceremony and land-based healing programs.

Healing, Continuity, and the Future

Western diagnostic labels can name suffering but often fail to address its relational and spiritual origins. Indigenous health self-determination is ultimately about liberation—liberation from colonial definitions of health, from imposed systems of care, and from narratives that diminish Indigenous knowledge. Land-based ceremony is a source of freedom, power, and resilience. It reconnects individuals to ancestors, restores relationships with land, and realigns communities with their original responsibilities as *iyiniwak*—the Original People. We are living in a time of resurgence. Young people are returning to ceremony. Elders continue to pray. New generations seek language, stories, and land teachings. The land still calls us home. Ceremony endures—not as a memory but as a movement. Through ceremony, we heal. Through ceremony, we remember. Through ceremony, we reclaim ourselves.

Ceremony, Choice, and the Ethics of Mental Health Healing

One of the most important teachings that emerges from our ceremonial life is that spirituality, like healing, cannot be forced. Kevin often reminds me that he was never pressured into any one path. As he describes it, his parents never once said, *"You're going to church,"* or *"You're going to Sundance."* There was no ultimatum, no spiritual coercion. Instead, he was gently loved, nurtured, and encouraged to find out who he was, and what these ceremonies, songs, and lodges were about. That freedom to choose—held within a context of strong kinship, language, and land—became a core part of his mental, emotional, and spiritual development.

He explains that, as a child and youth, he was drawn in by curiosity and relationships. He watched the singers, observed how they carried themselves, and listened intently to the ceremonial songs. Over time, he began to understand the meanings behind those songs: which spirit they were calling, which direction they were facing, which lodge they were connected to. He came to see that each ceremonial space has its own architecture of knowledge. Ten primary types of lodges, he tells me, can be named, but within each of those there are levels—layers of specialization, teachings, and responsibilities. Each lodge is a library. Each pole, a text. Each song, a chapter.

One of his Elders once told him, *"If you ever find somebody that knows everything, you have met the Creator. That's Creator you are sitting with."* That teaching stayed with him. It humbled him and reminded him that no one knows everything, and no one tradition holds all knowledge. There are many ways of doing things, many ways that ceremonies are carried out from community to community. He recalls thinking at one point that there was "only one right way" to conduct a lodge or a ceremony, but his Elders corrected him: "This is the way they do things here. When we are guests, we follow their lead. We do not come to force our ways. We are here to help and learn."

This ethic of humility, relational accountability, and non-imposition is also fundamental to decolonizing mental health practice. Just as we do not impose ceremonial forms on another community, we must refuse the imposition of singular Western models of mental health as the only legitimate means of healing. Ceremony teaches us that there is never just one pathway to wellness. There are multiple lodges, many songs, and countless relationships to ancestors and land that shape how a person might heal.

For the field of mental health research and practice, Indigenous land-based ceremony offers more than cultural insight—it offers an alternative epistemology of healing grounded in relational accountability, land ethics, and community governance. Translating these principles into research design, clinical training, and policy frameworks is not optional if decolonization is to move beyond rhetoric.

Naming Illness, Seeking Ceremony: The Limits of Western Systems

When Kevin talks about mental illness, he does not dismiss Western categories outright. He recognizes that in contemporary life people are given names—bipolar disorder, depression, PTSD, OCD, eating disorders, and addictions—to describe their suffering. These labels can sometimes help people make sense of their experiences, but they can also limit or stigmatize them. For many First

Nations people, such diagnoses cannot be understood without reference to intergenerational and transgenerational trauma: the mental, emotional, spiritual, physical, and sexual abuses that occurred in residential schools, and the colonial policies that followed.

In my own life, I have been diagnosed with bipolar disorder. I have spent time in the mental health ward, during some of my darkest periods, particularly after losing loved ones to suicide. I know what it means to be medicated, monitored, and clinically assessed. I also know what it means to sit in a lodge, to have an Elder pray for me, to have medicine people sing for my spirit, to be smudged and reminded of who I am and where I come from. These are not interchangeable experiences. They represent two very different epistemologies of healing.

My psychologist, Dr. Kathy Wheaton, once told me, *"I dislike labels."* She encouraged me to be cautious about how I internalized diagnoses such as "bipolar." She recognized that Western psychiatry, while sometimes helpful, can also become reductive, focusing more on symptoms than stories, more on pathologizing than understanding. By contrast, in our Cree teachings, mental and emotional struggles are understood within a larger spiritual and relational context. We ask: What has happened to this person? What histories are they carrying? Which relationships have been broken? Which ceremonies are calling them back?

Elders like Dr. Diana Steinhauer speak about how our ceremonies—including Sundance, Chicken Dance, Horse Dance, Pipe Ceremony, Sweat Lodge, and rites of passage—carry extensive natural law, medicine wheel teachings, tipi teachings, and more. Each ceremony is a complex curriculum, offering insight into how to live with balance across the mental, emotional, physical, and spiritual dimensions of life. In pre-contact times, we had our own healing ceremonies and plant medicines that addressed distress, grief, and imbalance. While there may always have been forms of suffering, our Elders insist that the intensity and prevalence of mental illness we see today is deeply tied to colonial trauma, rapid social change, disconnection from land, and the suppression of ceremony.

Ceremony as Restricted "Non-Therapy": Structural Injustice in Health Systems

One of the clearest examples of structural injustice is that Western institutions routinely accept Christian-based programs—such as 12-step addiction recovery rooted in biblical teachings—as legitimate therapeutic approaches, yet they often deny that Indigenous ceremonies are therapeutic. As I have experienced working as a mental health therapist under NIHB, there is a blatant hypocrisy. Biblical verses and church-based practices are recognized and funded as part of treatment programs, but our Sweats, our Pipes, our Sundances, our feasts, and our fasting ceremonies are not.

Kevin speaks about this injustice with both clarity and grief. He reminds us that religious institutions and clergy were deeply implicated in the sexual, emotional, spiritual, and physical abuse of Indigenous peoples, often using the Bible as a tool of control and violence. Yet these same institutions are still recognized today as legitimate healers, whereas it was illegal, for decades, for us to lift up our pipes, sing our songs, or travel to funerals across reserve boundaries. The pass and permit systems under the Indian Act restricted movement so much that even attending ceremonies or grieving with relatives could be criminalized.

He insists that this history must be named honestly. Indigenous people were imprisoned for practicing ceremony, while churches were funded and protected. Today, our people are not coming to us with tears in their eyes asking to be taken to church. They are asking to be smudged, to be sung to, to pray in our ways. They want to explore the ceremonial side of their identities as nêhiyawak. They want pipe, they want land, they want stories, they want laws like *pâstâhowin* and *ôcinêwin* to guide them.

The Cost of Not Having Ceremony-Based Programs

Kevin shares a story of a man who is no longer with us, a man who came to the ceremonial camp twice seeking help. He came alone, and Kevin did what many of us do as relatives: he listened, he smudged him, he sang for him, he reminded him who he was and where he came from. They spent three hours together in the tipi, talking about his goals. The man wanted to support his family. He wanted to live differently. But he needed more support than one conversation could provide.

Kevin reflects on how, if there had been a sustained, community-run traditional program—a place where this man could regularly sit with Elders, healthy men, healthy women, and ceremonial helpers—he might still be alive today. The need was not abstract. It was concrete: safe spaces, time, consistency, and structured ceremonial healing. Instead, he drifted between systems that did not fully understand him and ultimately ended his life.

This is not an isolated story. Many people carry deep suffering, often invisible to outsiders. They may express their pain as "not wanting to be here" anymore. They may feel caught between Western systems that label them and Indigenous systems that are underfunded, fragmented, or unsupported by policy. The absence of land-based programs and ceremonies embedded as core mental health services is not a small gap—it is a matter of life and death.

Lodges as Written Texts: An Indigenous Literacy of Healing

One of the most powerful metaphors Kevin offers is that our knowledge is written, but not necessarily in alphabetic form. It is written into the architecture of our lodges, our ceremonies, our songs, and our landscapes. When we look at a Horse Dance lodge or a Chicken Dance lodge, we are looking at a text. Every pole has meaning. The direction of the door, the placement of ribbons, the position of the drum, the structure of the circle: all of it is *writing*. It has always been written down; we simply forget, sometimes, how to read it.

To learn how to "read" lodges is to learn our healing curriculum. It is to recognize that the Chicken Dance lodge, for example, encodes teachings about gender, movement, life cycles, and communal responsibility. Sundance grounds encode teachings about sacrifice, endurance, and prayer. Sweat lodges encode teachings about rebirth, purification, and humility. But currently, we do not have enough safe, community-controlled spaces to systematically teach this literacy. As Kevin points out, we need places where we can gather, store, protect, and transmit this knowledge—places where Elders can teach without fear of misappropriation or violation of sacred laws.

The urgency is clear: Elders are aging, and with each Elder who passes, an entire chapter of a lodge's teachings may disappear. This reality calls for careful, community-led documentation—not in ways that expose sacred knowledge indiscriminately, but in ways that respectfully record what must be carried forward for future generations. The challenge is to balance protection with accessibility: How do we digitally or textually capture some parts of ceremonial knowledge while upholding Creator's laws, family laws, and community governance over how that knowledge is used?

Natural Law as Mental Health Guide: pâstâhowin *and* ôcinêwin

Kevin identifies two natural laws that are particularly central and, at the same time, seemingly simple: *pâstâhowin* and *ôcinêwin*. They may be easy to name, but are profoundly challenging to live.

Pâstâhowin speaks to the harms we cause through words and actions—speaking badly about others, spreading negativity, disrespecting our peers, violating relational responsibilities. It reminds us that our words carry spirit. Negative speech can create sickness, conflict, and emotional harm that reverberates far beyond the immediate moment.

Ôcinêwin, on the other hand, deals with harm to the more-than-human world. Polluting water, disrespecting trees, abusing four-legged relatives, and misusing medicines—all of these actions have consequences. The land remembers. The water remembers. These laws are not metaphorical: they describe the real, material, and spiritual effects of disrespecting relationships.

Together, these two laws govern the two-leggeds on Mother Earth. They are not limited by age, social class, or occupation. They apply equally to chiefs, CEOs, Elders, youth, and children. Walking the *sweetgrass road*—a life guided by these laws—creates the conditions for a good life: one marked by respect, hard work, reciprocity, and service to Elders, youth, family, and community.

From a mental health perspective, these laws offer a clear ethical compass. They help individuals navigate conflicts, manage emotions, and understand the relational consequences of their decisions. While they are "easy to teach," they are difficult to practice consistently—but they provide a profoundly grounding framework for mental, emotional, spiritual, and physical balance.

Elders' Prayer as First-Line Regulation

When I ask Kevin how ceremony is healing and therapeutic, he responds with both spiritual insight and practical clarity. He offers a simple example: imagine you are deeply worried about a loved one. You go to an Elder and share that worry. The Elder listens. They pray for you and for the loved one you are concerned about. Already, something shifts.

From a Western perspective, one could explain this shift through neurochemistry. Having someone you trust, someone with white hair who has lived a long life, speak words of care and prayer over you can physically calm your nervous system. It can help regulate the chemicals in your brain—serotonin, dopamine, adrenaline—that, when imbalanced, contribute to anxiety, depression, and distress.

From an Indigenous perspective, that prayer carries spiritual force. It calls in ancestors. It calls in the Creator. It invites the help of the unseen relatives who can support you and your loved ones. Healing occurs simultaneously at the neurological, emotional, and spiritual levels.

Kevin reminds us that life will never be permanently balanced. It is not meant to be "easy street." There are seasons—fall, winter, spring, summer—and each season brings shifts in energy, mood, and spiritual focus. Some times of year, you may feel more spiritually "high," more physically active, more emotionally excited. At other times, grief may be heavy, fatigue more present, and motivation more difficult to find. Ceremony does not eliminate these ups and downs; it helps us understand and move through them.

He explains that the things we work hardest for, the things that cost us effort, sacrifice, and sometimes pain, are the things we honor most. This is true for ceremony, for land-based work, and for healing. When we commit to the long road—to return to teachings, to sit with Elders, to walk the sweetgrass road, to confront our own trauma—we begin to experience mental health as an ongoing practice rather than a fixed destination.

Effort, Learning, and the Long Road of Healing

It's kind of funny how humans are, but it's like when you value something, there's always a little bit of pain involved. There's always a little bit of effort involved. Maybe it's mental, maybe it's spiritual, maybe it's physical, but it's like something that really sticks in your memory that you cherish will always test those boundaries. Now to have luck on your side, some people will say that's the effort that goes behind the people. Let's say I want to be a really good hide tanner. I really, really want to know how to tan hides, right? Nobody's going to see the late night that we spent yesterday trying to flesh out these buffalo hides and we never documented it. Right? We just did it because they needed to be done. And in order to be something to be really good at you have to go out and seek out those hides, seek out those buffalo hides, test yourself on the deer hide, test yourself on a moose hide. Get yourself blistered up, get yourself mixing the chemicals, the brains, all these different little tricks of the trade. Then that's what it takes to become a real master. And people will say, oh, you're lucky. Oh that, oh, that's just luck. No one sees the effort that goes behind the work that goes behind the studying that goes behind the research that goes behind something you become good at. Some people say, oh yeah, you're gifted. Yeah, you're gifted. But then how do you hone that gift? Like how do you really, really hone it where you can get any hide and then you'll be able to tan it. Right? I'm just using hide tanning for just an example, because we just finished that ten-day hide tanning camp here. That's just an example and you can do that with music. You can do that with ceremony. If you want to become a language speaker, if you want to be a storyteller, you got to put in your hours, you got to put in your hours learning, you put in your hours sharing, you got to put in your hours with that skill, that skillset, learning those skills, learning how to speak, learning how to share, learning how to learn.

Elders, Medicines, and Stories as Integrated Mental Health Care

When you're going to Elders, they'll give you medicines, even to help you, when you're tired, if your hands are hurting, you go to a medicine person and that person will give you medicine to put on your hand. You can continue working on those hides. You know, maybe they'll add on the spiritual side of things, maybe they'll say, okay, there's a story of the moose. There's all these stories and those are healing in themselves. Then maybe there's medicine that you can drink that an elder or a medicine person can give you that'll sustain you because it is hard work. You know, this journey that you're going to try to do. If it's mental health that you're trying to heal from trying to figure out what type of mental health it is and what's triggering it. Then they might even have a story of their own or they might have went through it themselves, where they are now, they might be able to guide you through that process because they went through that process themselves. It's such a big topic. It's such an amazing topic, the mind is such a complex organ. I don't even know if you want to call it an organ, but a gift, but it's figuring it out. Then how many people do you know that are, could be struggling with mental health disorders, right? You don't even know, because they don't even show it. They may look happy, you know, when you're meeting them, but then how are they coping at home? So those types of things too are pretty interesting when you start studying them. It's like we're just at the beginning, I'm really understanding how to incorporate Indigenous wisdom with, cognitive science and cognitive science in itself is pretty brand new as well, because you have MRIs, you have CT scans, brain injury, cognitive development. Now they're starting to map out the brain and then it was used to be left brain and right brain. Now they're going right into the chemicals. Now they're mapping out the brain where language development happens, where memories and cells develop neurons, where you're growing new neurons, that's a possibility. You can rewire your brain. If you had a brain injury and part of your brain is damaged, you can rewire and restructure your brain because that organ is, or that gift is that complex. Those type of things are just on the cusp of something pretty special here, but I think a lot of it, yes, there's science, we can include that. I think on the spiritual side of things, it feels good to be smudged by an elder. It feels good to be prayed for by someone when they pray, it feels special. You feel like that's a gift and then sooner or later you are going to be that elder. Then how are you going to pray for your grandchildren? She's already showed you how to do it on you. So that's how you're going to care for your children and grandchildren, the future. They're showing you already how to act as an elder. So that, and then, but of course you don't want to rush there either. You know, when the time comes, it comes, but it's good to have that, that exposure to those elders because they carry so much wisdom. Then when we reference people, when we reference our ancestors, the elders will say, this is something that I was taught, you know? Then here I'm gifting it to you, just like how it was gifted to me. And this is medicine specifically for somebody that's going through a mental health issue. Then you combine these two ingredients, and this is how you smudge with it or smoke or ingest or use it. Right. There's all those different ways that are out there. We have them and it's not like we never had mental disorders. I don't think probably not as much, but we did too have a very, very strong medicine society that were very, very powerful. And they are still there. They are still working on our people, but they're still very quiet and under underground. They don't trust the systems that are out there. They're capitalistic way of looking at medicine is kind of not good.

Liberation, Leadership, and Indigenous Authority in Mental Health

Judy: With all these mental illnesses that exist, as I had mentioned, we have to be careful in how we treat our people and how our people are labeled because we are the most pathologized race in this world, we're the most studied. We're the most researched, many non-indigenous people make money and profit off of researching and studying our people. It's time to take back our own, this has been a movement that has been in effect for the past 30 years, during the integration era. We got to step up and take care of our own people, work with our own people, heal our own people, because there is such a high percentage of our people that suffer from social-psychological issues or mental illnesses. We must be careful of labels. We need to heal and empower our people, like Jennifer Katz and Eduardo Duran explain, as well as Richard Katz explain, ensouling our people is a new method of counseling and therapy we must instill in our people. Furthermore, Kevin says there will be liberation of our people, we're in that era, right now, despite going through Covid for the past three years and living within that fear in isolation which has further caused other new mental illnesses. Do we believe in that labeling, or should we just continue on and make ourselves believe we are really that dysfunctional? We are a healthy nation, a healthy people, we're strong in our identity, in our language and in our culture and ceremony. So what are the next steps? Where do we see ourselves in 20 years? In 30 years or 40 years? Just in 2021 October, I lost my Auntie Judy to diabetes and she suffered for a long time. Her kidneys failed on her, her liver checked down and I asked her on her deathbed, I said, are you healed Auntie Judy? And she said, no. It breaks my heart to hear something like that because there's so many people who have gone before us that have not had that chance to heal wholeheartedly, that have gone to their deathbeds with all this hurt and pain locked inside them. I want to show our people a new way and sohkêyihta mina (you have strong faith, you have strong faith, you have strong will). Show them that new healing path. It's a lifelong learning path. I used to think we should start writing things down, but I don't think that anymore because like Kevin mentioned, you have to earn it. You have to put in the hours, it's a lifelong learning process. It just doesn't come to you like that. You have to, work for it. In the end you will reap the benefits. But I no longer want to see my people going to their graves unhealed. I want to see rich, empowered, healed…more so ensouled, healthy, thriving people. I hope I see that within my lifetime, within my own *wâhkôhtowin*/kinship circle. I hope to break these cycles. A question I would like to ask you, and the last question is, how do you think ceremony is liberating for our First Nations people as well healing and empowering for our people of Ministikwan Lake Cree Nation?

Liberation as Governance: "Being in the Driver's Seat"

Kevin: Well liberating. It's like liberation has to do with us being in the driver's seat. Liberation, to start with us, I think we have to be in the driver's seat and our own Indigenous researchers have to take the lead on it. Our own Indigenous healers have to take a lead on it. Then they also have to understand mental health. There's a lot of funding that's being placed toward mental health and healing. We have to figure out, you know, I don't know if it's scales or specialty or what type of compensation, those type of things to be considered because those are specialties. Everyone's going to be able to do mental health, let's say if there's a Sundance lodge holder, maybe that's all they know, or that's all the law lodge they're responsible for. They wouldn't have any time for any of those other different lodges, like a horse dance or round dance lodge, the old school round dance lodge, the sweat lodge, the different types of sweat lodges. The different types of healing lodges, they're going to make. All of those are inclusive. We also have what they call the shaking tent ceremony. So there's ways to heal. We have always had ways to heal, but it's in the Sundance lodge, reconciling hasn't happened yet though. Reconciliation, in terms of that we have to take that lead. We have to take that role. We have to start building capacity. How do we do research in a good way? How do our Indigenous researchers research our people to benefit our people? Internationally, I think we're seen as the lead in terms of healing, in terms of structuring our governance around healing. There is a lot of supporting documentation on it already, that are not non-Indigenous that are listening, that are researching, that are working on that process on all different levels. So the one that I liked was Dr. Bruce Perry, I like his literature. I like his research. I like his work. And he talks about using music. He talks about using our rattles, using our drums, and using ways to heal. And then you have Dr. Gabor Mate, he used the auhausca ceremony from the Andes, from the Inca people, from the jungles there. His success rates in these East Hastings in Vancouver, where real high percentages of preventing people relapsing back into hard addictions, like heroin, cocaine, or meth use. Those types of people are allies. Where you can lean on their research and their studies and not literature. Right. So, it's good to study people like that.

Traditional Medicine Person

In this work, Elders and medicine people play a central role. When someone is learning hide tanning and their hands begin to ache, they can go to a medicine person and be given a salve to rub into their skin, or a tea to drink that sustains their energy. They might also be given a story about the moose or the buffalo—a teaching about respect, sacrifice, and gratitude. The medicine is not only physical, but it is also emotional and spiritual. The story itself is healing because it situates the person within a web of relationships: to animals, to land, to ancestors, to Creator.

Medicine people, shaman, whatever you want to call them, but the lead, they were the leads, but it's also not him conducting and leading those ceremonies, but it was empowering those people that have grown up with it that know, know the powers of what that particular ceremony does. But then there's also study on people, really looking at the chemicals of the medicine of auhausca and then figuring out. Then we must ask ourselves what is that healing component or the chemicals that are helping people look within and then looking at childhood trauma and looking at the cognitive development, if you're have abandonment issues, when you're younger, if you have different abuses that one has gone through that show themselves later on in life. In whatever ways it could be cancer, it could be all sorts of different, different ways that they show those sicknesses later on in life. If you can get them early on in alternative ways, you know, there's also studies right now that are happening still continuously with cannabis, how is it helping? There's a lot of companies that are out there that have really brilliant people that are studying this. There's a lot of pilot projects that are going on right now studying the mental health side of things in Canada and probably around the world, for sure, all over the world. But it's really trying to figure out ways to study in a good way, in a respectful way. But you still say liberation will come from the leads, the leads of Indigenous leaders in science and in mental health, in medicines, college of medicines, college of studies, college of chemistry, college of physics, and then working respectively in how much they have uncovered or have started to understand deoxyribonucleic acid (DNA).

They're also starting to take, let's say Buffalo. We have the buffalo, when the domesticated cows started coming over to North America, there's a strain of tuberculosis that they brought with them. That's part of the bison now. What they're doing now is they can take that straight out in the fetus, in the DNA, the embryo. So already there's bison or buffalo in North America that don't have that strain that has been passed on from other generations. They already know that intergenerational trauma can be passed on right into the molecular structure of our makeup. Again, within that type of study, we need more people that are Indigenous, that can speak, that can sing, that can drum, that can dance, that are part of those lodges that take a lead, that understand the boundaries that are respectful. Yeah. I think the liberation movements that have been successful are helping our communities.

As we mentioned I'm very thankful and grateful for these wise words and knowledge that has been shared. I hope that this helps advocate on behalf of our people for mainstream society to acknowledge our ways, utilizing our ceremonial realm and higher power, our deeply rooted spirituality, to accept our ways as therapy. There are more non-Indigenous people seeking our ways of being and knowing, and as Herman Michell states "we must go back to the land as we are 'rooted', this is known as Indigegogy" (2018). Lastly, our ceremony is beautiful, graceful, humble, and full of lifelong teachings, natural law teachings that we must preserve for our future generations.

When we talk about healing, ceremony, and mental health, one teaching that keeps returning is that anything truly valuable in life comes with effort. Kevin often laughs gently when he explains this, because humans sometimes call it "luck" when they only see the end result and not the long road behind it. But as he says, when you value something, there is always some kind of pain, sacrifice, or commitment involved. Sometimes that effort is physical—aching hands, late nights, blistered skin. Sometimes it is mental or emotional—facing old memories, learning new teachings, confronting our own patterns. Sometimes it is spiritual—sitting in ceremony, fasting, or surrendering to a process we cannot fully control. Whatever it is, the things that truly stay with us, the teachings and skills that shape who we are, will always test our boundaries.

He uses hide tanning as a powerful metaphor. If someone wants to become a really good hide tanner, they cannot simply watch one demonstration and then claim mastery. They have to actively seek out the hides—buffalo, deer, moose—and test themselves repeatedly. No one sees the late nights, the hours spent fleshing out buffalo hides in the dark, hands numb and sore, bodies exhausted. No one documents every moment, every failed attempt or experimental mixture of brains and fats, every small breakthrough that leads to a better technique. From the outside, people may say, "Oh, you're so lucky," or "You're so gifted." But what they do not see is the discipline, the learning, the trial and error that went into becoming a master hide tanner.

The same is true of ceremony, language, and storytelling. You cannot become a fluent language speaker, a respected storyteller, or a ceremonial leader without putting in your hours—hours of listening to Elders, repeating phrases, asking questions, sitting in lodges, learning protocols, making mistakes, and being corrected. To really hone a gift, you must live with it over time. You must learn how to share it in a good way, how to be accountable for it. These teachings remind us that healing—especially from mental illness or trauma—is not instant. It is a lifelong learning process that requires patience, humility, and steady effort.

Healing as Medicine Through Elders

The same pattern applies to mental health. When someone is struggling with depression, anxiety, or other forms of distress, Elders may offer medicines to smudge with, to drink, or to carry. But they also offer stories—from their own lives, from community history, from the old people who came before them. Many Elders have walked through their own mental health struggles: grief, trauma, hardship, loneliness. They know what it means to carry pain. Because they have gone through their own healing process, they are able to guide others with compassion and wisdom. They are not speaking from theory alone; they are speaking from lived experience.

Kevin often remarks that mental health is an enormous topic, and that the mind is one of the most complex gifts we have been given. Some people struggle quietly and never show obvious signs. They may appear happy or calm in public, while silently battling intrusive thoughts, despair, or feelings of worthlessness at home. Others are more visibly struggling, moving through cycles of crisis, hospitalization, or addiction. We never fully know what someone is carrying inside.

At the same time, Western cognitive science and neuroscience are rapidly advancing. Researchers now use magnetic resonance imaging (MRI) and computed tomography (CT) scans to map brain injuries, cognitive development, memory formation, and neuroplasticity. Old ideas about left brain and right brain have been replaced by more nuanced understandings of how chemicals, neurons, and circuitry shape emotion, cognition, and behavior. Science now confirms what many Indigenous people have always believed: the brain can change, repair, and rewire itself. New neurons can form. Pathways damaged by injury or trauma can be partially rerouted. Healing at the level of the brain is possible.

For Kevin, this is where Indigenous wisdom, and cognitive science can meet. Western research can provide insights into how certain practices affect the brain's chemistry and structure, while Indigenous knowledge offers centuries of experiential learning about how ceremony, story, and medicine shape the heart, mind, and spirit. He insists, however, that science alone is not enough. On the spiritual side of things, it simply feels good to be smudged by an Elder, to be prayed for by someone who truly cares for you. That feeling of being held, blessed, and seen is itself a powerful form of medicine. Over time, those prayers shape how we, ourselves, become Elders. The way we are cared for now becomes a pattern for how we will care for our children and grandchildren in the future.

Elders often say, "This is how it was gifted to me, and now I gift it to you." When they share a teaching, a song, or a medicine specifically for someone going through mental health challenges, they are extending a long chain of relational knowledge. There may be instructions: combine these two plants and smudge with them, or use this medicine in drinking form, or use it in a certain lodge under the guidance of a particular ceremonial leader. These are sophisticated healing practices, tailored to specific conditions and guided by natural law.

It is not that Indigenous peoples never had mental disorders or psychological distress before contact. But many Elders argue that the intensity and frequency of certain illnesses are much higher today, due to compounded colonial trauma, rapid social changes, systemic poverty, and disconnection from land and ceremony. Historically, there were very strong medicine societies and ceremonial specialists who worked continuously to support the mental, spiritual, and emotional health of the people. These societies still exist, but many operate quietly, often underground, because they do not trust capitalist or colonial systems that would exploit, commodify, or distort their knowledge.

From my perspective as a Cree woman and a mental health therapist, I see how dangerous it is when Western systems dominate the conversation about mental illness. As I have mentioned elsewhere, we must be extremely careful about how we treat and label our people. Indigenous peoples are among the most pathologized, studied, and researched populations in the world. Many non-Indigenous scholars and institutions have built careers, secured grants, and gained prestige by researching Indigenous trauma, dysfunction, and "risk factors." Yet our communities have not always seen corresponding benefits, resources, or healing. It is long past time to "take back our own," as Indigenous scholars and activists have been insisting for decades.

This reclamation is not just intellectual; it is spiritual and practical. It means that Indigenous practitioners, Elders, and communities must lead their own healing initiatives, design their own programs, and define their own measures of wellness. It means shifting from viewing our communities as fundamentally broken or dysfunctional to recognizing that, underneath colonial damage, we remain strong, gifted, and resilient people with deep ceremonial traditions, languages, and teachings. Scholars such as Jennifer Katz, Eduardo Duran, and Richard Katz talk about "ensouling" our people—reconnecting them to spirit, meaning, and agency—as a vital alternative to purely diagnostic or deficit-based models of treatment. Rather than focusing only on illness, they emphasize re-storying, re-spiriting, and re-rooting individuals in community and land.

Reclaiming Indigenous Definitions of Wellness

Indigenous peoples must reclaim authority over how mental health is named, understood, and addressed, rather than accepting deficit-based labels imposed by colonial research and clinical systems. Kevin believes we are living in an era of liberation, even though we are still emerging from the collective trauma of COVID-19. The pandemic intensified fear, isolation, grief, and mental health crises in many communities. New anxieties and forms of distress have emerged. But alongside this, he sees a growing refusal among Indigenous peoples to accept imposed labels that frame them as inherently dysfunctional. Instead, there is a movement toward reclaiming health as identity: seeing we as a healthy nation, as capable, as grounded in culture, ceremony, and language.

For me, these questions are not abstract. In October 2021, I lost my Auntie Judy to complications of diabetes. Her kidneys failed, her liver shut down, and she had suffered for a long time. When I asked her on her deathbed, *"Are you healed, Auntie?"* she said, quietly, *"No."* That answer still breaks my heart. She, like so many of our relatives, carried immense hurt, pain, and unresolved trauma to the very end of her life. She did not have sufficient opportunities, time, or support to heal fully before passing on. I think of her, and of countless others who have gone to their graves carrying unspoken stories, buried emotions, and internalized shame.

I do not want this pattern to continue. I want our people to have access to the teachings, ceremonies, and supports that can help them heal wholeheartedly. I want us to walk *miyo-pimâtisiwin* together, to break cycles of violence and trauma, to embody the strength our ancestors prayed for. To do this, we must understand that healing is lifelong and not easily captured in books or written manuals. For a time, I thought the answer was to write everything down—to document every teaching, every protocol, every story. But as Kevin reminded me, there is a reason these teachings are earned. There is a reason they unfold slowly, through committed participation. Some knowledge cannot be simply downloaded or consumed; it must be lived into.

Still, we can create conditions where more of our people have access to these journeys. I long to see richer, empowered, healed—indeed, ensouled—Indigenous people in my lifetime: people who thrive spiritually, emotionally, mentally, and physically. I long to see this first within my own *wâhkôhtowin*, my kinship circle, and then radiating outward.

Liberation as Leadership: Indigenous Control of Healing, Research, and Funding

Liberation in mental health is not symbolic inclusion but Indigenous leadership over healing practices, research agendas, and the allocation of mental health resources. When I ask Kevin how he sees ceremony as liberating, healing, and empowering for our people—especially for Ministikwan Lake Cree Nation—he responds by returning to the notion of "being in the driver's seat." Liberation, he explains, means that we are the ones steering our own healing processes. Indigenous researchers, healers, and communities must lead. We cannot depend on external institutions to define liberation for us. At the same time, those Indigenous leaders must also understand the language of mental health, funding, program evaluation, and policy, because there is a great deal of money being directed toward mental health and healing. We need to ensure those resources are used in ways that reflect our values and serve our people.

He points out that within our ceremonial world, there is already specialization. A Sundance lodge holder may dedicate their life entirely to that lodge and have no time to hold a Horse Dance or a traditional Round Dance lodge. Other people may specialize in sweat lodges, or shaking tent ceremonies, or other forms of healing. All of these ceremonial forms are interconnected, but each one carries specific laws, songs, and responsibilities. If we are to build our own Indigenous mental health frameworks, we need to understand how these specializations work, and how to honor them without overburdening individuals or turning them into "service providers" in a purely Western sense.

Kevin also emphasizes that we can learn from non-Indigenous allies who are taking trauma, ceremony, and relational healing seriously. He mentions, for example, Dr. Bruce Perry's work on trauma and regulation, including the use of rhythm, drumming, and movement to support healing. He points to Dr. Gabor Maté's collaborations with ayahuasca practitioners from Indigenous communities in the Amazon, where ceremony, guided plant medicine, and deep attention to childhood trauma have produced remarkable shifts for people dealing with severe addictions. Importantly, in these models, the non-Indigenous clinician is not the one leading ceremony; instead, Indigenous ceremonial leaders take the lead while clinicians support and help translate the work into research languages that systems will recognize.

He notes that there is now extensive research being done on plant medicines like ayahuasca and cannabis, on their effects on the brain, on trauma processing, on cognition, and on long-term health outcomes. These studies, he believes, can be helpful—if they are conducted in respectful ways, and if Indigenous voices and ceremonial leaders are at the center rather than on the margins. Similarly, cutting-edge research on DNA, epigenetics, and intergenerational trauma is showing that the impacts of colonization, starvation, stress, and abuse can be passed on at the molecular level. Scientists can now identify and even remove certain harmful strains encoded in animal DNA, such as the tuberculosis strain passed from imported cattle to buffalo. This opens questions about how intergenerational human trauma might be addressed not only emotionally but also biologically.

For Kevin, the key is that Indigenous people must be at the forefront of these conversations—as scientists, as physicians, as psychologists, as ceremony people, as language speakers. We need Cree-speaking geneticists, nêhiyaw neuroscientists, and Indigenous psychiatrists who also Sundance and carry pipe. Liberation, he says, will come when Indigenous leaders in science, health, and ceremony work together, respecting both Indigenous and Western knowledges while always anchoring decisions in Indigenous values, natural laws, and community accountability.

As I close this part of the conversation, I feel deep gratitude for these teachings. They strengthen my resolve to advocate for our ceremonies to be recognized as legitimate therapy, not as mere cultural add-ons. More and more non-Indigenous people are seeking our ways of being and knowing, recognizing that Western systems alone cannot address the depth of human suffering. As Herman Michell writes, we must return to the land because that is where we are rooted; this land-based teaching practice is sometimes called Indigegogy. Our ceremonies—humble, beautiful, graceful, and full of natural law—carry the knowledge we need to guide future generations toward a more balanced and liberated life.

Conclusion

This chapter has argued that Indigenous land-based ceremony functions as a comprehensive mental health system—one that integrates emotional regulation, spiritual connection, community accountability, and lifelong learning. Rather than positioning ceremony as a cultural supplement to Western mental health services, the teachings shared here demonstrate that ceremony operates as its own ethical, relational, and therapeutic framework.

For students, researchers, and practitioners, the implications are clear. Decolonizing mental health research and practice requires more than cultural awareness or symbolic inclusion. It requires a fundamental shift in how healing is understood, who holds authority, and what counts as legitimate knowledge. Indigenous Elders, medicine people, and ceremonial leaders must be recognized not only as cultural advisors but also as knowledge holders and practitioners whose expertise has direct relevance for mental health care.

At the same time, this chapter highlights the importance of translation rather than extraction. Western neuroscience and cognitive science can offer complementary insights into how ceremony regulates the nervous system and supports healing, but such research must be conducted in respectful partnership, with Indigenous communities leading the questions, methods, and applications.

Healing, as these teachings remind us, is not a destination or a quick fix. It is a lifelong process that requires effort, humility, and commitment. Ceremony does not eliminate suffering, but it offers a way to move through it with guidance, meaning, and relational support. As Indigenous peoples reclaim authority over their healing systems, the task ahead is not to invent new ways to heal, but to protect, practice, and strengthen the ones that have always been there—for ourselves, our communities, and the generations yet to come.

We have always had ways to heal. Now, we are called to protect them, practice them, and lead with them—for ourselves, our children, and those yet to come.

7

WAPANIWIW ISKWEW

Land-Based Mental Health Healing Lodge Steps

Kevin Lewis with support from Ranjan Datta

This chapter presents the *Wapaniwiw Iskwew* Land-Based Mental Health Healing Lodge as a *model* rather than a fixed program. While grounded in the specific teachings, lands, and kinship structures of Ministikwan Lake Cree Nation, the Healing Lodge framework is offered here as a flexible, Indigenous-led approach that can inform mental health research, education, and practice across diverse Indigenous and non-Indigenous contexts.

Rather than prescribing a single intervention, the Healing Lodge model articulates core principles—land-based engagement, ceremonial grounding, kinship-centered care, and integration with mental health services—that can be adapted according to local protocols, Nations, and institutional settings. This chapter outlines those principles, demonstrates their application through seasonal and programmatic examples, and situates them within broader mental health and decolonizing research literatures.

Cree Phenomenology

With special attention to the members of Ministikwan Lake Cree Nation, it is important to recognize that this community continues to hold a remarkably strong foundation of language, culture, and ceremony. A high number of fluent nêhiyawêwin speakers live in the community, and many community members actively practice their traditional identity, participate in ceremonies, and uphold their responsibilities as a sovereign people. This is not simply cultural continuity in a general sense; it is an ongoing enactment of Cree law, Cree cosmology, and Cree philosophies of health, education, and governance.

DOI: 10.4324/9781003670308-7

In thinking through the development of *Wapaniwiw Iskwew* Land-Based Mental Health Healing Lodge (WILBMHHL), this chapter draws on phenomenological, cosmological, and philosophical terminology grounded in Cree knowledge systems. These theoretical lenses are not abstract add-ons from Western philosophy; rather, they help articulate what Elders have long taught: that traditional beliefs, morals, and values are lived, embodied, and transmitted relationally from generation to generation. Cree phenomenology is rooted in everyday lived experience—how we move on the land, how we perceive relationships, how we understand our place in the cosmos. Indigenous scholars have emphasized that culturally grounded healing frameworks are most effective when they align epistemology, practice, and governance rather than isolating "culture" as a supplemental intervention (Duran, 2006; Gone, 2013; Kingi, 2018).

Phenomenology, in this context, is intertwined with natural law teachings that guide us toward *miyo pimâtisiwin* (the good life). These teachings are expressed through the medicine wheel, tipi teachings, seasonal cycles, and natural law concepts such as *wahkohtowin* (kinship), *pâstâhowin,* and *ôcinêwin* (laws of consequence and relational responsibility). They provide a framework for understanding mental, emotional, physical, and spiritual wellness as interconnected rather than isolated domains. Walking the good life is not a metaphor; it is a lived process of aligning oneself with land, relatives, and spiritual responsibilities.

Elders as Indigenous Mental Health Practitioners

Our Elders are central to this philosophical, ethical, and therapeutic landscape. They carry enriched, sophisticated bodies of knowledge that might, in Western terms, be called psychology, philosophy, ecology, and theology all at once. They are our psychologists and counselors as much as they are our philosophers and ceremonial leaders. When individuals are in need of guidance or healing, they go to the Elders with protocol—offering tobacco, cloth, blankets, or honoraria. These offerings are not payment but expressions of reciprocity, humility, and respect, acknowledging that knowledge and healing are gifts, not commodities. Elders, in turn, provide teachings, stories, prayers, and sometimes medicines that support mental, emotional, spiritual, and physical health.

Our paradigmatic worldview is cosmological in nature. We understand ourselves not as separate individuals but as threads within a vast web of *wahkohtowin.* This kinship extends beyond human relatives to include the two-leggeds, four-leggeds, winged ones, swimmers, insects, plants, medicines, trees, rocks, stars, sky, and waters. All are interrelated and interdependent; one cannot exist in a healthy way without the others (Figure 7.1). This cosmological understanding is foundational to land-based healing because it reminds us that mental health cannot be separated from relationships with land, water, animals, and spirit (Figure 7.1).

FIGURE 7.1 The figure shows building land-based 3-week which is a 12-week program which brings to life out Indigenous teaching, Virties of the tipi are used to bide by and the First Nation Holistic Framework.

While these strengths are specific to Ministikwan Lake Cree Nation, the Healing Lodge framework does not require identical conditions to be effective. Other communities may draw on different languages, ceremonial systems, or kinship structures while applying the same foundational logic: grounding mental health care in Indigenous law, relational accountability, and place-based knowledge.

Revitalizing Kinship Language and Family-Based Healing

Another core aspect of *wahkohtowin* is our kinship system—how we name and relate to each other within families and communities. Elders teach that, traditionally, we did not primarily call each other by personal names; we called one another by our relationship. This form of address reinforced relational responsibility and mutual care. If you referred to your grandmother, you would say *nohkom*; your grandfather, *nimosôm*; your mother, *nikawiy*; your father, *nohtawiy*; your son, *nikosis*; your daughter, *nitânis*. If a mother passed on, her sister would often take on the role of *nikâwês*—the "little mother" who stepped in to provide love and care for that child. These kinship roles were not symbolic but practical; they structured childcare, discipline, emotional support, and the transmission of knowledge. Referring to one another through kinship language generated an everyday ethic of respect, responsibility, and connection. Extended family members were truly considered close family; aunties, uncles, cousins, and grandparents all held shared responsibilities for children's well-being. In the context of mental health, this collective, kinship-based approach ensured that no one was left entirely alone in their struggles.

At WILBMHHL, revitalizing this kinship-based way of relating is a central goal. Language is not just a communication tool; it shapes how we understand ourselves and each other. Elders often say there are meanings in Cree that cannot be fully translated into English. To know ourselves as *nêhiyawak* requires speaking, hearing, and feeling our language. Thus, the Lodge will work intentionally with fluent Cree speakers to create immersive spaces where kinship terms, prayer, ceremonial language, and everyday conversation are conducted in Cree as much as possible. This is not only language revitalization, but it is also mental, emotional, and spiritual healing.

Land as Teacher, Healer, and Relative

In mainstream mental health services, land-based programming is often framed as recreational or adjunctive. Within the Healing Lodge framework, land is understood as an active therapeutic agent. These reframing challenges clinical settings to expand definitions of evidence-based care beyond indoor, talk-based interventions.

The land-based program at WILBMHHL is designed to reconnect people with *mâmawi-ohkâwîmâw* (Mother Earth), recognizing that land itself is a primary healer. The land promotes the well-being of mind, body, spirit, and soul through direct sensory, emotional, and spiritual engagement. Being on the land—walking through the bush, feeling the breeze, smelling the soil, hearing the birds—helps release negative emotions such as anger, frustration, grief, sadness, and depression.

Even something as simple as a nature walk can reset energy, clear the mind, and shift emotional states. For Cree and Saulteaux peoples, this relationship with land is deeply historical: we are hunting, gathering, and fishing nations who have always flourished from what the land offers. Food, shelter, tools, stories, teachings, and medicines are all gifts from the land. This long-standing relationship means that land-based healing is not a new "intervention" but a return to an original way of being.

The land has unique and intrinsic characteristics that foster calm, peace, and spiritual presence. The quiet of the bush, the sound of leaves, the texture of moss, the taste of wild berries—these experiences create conditions where prayer and meditation come more easily. For many, it is far easier to pray, to talk to Creator, or to reflect deeply while sitting by a lake or walking among trees than in a clinical office. WILBMHHL recognizes this and will structure programs so that much of the healing work takes place outdoors, in direct relationship with the land.

Water, Spirit, and Environmental Responsibility

Water plays a particularly important role in Cree teachings. Elders say that water is intimately connected to our time in the mother's womb, where we are surrounded, held, and nourished. When we are near water—lakes, rivers, streams—our spirits feel lighter, freer, less burdened by the worries of the world. Water sustains physical life, but it also supports emotional and spiritual release.

The Lodge sits near a lake, and this proximity to water will be integrated thoughtfully and safely into healing programs. WILBMHHL will incorporate environmentally responsible, "green" practices related to drinking water, wastewater, and water purification. Clients will be involved in understanding and participating in these practices, helping them reconnect not only spiritually but also practically with their responsibility to care for the land and water.

Traditional teachings tell us that water has both female and male spirits. The grandmother water spirit, *nipiy-manitow iskwêw*, is said to live in the mountains in a sacred place on Turtle Island. She looks after us and provides life. If she is harmed, life on earth is endangered. There is also a male water spirit, *nipiy manitow*, whose teachings are particularly meaningful for male clients and youth. These teachings remind us that mental health cannot be separated from water protection and environmental stewardship. Climate change, water crises, and land degradation are not only ecological issues, but they are also spiritual and mental health issues.

Language, Identity, and Family-Centered Healing at WILBMHHL

Our traditional teachings—language, identity, culture, and ceremony—are inseparable. If one is lost, the others are weakened. Elders often say that without our language, we cannot fully function as a nation because our laws, our stories, and our spiritual teachings are embedded in words, metaphors, and expressions that English cannot fully carry. At WILBMHHL, fluent Cree speakers will play a central role in cultural programming. Clients will be invited into environments where Cree is used as the primary language of ceremony, teaching, and daily practice, with interpretation as needed. Through this approach, language learning becomes an integral part of mental health healing—not a side activity.

The Lodge will also function as a family-oriented space. Healing is not envisioned as an individual process detached from family and community, but as a collective journey. Programming will be designed to involve immediate and extended family members whenever appropriate, honoring the traditional teaching that "it takes a whole community to raise a child." This collective perspective recognizes that mental health challenges often ripple across family and community networks, and that healing must do the same.

Seasonal Education and Land-Based Activities

The seasonal activities outlined below are illustrative rather than prescriptive. Their purpose is to demonstrate how Indigenous education and mental health healing have historically followed ecological rhythms. Programs in other regions might substitute different plants, animals, or ceremonies while maintaining the same seasonal logic of preparation, endurance, renewal, and reflection.

Traditionally, Indigenous educational systems were year-round, guided by the four (sometimes six) seasons. Learning was not confined to classrooms or specific months of the year; it followed the cycles of land, animals, and weather. WILBMHHL will mirror this seasonal model, offering land-based cultural and healing activities throughout the year, aligned with natural rhythms. Summer activities will focus on harvesting, gathering, and plant teachings. These may include:

- **Medicinal harvesting:** learning how to identify, respectfully pick, prepare, and store medicines such as sweetgrass, sage, willow, and other healing plants
- **Berry-picking:** understanding protocols for taking only what is needed and giving thanks
- **Protocols about sacred plants and animals:** learning when and how to offer tobacco, how to approach animal remains, and how to treat all beings with respect
- **Traditional cooking:** preparing meals over open fires, learning recipes passed down through generations, and understanding food as medicine
- **Cultural camps:** multi-day gatherings that combine teachings, ceremony, language, and community-building
- **Wilderness survival skills:** fire making, shelter-building, navigation, and safety on the land
- **Picking tobacco, sage, sweetgrass, cedar:** teaching the sacred significance and proper uses of the four medicines

Fall activities will engage participants in preparation and reciprocity:

- **Muskeg and mint picking:** gathering plants specific to fall and learning their uses
- **Hunting, fishing, trapping:** supporting land-based food security and teaching ethical harvesting practices
- **Fire making and outdoor cooking:** deepening survival and community skills
- **Brain tanning hides:** teaching patience, resilience, and the value of hard work, as well as ceremonial protocols around animals
- **Meat harvesting and preservation** (dry meat, canning): emphasizing food sovereignty and winter preparation

- **Weather and migration teachings**: understanding animal migrations, changes in weather, and reading signs in the sky and land
- **Tool making**: crafting tools from natural materials, learning both historical and contemporary applications

Winter activities will focus on stories, endurance, and creativity:

- **Remembrance Day reflections:** honoring Indigenous veterans and community members who have passed on
- **Snowshoe making:** teaching traditional technologies and the ingenuity of winter travel
- **Winter snaring and trapping:** learning safe, respectful ways to harvest small animals
- **Winter shelter building and outdoor cooking:** fostering confidence, teamwork, and survival skills
- **Round dance:** participating in winter ceremonial dances that foster connection, joy, and healing
- **Ice fishing:** providing food and time on the land during the coldest months
- **Oral storytelling:** sitting with Elders to hear winter stories, laws, and histories
- **Traditional regalia, sewing, and beading:** promoting creativity, identity, and meditative focus
- **Moss-bag making:** teaching childcare practices and the sacredness of infants

Spring activities will celebrate renewal, law, and new growth:

- **Laws of Mother Earth:** discussing how to live in balance with land, water, and all our relations
- **Animal identification and tracking:** observing animal behavior as teachings about resilience and adaptation
- **Treaty teachings:** learning about historical and contemporary Treaty relationships and responsibilities
- **Making traditional toys and games:** integrating play, creativity, and intergenerational interaction
- **Powwow participation and teachings:** understanding the meaning of dance styles, songs, and regalia
- **Tipi teachings:** exploring the structural, spiritual, and gendered teachings of the tipi poles and canvas
- **Duck and rabbit hunting:** providing food and teaching respectful harvesting

Across all these seasonal programs, WILBMHHL positions land, language, kinship, and ceremony as the foundation of mental, emotional, spiritual, and physical wellness. By weaving together phenomenology, cosmology, kinship, environmental responsibility, and year-round land-based education, the Lodge aims to support individuals, families, and the wider community of Ministikwan Lake Cree Nation in walking *miyo pimâtisiwin*—the good, balanced, and collectively sustained life.

As discussed in earlier chapters, intergenerational trauma among Indigenous peoples is rooted in colonial policies that disrupted land relations, governance, and family systems. This section revisits those dynamics to demonstrate how the Healing Lodge framework responds not only to symptoms but also to the structural origins of distress.

Wapaniwiw Iskwew Land-Based Mental Health Healing Lodge focuses on the spiritual and ceremonial aspects of healing and helping the individual. With the incorporation of the sweetgrass road teachings, the tipi teachings, and the use of philosophies, beliefs, customs and traditional values this will provide key foundations to make this program more effective in helping to address the current problems within the Ministikwan Lake Cree Nation community. This program is unique and beneficial as it promotes the use of connecting one to the spiritual dimension through ceremony and promotes the use of Cree language immersion. WILBMHHL primary goals and objectives are to reintegrate and immerse the individual and family back into our Indigenous ways of being and knowing. Ceremony is one of the most important aspects of WILBMHHL, ceremony assists individuals in centering themselves and gives them strength to participate in a lifelong healing process. Ceremonies provide ways to discharge emotions through crying, yelling, talking, singing, dancing, and praying (Michell, 2011). These ceremonies offer and provide a way of life that is incomparable to any other.

WILBMHHL encourages the teachings of traditional roles and responsibilities of the community. It is important for the people to reintegrate the lost connections between community members. For example, in traditional societies, it was the men's role to hunt and provide for the community, as it was the women's role was to nurture and care for members of the community. The most important role was the connection between the Elder and the child as this is where the transmission of sacred knowledge took place. The reimplementation of roles and responsibilities encourages teaching healthier lifestyles, promotes self-esteem, and builds self-confidence. This also provides a basis for creating stronger and healthier communities as well as nations.

WILBMHHL offers programs all year-round and are offered in a four-day time frame, with a proposed 12-week program. Within this timeframe the programming involves land-based and task-based activities as well as ceremony using Second Language Methodologies. With the program typically running four-day camps, we could provide longer camps (12 weeks) for lasting results. The land-based activities could also be structured around the length of time participants request. The typical four-day camp consists of picking medicines, going on hikes, fishing, canoeing, dogsledding, snowshoeing, trapping, and making small projects such as drums and rattles. The activities will also depend on the season and the weather. Longer projects are hunting and fishing. Hunting allows for one to acquire knowledge of processing of an animal which includes skinning the hide, tanning, and smoking the hide. One will learn how to process the meat for preservation and learn how to cook the animal as well as making tolls, nothing ever goes to waste. Fishing includes taking students out to the lake and showing them how to set a net. This also includes the learning and acquiring of a new skill of cleaning and gutting the fish. One will learn how to prepare the fish to eat and store for later purposes. The camp is currently researching on a way to implement birch bark canoe building into a long-range plan within the healing lodge.

There are currently other programs that focus on the teachings of Cree ways of being and knowing. What makes this program unique from others is the use of ceremony, spirituality, and total Cree immersion. We are a deeply spiritual people who incorporate prayer meditation and fasting as a way to connect with Creator. WILBMHHL offers a different teaching methodology that is ingrained in outdoor land-based education which is key to Cree epistemology and ontology and further connects us with the land. Of course, we must all keep in mind that there is no single one cure for all, what WILBMHHL will offer is a cultural appropriate approach to healing and empowerment for the people.

WILBMHHL offers an authentic cultural appropriate approach that the First Nation people of the Ministikwan Lake Cree Nation community can use to help address the issues of lingering socio-psychological issues, which have affected our people for too long. It is believed that a connection to land, language, and ceremony play a pivotal role in the healing and empowerment of *nêhiyawak*. It allows people to reconnect with the land and receive traditional teachings from Cree epistemology, cosmology, philosophy, and phenomenology. It has been beneficial for the integration of other disciplinary insights to help alleviate and solve the current issues affecting First Nations. With *mâmitonihicikan* (the mind), *môsihtâwin* (heart), *acâhk* (spirit), *miyâw* (body) all in place we will be able to achieve healing and empowerment for our people.

Intergenerational trauma—shaped by both historical and contemporary colonial structures—has profoundly affected First Nations families and communities across generations. For the Saulteaux First Nation and neighboring Cree communities, these impacts are not abstract concepts but lived realities. The emotional, psychological, social, mental, spiritual, and sexual abuses endured during what many Elders call a "silent holocaust" continue to reverberate today. Colonial policies dismantled governance systems, outlawed ceremonies, severed land relationships, and tore families apart through residential schools and the Sixties Scoop. Over time, these assaults left many feeling powerless, disconnected, and robbed of spirit.

Today, the consequences of these colonial harms manifest in high rates of poverty, suicide, addiction, family violence, incarceration, gang involvement, and cycles of neglected parenting skills. These conditions are not inherent to Indigenous peoples; they are the predictable outcomes of sustained colonial trauma. The patterns often become learned behaviors, silently passed from one generation to the next, making them deeply challenging to interrupt without culturally grounded interventions.

WILBMHHL aims to address these cycles through a holistic program that integrates Cree ceremony, land-based learning, and Indigenized therapeutic practices. Rather than imposing external models of healing, the Lodge draws on traditional activities such as water ceremonies, Sundance, Sweatlodges, Pipe ceremonies, Horse and Chicken dances, and *pihtwawikamik* (thunderbird lodge teachings). These practices reconnect individuals to spirit, to land, and to the worldview that once sustained their ancestors.

Ceremony as Foundation for Healing

WILBMHHL places the spiritual dimension of healing at the center of its approach. Incorporating teachings from the sweetgrass road, tipi teachings, and other foundational Cree philosophies, the Lodge emphasizes traditional values such as humility, respect, gratitude, and relational accountability. These teachings form the baseline for all programming and provide individuals with strong moral and spiritual anchors during their healing journey.

What makes WILBMHHL particularly unique is its commitment to **total Cree language immersion** during cultural activities and ceremonies. Language is central to Cree epistemology and ontology; it shapes how people think, how they relate to others, and how they understand the world. By using the language of ceremony, prayer, and kinship, individuals reconnect with the worldview and identity that colonization tried to erase.

Ceremony plays a crucial role in centering individuals, restoring their sense of balance, and helping them access emotional release. As Michell (2011) notes, ceremonies enable people to discharge intense emotions through crying, yelling, talking, singing, dancing, and praying. These embodied practices move emotions that may have been stuck for decades. Ceremony also reminds individuals that healing is lifelong and relational—not a one-time event, but a continuous process supported by land, spirit, and community.

Reviving Traditional Roles and Responsibilities

Another key teaching at WILBMHHL is the revitalization of traditional roles within families and communities. Colonization disrupted gender roles, parenting practices, and intergenerational relationships, leaving many community members unsure of their responsibilities to one another. In traditional Cree societies, men were responsible for hunting and providing food, while women nurtured children and maintained the home. Elders served as the primary teachers of spiritual and cultural knowledge, maintaining a sacred relationship with children that ensured cultural continuity.

Reintegrating these roles encourages healthier lifestyles, builds self-esteem, and strengthens identity. Teaching youth their roles in relation to land, animals, and family promotes confidence and responsibility. Re-establishing Elder–child relationships is particularly important, as it ensures sacred knowledge continues to flow across generations. WILBMHHL fosters these connections intentionally through intergenerational programming and family-inclusive healing approaches.

Year-Round, Land-Based, Immersive Programming

WILBMHHL offers year-round programming designed around four-day land-based camps that can expand into 12-week intensive sessions for deeper healing. The structure is flexible so that participants can engage for the duration needed to support their wellness goals.

The typical four-day camp includes activities grounded in Cree land-based pedagogy, such as:

- Picking medicines
- Hiking and orienteering
- Fishing and canoeing
- Dogsledding and snowshoeing
- Trapping and winter survival
- Drum and rattle making

Programs adapt to the seasons, honoring traditional seasonal knowledge systems. For example, longer-term projects like hunting teach participants how to process animals in respectful and sustainable ways. This includes skinning, tanning, smoking hides, preserving meat, and cooking traditional foods. Nothing is wasted, and each step incorporates ceremonial protocols and teachings about respect for animal nations.

Fishing activities allow participants to learn how to set nets, gut and clean fish, and prepare meals from their catch. These practical skills build confidence, self-sufficiency, and a sense of pride in traditional knowledge systems. The Lodge is also exploring the addition of birch bark canoe building into long-range programming—an intensive learning experience requiring patience, teamwork, and respect for elders' teachings.

What Makes WILBMHHL Distinct

While other programs offer Cree cultural teachings, WILBMHHL stands apart because it integrates ceremony, spirituality, and full Cree immersion in every aspect of healing. The program does not treat culture as an "add-on" to Western therapeutic models. Instead, it positions Cree ceremonial knowledge as the central, authoritative pillar of healing. Participants learn through doing—following the land, engaging in ceremony, speaking the language, and participating in community life. The teaching methodology is grounded in outdoor land-based education, which is essential to Cree ways of knowing. The land is not a backdrop—it is an active relative and teacher. Healing emerges through relationship: with the land, with community, with Elders, with one's own spirit. Importantly, WILBMHHL acknowledges that there is no single cure for all mental, emotional, or spiritual pain. The program does not claim to heal everyone in the same way. Rather, it offers culturally grounded pathways that individuals can adapt to their own experiences, identities, and needs.

Building Stronger, Healthier Nations

WILBMHHL provides an authentic, culturally appropriate framework for addressing long-standing socio-psychological issues in Ministikwan Lake Cree Nation. It is built upon Cree epistemology, cosmology, philosophy, and phenomenology—providing a holistic approach that addresses not only symptoms but also root causes of trauma. Healing requires alignment of *mâmitonihicikan* (mind), *môsihtâwin* (heart), *acâhk* (spirit), and *miyâw* (body). When these four elements are in balance, individuals are better able to participate in community life, support their families, and walk the good life—*miyo pimâtisiwin*. Through its land-based, ceremonial, and immersive Cree-centered approach, WILBMHHL aims to support the emergence of empowered, connected, and spiritually grounded individuals who can contribute to stronger families and healthier nations for generations to come.

Twelve-Week Program: Integrating nêhiyaw Healing and Indigenized Clinical Practice

The 12-week program described below represents one possible configuration of the Healing Lodge framework. Rather than a fixed curriculum, it should be understood as a modular learning pathway that integrates ceremonial, land-based, and clinical elements. Communities, institutions, or practitioners may adapt the sequence, duration, and specific practices according to their own protocols, capacities, and ethical responsibilities.

The 12-week program at *Wapaniwiw Iskwew* Land-Based Mental Health Healing Lodge is designed as a holistic, intensive journey that weaves together traditional nêhiyaw (Cree) knowledge systems and carefully Indigenized Western clinical practices. It responds directly to the realities of intergenerational and transgenerational trauma, acknowledging that the harms of residential schools, the Sixties Scoop, and ongoing colonial policies have not disappeared—they live in bodies, families, lands, and nervous systems.

If these traumas are not addressed, the pain we carry into adulthood often transforms into sickness, mental illness, addiction, and chronic disease. Too many of our ancestors, parents, aunties, uncles, and community members passed away without having access to meaningful healing paths or culturally grounded coping strategies. This 12-week program is one response to that reality: a structured, land-based, and ceremonial pathway that helps participants reclaim their well-being within their lifetime, for themselves and the generations who follow.

Each week of the program introduces a different set of teachings and practices. Together, they form a comprehensive healing framework that honors mind (*mâmitonihicikan*), heart (*môsihtâwin*), spirit (*acâhk*), and body (*miyâw*).

Week One: Life Skills and Walking in Two Worlds

In today's context, many *nêhiyawak* and Saulteaux community members must constantly move between two worlds: the world of the reserve and the world of towns and cities; the world of Indigenous laws and the world of Canadian institutions. For some, leaving the reserve is necessary to pursue post-secondary education, employment, trades training, or extracurricular activities such as sports and dance. For others, obligations to family, homelands, and community make it difficult or unappealing to leave.

Week One recognizes this complexity. Life skills are not just about individual success; they are about supporting families and communities to survive and thrive in both Indigenous and Western systems without losing their identity. Participants learn to structure daily routines for the whole family:

- waking up at a consistent time
- showering and brushing teeth
- preparing and eating a nourishing breakfast
- organizing healthy lunches
- returning home to chores, homework, and cooking supper
- making space for evening hobbies, recreation, or ceremony

These may seem like simple tasks, but many did not grow up in stable households where such routines were modeled. Colonization interrupted parenting, family cohesion, and everyday life patterns. Restoring rhythm and routine is therefore part of restoring dignity and control.

Life skills teaching also includes practical knowledge rarely taught in schools:

- budgeting and managing money
- paying rent, utilities, and loan payments
- grocery shopping and meal planning
- arranging childcare and navigating systems

A major focus is on healthy eating and physical activity. In pre-contact times, our people were highly active on the land, eating traditional foods that supported strong bodies. Today, processed foods and sedentary lifestyles have contributed to alarming rates of diabetes and obesity. Participants are encouraged to reconnect with traditional foodways, physical exercise, and land-based movement as part of a positive, healthy lifestyle. Spiritual practices—such as morning smudging and prayer—are integrated into these routines, reminding participants that each day is a gift and an opportunity to walk *miyo pimâtisiwin*, the good life.

Week Two: Mental Illness, Education, and De-Stigmatization

Week Two focuses on mental health literacy and de-stigmatizing mental illness in First Nations communities. Many Indigenous people live with conditions such as bipolar disorder, depression, anxiety, PTSD, OCD, schizophrenia, eating disorders, and addictions. During COVID-19, existing struggles intensified as isolation, grief, and uncertainty compounded pre-existing trauma. Participants learn about mental illness not as a personal weakness but as a complex outcome of:

- systemic racism and discrimination
- the residential school system
- the Sixties Scoop and ongoing child apprehensions
- community-level poverty, violence, and substance use
- unresolved grief and intergenerational trauma

Residential schools subjected children to emotional, psychological, spiritual, sexual, and physical abuse. These harms were rarely acknowledged or treated at the time, leaving survivors to carry enormous pain into adulthood. Many coped the only way they knew how—through alcohol, drugs, dissociation, or shutting down emotionally. Their children and grandchildren then inherited not only the trauma but also the coping patterns.

Week Two helps participants connect the dots between early childhood trauma, soul-wounding, and mental illness. It also teaches them that healing is possible. Through discussion, sharing circles, and ceremony, participants explore culturally grounded strategies for managing triggers, processing grief, and moving away from harmful coping strategies. The aim is to replace shame and stigma with compassion, understanding, and collective responsibility.

Week Three: Advanced Wilderness & Remote First Aid

In Week Three, participants are introduced to Advanced Wilderness & Remote First Aid. This component serves multiple purposes. On a practical level, it builds confidence and competence in responding to emergencies on the land. On a deeper level, it reinforces the value of being able to care for one another in remote settings, where access to hospitals or clinics may be limited.

Training topics include:

- legalities and ethics of first aid
- planning and risk assessment
- primary and secondary assessment of injuries
- managing choking, circulation emergencies, and shock
- CPR and AED use
- breathing emergencies
- wound care and infection prevention
- head, neck, and spinal injuries
- bone, muscle, and joint injuries
- sudden medical emergencies (e.g., stroke, heart attack, diabetic crisis)
- environmental illnesses and injuries (e.g., hypothermia, heatstroke, frostbite)
- dealing with poisons and toxic exposures

By the end of the week, participants have tangible skills they can use to protect their families and communities. This builds self-esteem and supports the broader goal of community resilience.

Week Four: Outdoor Survival Skills and Land-Based Knowledge

Week Four centers on land-based survival skills. Participants learn not just how to survive in the bush but how to live in respectful, reciprocal relationship with Mother Earth, as their ancestors did. Skills taught include:

- fire making and safe extinguishing
- chopping wood and managing fuel
- building a variety of outdoor shelters
- bushwhacking and navigation
- setting snares and traps
- basic hunting practices and safety
- basic canoeing techniques
- setting up a tipi and a trapper's tent
- harvesting medicinal herbs (chaga, mint, muskeg tea, diamond willow fungus, dandelion)
- identifying plants, trees, and animal tracks
- learning about migration patterns
- compass reading and GPS basics

Elders explain that we must return to the old ways not out of nostalgia but out of necessity. Climate change—manifested in wildfires, flooding, late cold winters, and extreme temperatures—reminds us that the earth is in crisis. Land-based skills reconnect participants to ancestral knowledge and teach them that Indigenous ways of living lightly and respectfully on the land are urgently needed today.

Outdoor survival training also supports mental health. Time on the land reduces anxiety, reorients people physically and spiritually, and helps them remember that they belong to an old and enduring story on Turtle Island.

Week Five: Ceremony Protocols and Sacred Conduct

At *Wapaniwiw Iskwew* Land-Based Mental Health Healing Lodge, ceremony is not a decorative element; it is the central pillar of the entire program. Week Five focuses on ceremony protocols so that participants can engage safely, respectfully, and with confidence.

Local Elders, knowledge keepers, and *oskâpêwisak* (ceremonial helpers) are invited to lead and teach. Participants learn:

- how to offer tobacco, cloth, and other offerings
- when and how to ask for ceremony
- appropriate clothing and conduct (e.g., women wearing dresses in the lodge)
- protocols for entering and exiting Sweatlodges
- expectations around fasting, prayer, and song

Elders explain why certain protocols matter. For instance, some teach that when a woman does not wear a skirt or dress in the Sweatlodge, the spirits may not recognize her clearly as a woman. These teachings are not about shaming the body; they are about clarity, respect, and energetic roles within ceremonial space.

Participants are introduced to, or deepening their knowledge of:

- Sundance
- *pîhtwâwikamik* (thunderbird lodge)
- Pipe ceremony
- Horse dance
- Chicken dance
- Sweatlodges
- Round dances

Prayer is emphasized as powerful medicine. Participants learn that in ceremony, they pray not only for themselves but also for their families, communities, nations, and all other beings. Ceremony grounds the soul, helps discharge emotional energy, and strengthens spiritual resilience.

Week Six: Traditional Parenting and Generational Healing

Week Six focuses on traditional parenting teachings, drawing on the work and wisdom of the late Janet Fox from Maskwacis First Nation. Traditional Cree parenting views children as gifts loaned by Creator. Elders teach that before birth, an unborn spirit chooses their parents, arriving with specific gifts and purposes.

The program covers all stages of childhood development:

- conception and prenatal life
- birth and infancy
- toddler and early childhood
- adolescence and early teenage years
- young adulthood

Residential schools brutally disrupted these relationships. Children were taken from their parents and grandparents, denied affection and love, and exposed to violence and abuse. As adults, many survivors did not know how to express love, gentleness, or healthy discipline because they themselves had never received it. Others were overwhelmed by trauma and addictions. Outsiders then pathologized Indigenous parents as "deficient" or "unfit," ignoring the root causes.

Traditional parenting teachings help participants reclaim their roles as caregivers, aunties, uncles, grandparents, and community members. They learn how to nurture, how to set boundaries, how to listen, and how to guide children in walking *miyo pimâtisiwin*. This is not only about individual families, but it is also about rebuilding the conditions for cultural and spiritual continuity.

Week Seven: Swing Therapy and Returning to Comfort

In Week Seven, an Indigenous healer trained in cradle-based and song-centered therapeutic practices. Dr. Darlene Auger is invited to share her powerful modality known as Swing Therapy. As she describes, this healing method came to her in a dream. She saw a large swing strong enough to hold an adult, and she was instructed that it could be used to heal people through song and gentle rocking.

During Swing Therapy, adults are cradled in a swing while Darlene sings soft lullabies in Cree. The experience mirrors the comfort of being rocked and sung to as a child. Many participants have never experienced this kind of safe, nurturing touch and sound. Swing Therapy speaks directly to the nervous system, soothing the body, calming the mind, and reawakening a sense of being loved and held.

This intervention is deeply Indigenous in its use of language, song, rhythm, and relational presence. It offers a way to reconnect with preverbal parts of the self that may carry early childhood trauma, loneliness, or abandonment.

Week Eight: Moss Bag Teachings and Infant Care

Week Eight is guided by Dr. Lillian Gadwa, who shares moss bag teachings. Historically, moss bags were used to cradle babies, replicating the secure feeling of the womb. The snug wrapping helped babies feel content, safe, and loved. The moss bag also fostered close bonding between mother (or caregiver) and child. Sylvia McAdam and other knowledge keepers teach that the string on the moss bag symbolizes the umbilical cord, tying mother and child together. The baby's belly button is understood as a sacred site that signifies where one comes from. The moss bag often attaches to a backboard; women could carry their babies while berry-picking, harvesting, or traveling, leaning the baby against a tree while they worked. These teachings are more than history. They show that Indigenous infant care was—and is—highly sophisticated, promoting emotional security and physical development. Participants learn the cultural significance of the moss bag, as well as how to design and sew one in ways that honor family lineage and clan identity.

Week Nine: Traditional Regalia and Embodied Identity

Week Nine explores traditional regalia and dance as living forms of healing, memory, and identity. While contemporary powwow culture has evolved over time, its roots lie in ancient ceremonial and social practices. Participants learn about different dance styles and the regalia associated with them, such as:

- men's and women's traditional
- fancy dance
- grass dance
- jingle dress
- chicken dance

Each style carries unique teachings. For example, the jingle dress dance is widely recognized as a healing dance that emerged in response to illness in the community. Women's jingle dresses, adorned with metal cones, create a distinctive sound as they move. That shaking sound is itself a prayer, a healing vibration.

By making regalia, participants connect with the animals and materials that help protect and guide them. Feathers, hides, beadwork, and colors all carry meaning. Regalia-making also nurtures focus, patience, creativity, and pride.

Week Ten: Inner Child Therapy—Indigenized Clinical Practice

Week Ten introduces Inner Child Therapy, a Western therapeutic approach that has been Indigenized to honor First Nations worldviews. Over an intensive four-day period, participants engage in:

- physical exercise and breathwork
- meditation and grounding practices
- TRE (Tension & Trauma Releasing Exercises)
- guided imagery and visualization
- journaling and art therapy
- grief and loss work
- land-based activities such as hunting, snaring, and trapping
- canine therapy
- ceremony and one-on-one counseling

The core goal is to reconnect with one's inner child—the part of the self that may still carry fear, shame, grief, and unmet needs. Participants learn how to "re-parent" themselves: to offer the love, safety, and protection they may not have received when they were young. This is about reclaiming responsibility and tenderness toward oneself, while not blaming the child-self who lacked power at the time.

Week Eleven: Family Group Counseling and Reclaiming Wahkohtowin

Week Eleven uses Family Group Counseling, an approach developed in the 1950s and now Indigenized to align with Cree values. This week focuses on:

- medicine wheel teachings
- tipi teachings
- sharing circles and group processing
- exploration of traumatic events and their impacts
- psychodrama and role-play
- one-on-one counseling
- land-based activities with family members
- ceremony and Elder guidance

The central concept is *wahkohtowin*—the sacred web of family and kinship relations. Participants reflect on their roles within their family and community, and how those roles have been distorted by colonialism. The goal is not to assign blame but to strengthen each individual in their relational responsibilities.

This approach challenges the Western nuclear family model by honoring extended family involvement. It restores the understanding that "it takes a community to raise a child," and that healing must be collective to be sustainable.

Week Twelve: Seven Stages of Life and Lifelong Responsibilities

The final week introduces or revisits the Seven Stages of Life teachings, drawing on the work of the late Danny Musqua and other Elders. While many Cree teachings emphasize four primary life phases—childhood, adolescence, adulthood, and Elderhood—these can also be understood in more detailed stages. Participants learn about:

- birth and naming
- childhood learning and play
- adolescent rites of passage
- young adulthood and responsibility-taking
- full adulthood and community leadership
- Elder years as wisdom-sharing
- the final journey into the spirit world

These teachings place each person's life within a larger cyclical framework. They remind participants that they are part of an unbroken chain of ancestors and descendants. Each phase carries specific responsibilities and gifts.

By the end of Week 12, participants have walked through a full cycle of teachings—ceremonial, clinical, land-based, and relational. The 12-week program does not promise that all pain will be gone. Instead, it offers tools, teachings, community, and spiritual grounding so that participants can continue walking their healing path with more strength, clarity, and hope.

From Program to Framework: Implications for Mental Health Research and Practice

The Healing Lodge framework offers more than a localized intervention; it provides a conceptual and practical model for reimagining mental health care through Indigenous law, land-based pedagogy, and relational accountability. When adapted respectfully, this framework can inform clinical training programs, community wellness initiatives, and decolonizing research methodologies.

For practitioners, the model emphasizes slowing down, working within seasonal rhythms, and privileging relational ethics over efficiency. For researchers, it challenges extractive approaches and calls for community-led design, evaluation, and knowledge governance. For institutions, it raises urgent questions about how Indigenous healing practices can be meaningfully embedded—rather than symbolically included—within mental health systems.

8

SOHKÊYIHTAMOWIN

Cree Masculinity, Fatherhood, and Land-Based Wellness

Kevin Lewis with support from Ranjan Datta

This chapter sets out an intensely transformative intellectual, cultural, and community-centered goal: to reclaim and restore Cree masculinity—*nâpêwiwin*—through land-based practices, ceremonial re-engagement, and kinship responsibilities. This chapter challenges the colonial misrepresentations of Indigenous masculinity and brings forward a powerful counter-narrative that redefines strength through Cree Natural Law, emotional depth, relational accountability, and ancestral teachings. Its central goal is to document, theorize, and revitalize Cree men's roles within families, communities, and ceremonial life by foregrounding *sohkêyihtamowin*—strength of mind, body, spirit, and heart. Within the Mental Health Healing Lodge framework, Cree masculinity functions as a connective force between the lodges of Land, Body, Spirit, and Kinship. This chapter specifically focuses on how restoring *nâpêwiwin* strengthens men's capacity for regulation, caregiving, and leadership—capacities essential for both individual healing and collective wellness.

We aim to provide a scholarly and community-grounded critique of colonial disruptions that targeted Indigenous men through residential schools, policing, incarceration, Christian patriarchy, and systemic anti-Indigenous racism. Tracing how these institutions disconnected men from fathers, land, ceremony, and emotional expression, this chapter illuminates the structural violence that produced cycles of trauma—silence, addiction, aggression, hopelessness, and emotional suppression. However, the goal of this chapter is not only diagnostic but it is also futurist and reparative. It offers pathways for Cree men to reconnect with their original identities grounded in relationality, humility, and kinship. Another key goal is to document the role of land-based wellness

DOI: 10.4324/9781003670308-8

practices—hockey, dogsledding, canoeing, running, hide scraping, hunting, trapping, and sweatlodge participation—as central teachings that rebuild Indigenous masculinities. These activities are framed not as recreational but as ceremonial sites of pedagogy, healing, and identity restoration. This chapter teaches that movement itself is medicine, that the land is a healer, and that sports operate as social and emotional infrastructures for rebuilding Indigenous men's self-esteem, resilience, and belonging. A further goal is to theorize Cree fatherhood as a relational responsibility that extends beyond biological ties. Fatherhood is presented as a communal, intergenerational, and ceremonial role involving mentorship, protection, emotional guidance, and spiritual caregiving. By grounding fatherhood in Cree Natural Law, this chapter emphasizes the importance of returning men to their responsibilities as teachers, caregivers, oskâpêwisak (ceremonial helpers), and protectors who lead with humility rather than dominance.

In this chapter, we also seek to elevate the role of ceremony—sweat lodge, pipe, fasting, water ceremonies, and rites of passage—in shaping emotionally grounded and spiritually aligned Indigenous men. Through ceremony, men learn discipline, humility, vulnerability, and courage, ultimately reconnecting with ancestral teachings that shape their identities. Finally, this chapter has a methodological and political goal: to affirm that Indigenous masculinity must be healed in relation—to partners, children, Elders, land, and community. Healing is framed as both an individual and collective responsibility, shaped by ongoing decolonization, gender resurgence, and kinship restoration. Through these scholarly, ceremonial, and relational goals, Chapter 8 becomes a blueprint for reclaiming Cree masculinity in ways that honor ancestral strength, cultural continuity, and community well-being.

Cree masculinity—*nâpêwiwin*—has long been one of the most misunderstood and misrepresented concepts within Indigenous studies, especially through the lens of colonial anthropology and Western gender frameworks. Too often, Indigenous men have been portrayed through deficit narratives that obscure the complexity, tenderness, resilience, and cultural depth that define nêhiyaw masculinities. In Cree worldview, a strong man is neither dominant nor detached. Instead, he embodies *sohkêyihtamowin*—a strength grounded in the mind, body, spirit, and heart. This strength emerges from responsibility, humility, service, and relational accountability, not from displays of power or emotional stoicism. Traditionally, Cree masculinity was nurtured through land-based mentorship, kinship teachings, and intergenerational relationships with fathers, uncles, grandfathers, Elders, and animal nations. Boys learned to hunt, gather, build, paddle, and protect—but just as importantly, they learned to comfort, pray, listen, cook, carry babies, sing, help Elders, and express emotion. They learned that leadership did not come from speaking loudly but from speaking truthfully, walking gently, and caring deeply.

Yet colonialism targeted Indigenous men with precision. Through residential schools, Christian patriarchy, policing, incarceration, welfare systems, and anti-Indigenous racism, Indigenous masculinities were distorted, shamed, and disconnected from cultural sources of strength. Entire generations were denied the teachings of *nâpêwiwin*. Many Indigenous men were raised without fathers, without ceremony, and without the land to guide their identities.

This chapter reflects on the complexity of restoring Indigenous masculinity in this era of return—of coming home to land, spirit, kinship, and responsibility. I write as a Cree father, partner, *oskâpêwis*, land-based educator, athlete, and community member who continues to navigate the lifelong healing journey that accompanies reclaiming *nâpêwiwin*. Through stories of sport, movement, ceremony, and fatherhood, I explore how land-based practices revive Cree men's identities and provide pathways toward well-being grounded in Cree Natural Law.

Cree Fatherhood: More Than a Role, a Relational Responsibility

In Cree societies, fatherhood extends far beyond a biological connection. A *nôhtawiy* is a teacher, caretaker, guide, mediator, and protector. He contributes to the collective well-being of all children in his circle, including nieces, nephews, cousins, students, and young community members. Traditional Cree fatherhood was communal, guided by protocols of respect, kindness, humility, and generosity.

A father's responsibility was to prepare the next generation for life's challenges—not only physical challenges like hunting, building, and navigating the land but also emotional ones such as grief, disappointment, conflict, and transformation. Fathers taught boys the protocols of ceremony, how to listen to Elders, how to protect their siblings, how to honor their bodies, and how to walk in beauty with all living beings. They taught sons to cry without shame, to feel emotion fully, and to stand firmly in love, not fear.

My own father, *nohtawiy-pan* Andrew Lewis, embodied these teachings with quiet strength. He was not a man of many words, but he was a man of presence. He visited often. He cared deeply. He socialized, laughed, listened, and held responsibilities without complaint. His teachings were transmitted through example: how to greet people, how to sit with Elders, how to take care of grandchildren, and how to remain grounded in the face of hardship. His legacy reminds me daily that Cree fatherhood is less about authority and more about relational endurance—being there, being steady, being teachable, and always remaining connected to the land.

Fatherhood is inseparable from ceremony. Men learn to carry the pipe, support the lodge, fast, pray, and offer thanksgiving. Through ceremony, fathers receive teachings that guide them through loss, conflict, identity challenges, and healing. When men lose connection to ceremony, they lose connection to one of their greatest sources of grounding, clarity, and responsibility.

Colonialism interrupted Cree fatherhood in devastating ways. Residential schools severed sons from fathers, taught boys that emotional expression was weakness, and punished traditional roles. Many Indigenous men grew up without healthy models of masculinity, without language, and without the spiritual teachings that once shaped their identities. This disconnect created cycles of trauma—anger, addiction, withdrawal, silence, fear of vulnerability—that continue today.

Healing Cree fatherhood requires restoring relationships between men and the land, men and ceremony, men and Elders, and men and their own spirits. When men reconnect to these sources of knowledge, they rediscover the sacred role of *nâpêw*—a man whose strength comes from care, balance, and relational accountability. This understanding aligns with Indigenous well-being frameworks identified by Kingi (2018), which emphasize balance, relational accountability, and collective responsibility rather than symptom reduction alone. Unlike Western cognitive-behavioral approaches that prioritize individual cognition, land-based Cree practices operate at the level of nervous system regulation, attachment repair, and spiritual meaning-making simultaneously.

Healing Indigenous Masculinity Through Land-Based Wellness

To heal Indigenous masculinity, we must understand that colonialism targeted not just Indigenous people but Indigenous gender systems, emotional systems, and ceremonial responsibilities. Many of the behaviors associated with "toxic masculinity" came not from Indigenous traditions but from colonial institutions that enforced shame, punishment, hierarchy, and violence.

Indigenous men today carry the profound burden of intergenerational-trauma-induced identities: silence, aggression, hopelessness, addictions, fear of failure, and suppressed grief. The resurgence of Cree masculinity requires land-based healing, language revitalization, and embodied practices that reconnect men to spirit and identity. Land-based wellness is not recreational; it is ceremonial and therapeutic. Through hunting, canoeing, trapping, running, dogsledding, hide scraping, fire building, and sweatlodge participation, Cree men rediscover their original roles and responsibilities. The land teaches patience, humility, courage, discipline, and relationship-based leadership. For many Indigenous men, healing begins by reconnecting with their bodies. Colonialism taught men to numb emotions, detach from their bodies, and internalize shame. Sports, physical activity, and movement counter this. They help regulate emotions, release trauma, and build confidence. They teach teamwork, perseverance, communication, and mental discipline—all important aspects of healthy masculinity.

Land-based activities nourish the spirit. In the quiet of a forest, a man hears the teachings of his ancestors. In the rhythm of paddling, he feels his spirit strengthened. In the chill of winter air on a dogsled trail, he reconnects with his inner child. Through sweat, exhaustion, and prayer, clarity emerges. The land remembers him, and he remembers himself.

Sports, Movement, and Ceremony as Healing Pathways

For many Cree communities, sports have long served as one of the most accessible, consistent, and meaningful forms of mentorship. Hockey, softball, basketball, track and field, canoeing, cross-country skiing, and running were not merely pastimes—they were wellness systems, social networks, and identity builders.

Sports teach many of the same principles as ceremony:

- Breathing and grounding
- Discipline and humility
- Teamwork and relational support
- Perseverance during hardship
- Respect for oneself and others
- Courage, vulnerability, and accountability

Growing up playing hockey, running long distances, and navigating the lakes and trails, I learned that movement itself was medicine. Physical exertion clears the mind. Competition builds resilience. Training teaches patience. And team sports create the sense of belonging many Indigenous men crave.

Dogsledding, particularly, is a powerful teaching. When running a team of dogs, men learn responsibility, connection, and communication. They learn that leadership does not require dominance but trust, care, and consistency. Each dog has a role. Each dog depends on the musher. This relationship models Cree leadership and masculinity—mutual respect, calm direction, and ongoing responsibility.

Hunting is another form of prayer. As a man walks the land, reads tracks, and prepares offerings, he enters a ceremonial relationship with the animal nation. Hunting teaches humility, gratitude, and patience. It anchors men in their roles as providers—not providers in the capitalist sense, but providers of love, nourishment, protection, and story. Canoeing brings focus and endurance. It teaches balance, rhythm, and cooperation. It allows men to experience the land through water, which is itself a ceremonial teacher. Running connects breath to land, heartbeat to earth, and spirit to memory. The trials remind men where they come from and who they must become. These activities are not hobbies; they are healing practices that reconnect Indigenous men with *nêhiyawiwin*—the Cree way of being.

sohkêyihtamowin: Strength of Mind, Body, Spirit, and Heart

Cree strength is holistic. A man is strong when he is emotionally grounded, spiritually clear, physically healthy, and mentally disciplined. Colonial systems disconnected these teachings, but Indigenous men are reclaiming them.

Mind: Strength means clarity, introspection, humility, and the ability to regulate thoughts.
Body: Strength emerges through movement, labor, nutrition, and land-based skill.
Spirit: Strength comes from ceremony, prayer, dreams, and ancestral connection.
Heart: Strength means compassion, love, vulnerability, and accountability to family and community.

A Cree man becomes strong not when he suppresses emotion but when he learns to carry emotion with balance. True strength emerges when a man can speak honestly, admit mistakes, seek healing, protect without harming, lead without dominating, and express love without shame.

Restoring Cree Masculinity for Future Generations

Healing Cree masculinity is not only about individual transformation but also about transforming systems—family systems, community systems, land-use systems, and ceremonial systems. Young boys need men who are emotionally honest, spiritually grounded, physically active, and deeply connected to land-based practices. They need uncles, fathers, grandfathers, coaches, oskâpêwisak, and ceremonial leaders who model *nâpêwiwin*.

The resurgence of Cree masculinity requires:

- Restoring father-child relationships disrupted by colonialism
- Returning men to ceremony and language
- Rebuilding land-based cultural camps for boys and young men
- Supporting Indigenous men's mental health through culturally grounded programming
- Recognizing sports, movement, and outdoor activity as healing
- Teaching men to express love, grief, and vulnerability without shame

Through these pathways, Cree masculinity becomes not a site of harm but a force of healing.

To speak of Cree masculinity today is to speak of recovery, resurgence, and relational restoration. The work of decolonizing Indigenous masculinities is both ancestral and emergent, grounded in teachings passed down for generations and renewed through contemporary land-based practices. Through ceremony, movement, sports, fatherhood, and kinship, Indigenous men reclaim their identities, responsibilities, and spiritual roles.

Cree masculinity begins and ends with love. Love for land, love for children, love for future generations, love for community, and love for Creator. When we restore *sohkêyihtamowin*—strength of mind, body, spirit, and heart—we restore our nations. The trees, as our Elders say, are still dancing. So too are our men. They rise again—slowly, steadily, ceremonially—returning home to themselves, to their families, and to the land that has been waiting for them.

Dogsledding: A Teaching of Responsibility, Balance, and Spirit

For over a decade, dogsledding has been central to our family life, our cultural camps, and the teachings we pass down to youth. What may appear from the outside as a sport or recreational activity is, in reality, a profound ceremonial practice that shapes the emotional, spiritual, and relational development of Cree men and boys. Dogsledding is one of the most powerful teachings of *nâpêwiwin* because it cultivates discipline, humility, emotional regulation, and relational accountability—qualities essential to restoring Indigenous masculinity after generations of colonial violence.

In Cree understandings, animals are not subordinates; they are teachers, relatives, helpers, and guides. The dogs we work with are kin. They sense our emotions, intentions, and the state of our spirit long before we speak. When you approach a dog team with a heavy mind or a troubled heart, the dogs respond. They hesitate. They look back. Their bodies mirror your uncertainty. When you bring clarity, grounded breathing, and confidence, they rise to meet your energy. In this way, dogsledding becomes ceremony. It forces a man to confront himself—to feel what he is carrying and to adjust his spirit before asking the dogs to run with him.

Working with a dog team teaches the kind of leadership Cree boys once learned through land-based apprenticeship with fathers, uncles, and Elders. Leadership is not domination. It is consistency, calmness, clarity, and the capacity to maintain balance even under stress. A dog team listens to tone, rhythm, patience, and energy. It responds to your breath. It mirrors your state of mind. A frustrated musher creates a chaotic team; a grounded musher creates harmony. These lessons extend far beyond the trail.

Dogsledding also brings stories of *wîsahkêcâhk*, the trickster-transformer whose interactions with wolves and dogs teach us about humility, responsibility, and the dangers of arrogance. In our stories, the wolves represent intelligence, cooperation, loyalty, and endurance. A dog team reflects these teachings—each dog has a role, each depends on the others, and each carries responsibility for the group. The lead dog must think ahead, the team dogs must work in unison, and the wheel dogs must anchor the strength of the sled. This structure teaches Cree boys about kinship, hierarchy based on expertise rather than dominance, and the importance of recognizing everyone's gifts.

Dogsledding also connects us to *onitawâhtwâwak*—the explorers and researchers of our nations. Long before the term "scientist" existed, Cree hunters and trappers were scientists of snow, ice, animal behavior, wind patterns, and land-based medicine. The musher, guiding the dogs through storm, darkness, or difficult terrain, becomes part of this lineage. Dogsledding reconnects Cree men to ancestral intelligence, reminding them that they come from mobile societies whose survival depended on deep land knowledge, careful observation, and cooperation with non-human relatives. Through these relational teachings, dogsledding becomes more than an activity. It becomes a healing methodology, a cultural pedagogy, and a spiritual responsibility.

Hockey and Modern Indigenous Wellness

Hockey occupies a special place in many Indigenous communities. Rinks—frozen lakes, community arenas, outdoor patches of ice—have long served as gathering spaces for youth, families, and entire nations. Hockey is a modern teaching lodge, a site where Indigenous youth learn discipline, teamwork, emotional regulation, and perseverance. For many, it is one of the few consistent structures remaining in communities disrupted by colonialism. As a father of hockey players, I have witnessed how the hockey arena becomes a place of emotional release. Children express joy, frustration, triumph, exhaustion, and heartbreak—and all of it is healthy when held in a circle of support. Hockey requires physical stamina, mental resilience, and emotional adaptability. It demands early mornings, late-night practices, financial sacrifice, and community fundraising. These efforts build character in both players and families. They create routines, encourage healthy living, and strengthen kinship ties.

Hockey teaches Cree boys and girls how to:

- work as part of a team
- listen to mentors and coaches
- respect opponents
- push their physical limits safely
- experience failure as learning
- practice discipline and time management
- make healthy food choices
- care for their bodies through movement

But hockey also carries cultural importance. It creates belonging. It provides identity and self-esteem. It becomes a pathway for Indigenous youth to shine, to lead, to mentor younger siblings, and to make their ancestors proud. Hockey transforms potential loneliness into community, potential disengagement into passion, and potential despair into purpose.

Hockey is ceremony in motion. It is a place where Indigenous youth build the emotional and physical endurance needed to navigate the challenges of contemporary life—racism, trauma, poverty, family instability, and the weight of intergenerational memory. Hockey teaches youth to keep moving, no matter the obstacles in front of them.

Partners in Healing: Walking the Difficult Road Together

Healing as a Cree man is not a solitary undertaking. While individual reflection, ceremony, and land-based activities are important, healing must happen in relationship. Colonialism did not only disrupt Indigenous families, but it also fractured our relational systems—teaching men to isolate themselves, suppress emotion, or avoid vulnerability.

Walking a healing journey with a partner requires courage, honesty, humility, and patience. Intergenerational trauma affects communication, emotional expression, trust, and conflict resolution. It impacts how we parent, how we respond to stress, how we interpret love, and how we manage fear. But when Cree men commit to relational healing, they reclaim original principles of nêhiyaw identity: reciprocity, deep listening, mutual responsibility, and gentle care.

A partner does not fix you—they walk beside you. They witness your transformation. They remind you who you are when you forget. They help you sit with uncomfortable teachings, encourage your growth, and accompany you to ceremony. Healing becomes a shared journey, a path braided with two spirits, influenced by Elders, held by community, and strengthened by land. Healing with a partner means recognizing that our relationships mirror our spiritual work. They reflect what we have not yet resolved, the wounds we still carry, and the responsibilities we have yet to reclaim. When approached with humility, partnership becomes a ceremonial space where both individuals grow, witness, teach, and transform one another.

Breaking Cycles Through Intentional Fatherhood

Intentional fatherhood is one of the most powerful tools for breaking cycles of intergenerational trauma within Indigenous communities. Colonialism disrupted Indigenous fatherhood—through residential schools, wage labor migration, incarceration, systemic racism, and ongoing resource extraction that keeps men away from their families. Many Indigenous men grew up without nurturing fathers, without emotional guidance, and without ceremonial mentorship. Today, intentional fatherhood becomes a radical act of decolonization.

When a Cree father chooses patience instead of anger, presence instead of absence, prayer instead of silence, and emotional availability instead of withdrawal, he interrupts the colonial script. He becomes a cultural transformer, restoring teachings that were once nearly severed.

Intentional fatherhood involves:

- speaking Cree words to children daily
- introducing children to ceremony, one step at a time
- letting them observe our healing
- teaching them about land, plants, animals, weather, and water
- cooking for them and nourishing their bodies
- making time to play, laugh, and be silly
- showing love openly, not conditionally
- offering soft guidance, not harsh criticism
- protecting their spirits from lateral violence and shame
- inviting them into safe cultural spaces where identity can flourish

Practicing these teachings, Cree men begin to repair the ruptures caused by colonialism. They teach children how to carry themselves with balance, humility, and gentleness. They show them that strength does not require silence or harshness, but comes from emotional stability and spiritual grounding.

Through fatherhood, healing becomes intergenerational.

The Role of the *oskâpêwis:* Ceremony as Masculine Transformation

The role of the *oskâpêwis*—the ceremonial helper—is one of the most important pathways for Indigenous men to learn humility, discipline, and service. Becoming an *oskâpêwis* means surrendering ego, following instructions, and supporting Elders and knowledge keepers without expectation of recognition.

An *oskâpêwis* learns:

- to anticipate the needs of others
- to maintain composure under pressure
- to carry heavy responsibilities quietly
- to handle sacred items with respect
- to understand ceremonial law
- to practice emotional self-control
- to protect ceremonial space
- to help others before helping oneself

These teachings challenge the colonial distortions of masculinity that promote dominance, aggression, or stoicism. Instead, the *oskâpêwis* role models a masculinity grounded in care, reflection, vulnerability, and softness. Ceremonial helpers learn that true leadership is service. True power is humility. True strength is gentleness guided by spiritual discipline. The *oskâpêwis* emerges from ceremony not only with knowledge but also with identity—an understanding of who he is, his place in the world, and the responsibilities he carries as a Cree man.

Cree Masculinity Reborn Through Land, Ceremony, and Kinship

Cree masculinity is in a profound moment of return—return to land, return to ceremony, return to kinship, return to emotional honesty, and return to the teachings that once shaped generations of strong, gentle, spiritually grounded Cree men. The work of reclaiming *nâpêwiwin* requires courage, vulnerability, and ongoing commitment to *sohkêyihtamowin*—the strength of mind, body, spirit, and heart. Through dogsledding, hockey, physical wellness, partnership, fatherhood, and ceremonial work, Indigenous men are rediscovering who they were always meant to be. They are remembering ancestral teachings. They are becoming emotionally available to their families. They are cultivating healthier bodies, clearer minds, and balanced spirits. They are guiding youth onto good paths. They are healing themselves and, in doing so, healing their communities. Cree masculinity is not being invented; it is being remembered.

It is rising again from the land. It is carried by the breath of dogs on a cold morning trail, by the rhythm of skates cutting across ice, by the laughter of children in a warm kitchen, and by the prayers whispered into lodge stones. Through movement, ceremony, land, and kinship, Indigenous men reclaim their purpose. They become protectors who do not harm, leaders who do not dominate, fathers who nurture, partners who walk in honesty, and helpers who carry the teachings with quiet dignity. This is *nâpêwiwin*. This is *sohkêyihtamowin*. This is the rebirth of Cree masculinity: grounded in love, strengthened by land, and guided by ancestors toward *miyo-pimâtisiwin*—the good life.

In this chapter we stand as one of the most emotionally resonant and theoretically compelling sections of this manuscript. It weaves together personal testimony, Cree philosophy, land-based pedagogy, and decolonial gender analysis to articulate a vision of Indigenous masculinity that is profoundly different from Western constructs. This chapter is deeply significant because it demonstrates that Cree masculinity is not a site of deficiency—as colonial narratives have long insisted—but a site of profound cultural knowledge, emotional capacity, and relational strength.

One of the strongest contributions lies in its rejection of colonial gender binaries and pathologizing frameworks. It exposes how residential schools and state violence deliberately dismantled Indigenous gender systems by removing children from fathers, suppressing men's emotional expression, and disrupting Indigenous mentorship structures. This reflection challenges readers to understand Indigenous men's struggles not as individual failings but as systemic injuries created by colonialism. In doing so, this chapter reframes trauma as a political, communal, and historical issue rather than a set of isolated psychological symptoms.

The engagement with land-based wellness is another powerful contribution. It situates sports—particularly hockey—and land-based practices such as dogsledding, running, canoeing, and hunting as more than physical activities. They are presented as ceremonial infrastructures that rebuild emotional regulation, self-confidence, and a sense of belonging. This reconceptualization broadens the field of Indigenous mental health research by demonstrating that healing does not occur solely within clinical spaces but emerges from movement, land connections, and relational experiences. The description of dogsledding, for instance, positions animal nations as teachers who reflect a man's emotional state and guide him toward balance and humility. This represents a profound decolonial ethic: non-human relatives serve as co-therapists and co-researchers in Indigenous wellness.

We also offer an important reflection on Indigenous fatherhood as a site of both loss and resurgence. It honors the ancestral roles of fatherhood while acknowledging the ruptures caused by colonialism. Yet it does not dwell in grief; instead, it presents Cree fatherhood as a powerful mechanism for breaking cycles of intergenerational trauma. Reading about intentional fatherhood—speaking Cree to children, inviting them into ceremony, modeling healing and emotional availability—underscores how everyday acts of love can become revolutionary forms of decolonization.

We emphasize on the *oskâpêwis* role is particularly meaningful. By framing ceremonial helper responsibilities as pathways toward humility, discipline, and service, it redefines leadership in Indigenous communities. This challenges Western patriarchal definitions of masculinity rooted in dominance, autonomy, and control. Instead, Cree masculinity emerges as service-oriented, relational, and spiritually accountable. Another key reflective point is the balance this chapter strikes between personal narrative and collective teachings. The stories about the author's father, sports experiences, and ceremonial learning create emotional depth while reinforcing the broader cultural analysis. These narratives embody Wilson's (2008) relational accountability framework, demonstrating that Indigenous knowledge is always grounded in lived experience rather than abstraction.

This chapter finally invites readers to witness a resurgence in motion. It shows Cree men not as victims of colonial harm but as active agents reclaiming their identities through ceremony, movement, kinship, and love. This transformation is not romanticized; it is presented as challenging, ongoing, and relationally demanding. Yet it is precisely this honesty that makes this chapter so compelling. It offers a hopeful, grounded vision of Indigenous masculinity restored—shaped not by colonial expectations but by Cree Natural Law and ancestral teachings.

9

KINSHIP ECONOMIES AND EDUCATIONAL SOVEREIGNTY

Rebuilding Nations through Cree Teacher Education and Indigenomics

Kevin Lewis with support from Ranjan Datta

This chapter examines how Cree nationhood is sustained through the integration of educational sovereignty and economic sovereignty. Building on earlier discussions of land-based healing, mental wellness, and ceremonial frameworks, this chapter shifts focus from individual and familial healing toward collective, institutional, and structural transformation. It argues that long-term mental health and cultural resurgence require Cree-led educational systems, kinship-based economies, and governance models grounded in wâhkôhtowin. Specifically, this chapter offers: (1) a framework for Cree educational sovereignty through teacher education and land-based pedagogy; (2) an applied discussion of Indigenomics and kinship economies; and (3) implications for mental health systems, universities, and community-based institutions.

This chapter's central goal is to articulate a comprehensive model of Cree sovereignty that integrates two mutually reinforcing domains: educational sovereignty and economic sovereignty. Educational sovereignty ensures that Cree children learn through language, land, kinship, ceremony, and local governance rather than colonial curricula that privilege Euro-Western epistemologies. Economic sovereignty ensures that communities have the resources, infrastructure, and stable livelihoods necessary to sustain cultural resurgence, teacher training, youth programming, land-based healing, and Elder-led knowledge systems.

Another important goal is to reposition Cree pedagogy—land-based learning, experiential teaching, Elder-led governance, ASLA, TPR, and immersion schooling—as advanced knowledge systems rather than cultural supplements. By demonstrating how Cree educational institutions cultivate leaders, researchers, healers, and language experts, this chapter asserts that Cree teacher education is itself a form of nation-building.

DOI: 10.4324/9781003670308-9

A further goal is to illustrate how Indigenomics and kinship economies revitalize the economic infrastructures that colonization dismantled. This chapter shows that economic development rooted in kinship, stewardship, reciprocity, and long-term planning has the power to strengthen mental health, reduce dependency, increase community pride, and create sustainable opportunities for youth and families. Unlike capitalist models that prioritize extraction and individual accumulation, Cree economic resurgence cultivates collective wellness and intergenerational accountability. This chapter also aims to show that decolonizing universities from within is an essential political and intellectual strategy. Cree scholars, Elders, and language keepers working in universities are rebuilding pathways for Indigenous knowledge systems to flourish, ensuring that academic institutions evolve beyond symbolic inclusion toward structural change. The goal of Chapter 9 is to weave together language, land, pedagogy, ceremony, innovation, and Indigenous economics into a coherent framework of Cree nationhood—one that honors wâhkôhtowin and prepares future generations for lives grounded in Cree identity, sovereignty, and purpose.

Education and economy—learning and livelihood—have always been inseparable in Cree society. Long before colonial schooling systems attempted to reshape Indigenous cognition and community life, the nêhiyawak sustained themselves through highly advanced models of land-based learning, kinship-driven governance, and reciprocal economies rooted in ethical relations. Children learned not in isolated classrooms but through movement, observation, direct participation, and ceremonial responsibility. The bush, the lakes, the lodges, the camps, the traplines, the stories, and the Elders formed a complete educational ecosystem. Our economies were equally complex. They were based on Natural Law: wâhkôhtowin (kinship), miyo-wîcêhtowin (living in good relation), pimâtisiwin (the good life), sharing, humility, responsibility, and collective well-being. These were not metaphors—they were the infrastructure of Cree nationhood. In our contemporary context, Cree communities are once again rebuilding these foundations by asserting two interrelated forms of sovereignty that colonial systems have intentionally disrupted:

1 **Educational Sovereignty:** The inherent right and responsibility to educate our children in our own language, worldview, pedagogy, and ceremonial practices.
2 **Economic Sovereignty:** The right to rebuild sustainable, land-based, culturally aligned economies that strengthen community resilience and independence.

These forms of sovereignty cannot be separated. Education shapes the future workforce, governance, and leadership; economics shapes the material conditions that allow communities to thrive. This chapter examines how Cree teacher education, land-based pedagogies, and Indigenomics (First Nations-driven economic theory) work together to restore nationhood, rebuild kinship, and re-establish the systems of self-determination that sustained our ancestors for millennia.

Within contemporary mental health systems in Canada and the United States—such as school-based counseling, community wellness programs, child and youth mental health services, and addictions treatment—education remains one of the most influential determinants of long-term well-being. Cree educational sovereignty directly affects mental health outcomes by shaping identity development, language continuity, community belonging, and cultural continuity. Teacher education programs thus function not only as academic initiatives but also as preventative mental health interventions that reduce disconnection, internalized colonialism, and intergenerational trauma.

Reclaiming Educational Sovereignty: Language, Land, and Teacher Training

Cree education is not a "new" innovation—it is a *renewed* system that predates colonial schooling by thousands of years. Our ancestors studied ecosystems, tracked seasonal cycles, memorized star maps, built engineered hunting structures, governed trade routes, and maintained sophisticated forms of diplomacy. These intellectual traditions were carried through language and kinship.

nêhiyawêwin is more than a communication system; it is a living archive of philosophy, law, governance, land-based knowledge, and ceremonial teachings. Our verbs contain entire worldviews. Our kinship terms encode governance principles. Our stories transmit science, ethics, and history.

When colonial schools removed generations of Cree children from their lands, languages, and families, they severed the intergenerational transmission of Cree pedagogies. Today, reclaiming educational sovereignty means restoring this pathway through:

- Cree-led teacher education programs
- Land-based learning initiatives
- Language immersion curricula
- Cultural camps and seasonal schools
- Community-driven policies and standards

Educational sovereignty is not just about correcting historical injustice; it is about rebuilding nations.

Teacher Education as Nation-Building

Cree teacher education programs—such as the Indigenous Language Certificate, Bachelor of Arts in nêhiyawêwin, and the forthcoming five-year BA/BEd dual program—represent some of the most important investments in long-term nation-building. These programs do not merely train classroom teachers; they cultivate:

- Fluent and confident language speakers
- Land-based educators
- Pedagogical innovators
- Researchers rooted in community
- Counselors and youth mentors
- Cultural practitioners and ceremonial helpers
- Future leaders in governance and policy

A Cree teacher operates far beyond the traditional Western role of "instructor." A Cree teacher is a knowledge carrier who transmits worldview, identity, kinship responsibilities, ceremonial protocols, and ways of being. In Cree communities, teachers stand at the nexus of youth empowerment, community healing, and language revitalization. Through teacher education, entire kinship networks are strengthened, repaired, and extended across generations. These outcomes align with Indigenous education scholarship demonstrating that culturally grounded teacher education strengthens student engagement, improves mental health outcomes, and supports community resilience (Battiste, 2013; Kirkness & Barnhardt, 2001).

Land-Based Pedagogy: Learning Through Doing

At the heart of Cree education lies land-based pedagogy. Land-based learning is experiential, embodied, relational, seasonal, and spiritual. It draws from five primary knowledge sources:

1 **Land**
2 **Language**
3 **Elders**
4 **Ceremony**
5 **Kinship**

At kâniyâsihk Culture Camps and kâ-nêyâsihk mîkiwâhpa immersion school, these principles guide year-round learning. Children, youth, and educators engage directly in activities that teach Cree science, mathematics, engineering, governance, medicine, and ethics:

- Scraping, tanning, and smoking hides
- Fishing with nets, filleting, drying, and preserving

- Hunting, snaring, tracking, and field processing animals
- Canoe building, snowshoe making, and survival skills
- Sewing, beading, regalia-making, moss bags, and cradleboards
- Tipi teachings, fire teachings, star knowledge
- Year-round ceremonies, feasts, and rites of passage
- Traditional parenting and Elder-youth mentorship
- Seasonal ecological learning

This is not "alternative" education. It is Indigenous science. It is Indigenous engineering. It is Indigenous governance. It is the original system of teaching that sustained Cree nations for thousands of years. Cree pedagogy teaches that learning is not simply the transfer of information—it is the cultivation of identity, ethics, spirit, and relationships.

From a comparative pedagogical perspective, land-based Cree education aligns with experiential learning theory, embodied cognition, and ecological psychology, while extending beyond them through ceremonial accountability and kinship governance. These pedagogical models challenge Western schooling systems by redefining assessment, authority, and curriculum as relational rather than hierarchical.

ASLA, TPR, Drama, Singing, and Drumming: The Future of Language Learning

Modern language revitalization does not abandon ancestral practice—it expands it with current tools. Accelerated Second Language Acquisition (ASLA), Total Physical Response (TPR), drama-based learning, singing, dancing, and digital storytelling have been integrated into Cree immersion classrooms with overwhelming success.

ASLA and TPR replicate natural learning environments:

- Students respond physically to commands
- They acquire vocabulary through action and repetition
- Fear and anxiety decrease
- Fluency increases rapidly

Drama, singing, and drumming build emotional, cultural, and linguistic confidence. Students become active participants in their own learning rather than passive recipients. When combined with land-based pedagogy, these methods recreate the immersive learning environments our ancestors relied on.

For practitioners and institutions seeking to adapt these approaches, key implementation principles include: (1) embedding language learning within daily physical activity; (2) prioritizing emotional safety over correction; and (3) involving fluent speakers and Elders as co-educators rather than consultants.

Indigenomics: Reclaiming Economic Sovereignty

Education alone cannot rebuild nations without parallel economic transformation. Colonization disrupted Indigenous economies by restricting land access, undermining trade routes, banning cultural practices, and imposing cash-based dependence structures through the Indian Act. Indigenomics—coined and advanced by Carol Anne Hilton—offers a pathway for restoring economic sovereignty by applying Indigenous worldviews to modern economic development. In Cree contexts, Indigenomics emphasizes:

- Ethical resource stewardship
- Community-owned enterprises
- Sustainable cultural tourism
- Land-based economies (trapping, crafts, harvesting, guiding)
- Renewable energy and eco-governance
- Food sovereignty and agricultural revitalization
- Youth training and workforce development
- Investment in Indigenous innovation

Economic sovereignty ensures that communities have the infrastructure and resources needed to sustain educational and cultural resurgence. Research in Indigenous health consistently demonstrates that economic security, meaningful work, and community ownership are protective factors against depression, addiction, and suicide. Indigenomics thus functions not only as an economic model but also as a population-level mental health intervention.

Kinship Economies: The Original Cree Economic System

Before colonization, Cree economies were built on kinship networks that shared resources, redistributed wealth, and ensured no one was left behind. These were sophisticated systems of:

- Seasonal labor organization
- Knowledge exchange
- Communal harvesting
- Treaty-making and diplomacy
- Long-distance trade networks
- Ethical governance

Kinship economies were rooted in reciprocity, not extraction; responsibility, not accumulation. Reviving kinship economies today means:

- Prioritizing community well-being over profit
- Supporting local artisans, hunters, and knowledge keepers
- Creating youth mentorship systems tied to economic activities
- Ensuring Elders guide economic decision-making
- Building partnerships that respect Indigenous rights and sovereignty

Indigenomics and kinship economies are compatible frameworks. Together, they allow Cree communities to reclaim ownership of their economic futures.

Educational Sovereignty + Economic Sovereignty = Nationhood

The central argument of this chapter is that Cree teacher education and Indigenomics cannot be separated. They form a dual foundation for rebuilding nations:

- **Education** restores identity, language, culture, governance, and leadership.
- **Economics** restores independence, infrastructure, resources, and long-term sustainability.

Without economic sovereignty, educational sovereignty lacks material support. Without educational sovereignty, economic sovereignty lacks cultural grounding.

Cree nations thrive when both systems are aligned with cultural teachings and governed through wâhkôhtowin.

We emphasize that rebuilding Cree nations requires a return to the principles that sustained our ancestors:

- Land-based learning
- Kinship-driven economies
- Ceremonial governance
- Language revitalization
- Community accountability
- Indigenous innovation

Through Cree teacher education and Indigenomics, we reclaim not only knowledge and livelihoods but also the spirit of Cree nationhood itself. This chapter demonstrates that sovereignty is not merely political—it is educational, economic, cultural, and deeply relational. Rooting our systems in Natural Law, Cree pedagogy, and kinship economies, we prepare future generations to live miyo-pimâtisiwin—the good life—grounded in identity, wellness, and collective strength.

Decolonizing Universities from Within

As more Indigenous scholars, Elders, and language keepers assume roles within Canadian universities, the academic landscape is undoubtedly shifting. However, genuine decolonization requires far more than representation. It demands structural transformation—intellectual, cultural, pedagogical, and administrative. Inclusion alone can still replicate colonial hierarchies if Indigenous presence is only symbolic or confined to consultation roles rather than decision-making power. For Indigenous scholars working within these institutions, the work becomes both liberatory and exhausting: we are expected to dismantle the very systems that simultaneously require our labor yet resist transformative change. To truly decolonize universities from within, Indigenous scholars must confront entrenched systems designed to privilege Euro-Western knowledge. This means rewriting curricula so that Indigenous epistemologies, ceremonial philosophies, land-based sciences, and kinship ethics are not supplementary modules but intellectual foundations alongside Western theories. It requires challenging outdated academic policies that restrict land-based instruction, ceremonial time, and Indigenous language learning. For example, Cree immersion courses should not be perceived as "electives" but as essential intellectual frameworks that shape worldviews, governance, relationships, and ethical decision-making.

Decolonization also requires the recognition of ceremonial knowledge as legitimate research. Sweatlodge teachings, pipe ceremony reflections, moon teachings, rites of passage, and Elders' narratives carry philosophical, scientific, ecological, and medicinal dimensions that cannot be captured through Western academic methods alone. Universities must expand what counts as "evidence," "methodology," and "theory" to honor Indigenous ways of knowing. This also includes developing appropriate ethical protocols that respect ceremonial confidentiality, sacred law, and community ownership of knowledge.

In addition, non-Indigenous faculty must be trained in cultural safety and anti-racist pedagogy—not as optional workshops but as mandatory components of academic training. Too often, Indigenous scholars carry the labor of educating colleagues about racism, land acknowledgments, gendered colonial violence, Indigenous sovereignty, treaty relationships, and epistemic harm. True decolonization means redistributing this institutional responsibility.

Finally, Indigenous languages must become pillars of universities, not marginal departments threatened with closure. nêhiyawêwin holds our legal systems, humor, metaphors, philosophies, kinship structures, and cosmologies. To lose the language is to lose the architecture of Cree thought itself. Our work within universities is not assimilation; it is reclamation. Each Indigenous scholar inside the academy is a doorway through which ancestral knowledge re-enters institutional spaces designed to exclude it. We are not guests—we are restoring intellectual systems that long predated Western academia. Within a Mental Health Healing Lodge framework, universities function as contested but necessary sites of transformation. Decolonizing academic institutions enables Indigenous-led research, evaluation, and training pathways that support community-based healing lodges, teacher education programs, and land-based mental health initiatives.

Indigenomics: Economic Sovereignty Rooted in Kinship

While educational sovereignty strengthens cultural and intellectual nationhood, **economic sovereignty** fortifies the material and social foundations that make self-determination possible. This is where Indigenomics, inspired by Carol Anne Hilton's transformative economic framework, becomes essential. Indigenomics is not simply Indigenous participation in mainstream economic systems; it is a reorientation of economic design based on Indigenous worldviews, kinship obligations, ecological ethics, and collective responsibility.

At **kâniyâsihk Culture Camps**, Indigenomics is already taking shape through community-led, land-based ventures that honor Cree values. These include:

- Year-round land-based culture camps
- Cree immersion education programs
- Hide-tanning and craft-making camps
- Summer and winter cultural gatherings
- Sports academies rooted in Cree teachings
- Craft sales featuring hides, beadwork, drums, and traditional tools
- Greenhouses and food sovereignty initiatives
- Tourism rooted in ceremony, land-based learning, and seasonal teachings
- Future community-owned social enterprises

These initiatives do far more than create revenue—they rebuild the kinship economies that once sustained entire nations. They create spaces where Elders pass knowledge to youth, where language is spoken naturally, where community members practice skills grounded in seasonal cycles, and where culture becomes the foundation of economic renewal.

Indigenomics teaches us that economic sovereignty does not come from assimilation into capitalist structures but from building economies that reflect Indigenous ethics: reciprocity, relationality, environmental stewardship, and long-term thinking. These principles guide not only financial decision-making but also community well-being, governance, and intergenerational responsibility.

Economic Health as Mental Health

Economic sovereignty is deeply connected to mental health, healing, and community well-being. For generations, colonial policies—land dispossession, the reserve system, residential schools, the pass system, and the wage labor economy—destroyed Indigenous livelihoods, creating dependency and poverty. When communities regain control over their economic futures, they experience profound psychological and social benefits:

- **Reduced dependency**
- **Increased self-esteem and community pride**
- **More stable family environments**
- **Higher youth engagement and hopefulness**
- **Decreased violence, addiction, and despair**
- **Improved mental, emotional, and spiritual health**

Economic health is mental health. It restores a sense of purpose, belonging, dignity, and agency. When Cree people are able to sustain themselves through culturally aligned work—hide tanning, fishing, guiding, teaching, crafting, trapping, cultural tourism, language revitalization—they heal spiritually because they are returning to their ancestral roles.

Colonial systems sought to destroy Indigenous economies precisely because they knew that economic autonomy meant political autonomy. Today, reclaiming economic sovereignty is part of breaking intergenerational cycles of trauma.

Kinship Economies: The Cree Framework

The Cree economy is not extractive—it is relational. This is what distinguishes it from capitalist models that prioritize accumulation and profit over people and land. Kinship economies rely on:

- **Reciprocity**
- **Redistribution**
- **Stewardship of land and water**
- **Shared responsibility and communal labor**
- **Long-term planning based on ancestors and future generations**

A healthy Cree economy is not measured by individual wealth but by the collective well-being of the nation. Indicators of success include:

- A thriving language
- Good relationships with the land
- Strong, healthy children

- Elders who are honored and cared for
- Youth who feel hopeful for the future
- Families who support one another
- People who understand their cultural roles

Our economic systems do not chase profit—they cultivate wellness. They generate relationships, not commodities. They build communities, not corporations.

Sports Academies and Youth Empowerment

Sports have become one of the most powerful tools for Indigenous resurgence, identity formation, and nation-building. For many Indigenous youth, hockey, lacrosse, soccer, volleyball, canoeing, MMA, dogsledding, and archery are not simply recreational activities—they are pathways back to themselves. A **Cree Sports Academy**—rooted in ceremony, land-based learning, kinship, and cultural identity—would:

- Build emotional resilience and confidence
- Strengthen leadership and teamwork
- Enhance physical and mental health
- Create positive mentorship relationships
- Support language revitalization through sport
- Offer youth alternatives to addiction, violence, and hopelessness
- Create economic opportunities through coaching, training, and local tournaments

Sport becomes ceremony. It teaches humility, discipline, relationship-building, and perseverance—values that align with Cree teachings and support lifelong wellness.

When youth skate, run, paddle, or race dogs across the land, they feel their ancestors moving with them.

Creating Sustainable, Community-Led Systems

Educational sovereignty and economic sovereignty must develop together. Without one, the other remains incomplete. Teacher education programs ensure the transmission of language, history, governance, and cultural knowledge. Indigenomics ensures that communities have the economic infrastructure to sustain these systems long-term.

Together, they create:

- community-run schools
- Elder-led culture camps
- land-based healing lodges

- sustainable businesses
- language and arts centers
- food sovereignty programs
- sports and recreation facilities
- tourism grounded in Cree ethics
- research centers led by Cree scholars

In these integrated systems:

- **The community becomes the classroom**
- **The land becomes the teacher**
- **The language becomes the law**

This is what nationhood looks like.

Rebuilding Nations Through Kinship

Kinship economies and educational sovereignty are inseparable forces that shape the future of Cree nationhood. Together, they restore what colonial systems attempted to erase: identity, governance, land-based knowledge, language, ceremony, and relational responsibility.

Through Cree teacher education, land-based pedagogy, Indigenomics, sports academies, community enterprises, and culturally grounded leadership, we are building a world where Cree children grow strong in their language, confident in their identity, and grounded in their purpose.

This is more than resurgence. This is nation rebuilding.

This is wâhkôhtowin in action—living our relationships in ways that honor our ancestors and protect future generations. Our ancestors prayed for our return to this path. Today, we walk it with them, guided by language, land, kinship, and ceremony.

In this chapter we establish a deeply relational, land-based, and transformative approach to Cree healing, grounded in wâhkôhtowin, ceremony, kinship, and intergenerational accountability. It calls for a paradigm shift in mental health, education, governance, and community well-being by returning to Cree Natural Law and ancestral teachings. We directly extends this foundational vision by demonstrating how healing extends into the economic and educational structures that shape collective life. Where the Introduction focuses on cultural resurgence, identity restoration, and the reawakening of Cree knowledge systems, we show how these revitalizations must be institutionalized through Cree-led schools, teacher education programs, land-based pedagogies, community-run camps, and kinship-based economic models. It translates the Introduction's philosophical commitments into practical systems capable of sustaining Cree nationhood long-term.

We emphasize that healing is not merely psychological but relational, embodied, territorial, and ceremonial. It echoes this by arguing that Cree education must be rooted in the land, in seasonal cycles, in Elders' teachings, and in kinship governance. It reinforces the idea that learning must be experiential, spiritual, and participatory—children scraping hides, harvesting medicines, building canoes, speaking Cree, participating in ceremonies, and learning from the natural world. In this way, Chapter 9 provides the educational infrastructure needed to support the relational healing practices introduced at the beginning of this book. At the same time, the Introduction critiques colonial systems—residential schools, the Indian Act, child welfare, and resource extraction—that dismantled Cree governance and disrupted family and community roles. We respond by outlining the mechanisms through which Cree nations can reclaim these spheres of authority. Educational sovereignty restores control over what, how, and why children learn. Economic sovereignty restores the material autonomy necessary to ensure long-term survival and cultural resurgence.

We highlight the necessity of addressing intergenerational trauma and fostering cultural revitalization. We demonstrate that such revitalization requires stable, culturally aligned economic structures. When Cree communities build their economies around land-based activities, cultural tourism, crafting, hide tanning, harvesting, sports programs, and language revitalization, economic health becomes intertwined with mental and spiritual wellness. This reflects the Introduction's teaching that healing is holistic and must address the entirety of community life. Another strong point of connection lies in the Introduction's emphasis on relational accountability and community responsibility. Chapter 9 operationalizes these teachings through kinship economies—economic systems that prioritize reciprocity, relational ethics, Elder guidance, and shared governance. These are the same principles that grounded Cree societies prior to colonization, illuminating how cultural teachings translate into sustainable economic systems. The Introduction calls upon readers to rethink what counts as knowledge, teaching, healing, and leadership. We build upon this call by asserting that Indigenous scholars must reshape universities from within, asserting Indigenous languages, ceremonies, and methodologies as legitimate academic foundations. This reflection reinforces the Introduction's broader project of restoring Indigenous intellectual sovereignty.

This chapter is the structural embodiment of the introduction's vision. The introduction declares the necessity of healing through land, language, ceremony, kinship, and relational accountability. We show how these teachings can shape community-based educational and economic systems capable of sustaining Cree nationhood for generations. Through teacher education, Indigenomics, kinship economies, and cultural resurgence, this chapter operationalizes the holistic healing framework introduced at the beginning of this book, demonstrating that nationhood is not only possible but is also already unfolding through Cree leadership, land-based innovation, and community-driven sovereignty. This chapter demonstrates that Cree nationhood is rebuilt through the alignment of educational sovereignty, economic sovereignty, and mental health practice. For researchers, educators, and practitioners, this means: (1) designing mental health services that are land-based and language-centered; (2) investing in Cree teacher education as preventative mental health infrastructure; (3) supporting kinship-based economies as healing systems; and (4) ensuring Indigenous leadership governs research, funding, and evaluation. Together, these principles move decolonization from theory into practice and restore Cree self-determination as a lived reality.

10

CONCLUSION

Reaffirming Cree Ways of Knowing and Being

Ranjan Datta (with support from Kevin Lewis and Jody Houle)

We reaffirm throughout this book that Cree ways of knowing and being are not simply culturally relevant—they are vital, sophisticated, and urgently needed frameworks for restoring wellness, justice, and balance in Indigenous communities today. Rooted in the land, upheld through ceremony, and carried through kinship relations, Cree epistemologies offer a holistic and relational understanding of health that Western clinical systems have rarely acknowledged. At the heart of this worldview is wâhkôhtowin, a foundational Cree Natural Law that describes the sacred web of kinship linking all beings—humans, animals, waters, plants, ancestors, and cosmological entities. This kinship is not symbolic but embodied and enacted every day. It shapes how we speak to one another, how we heal, how we raise our children, how we pray, and how we walk in the world with humility and responsibility.

Across our chapters, we trace how colonial systems—particularly residential schools, the Sixties Scoop, and contemporary child welfare and justice systems—violently disrupted these kinship networks. These disruptions produced profound mental, emotional, spiritual, and physical harms that continue to reverberate across generations. Yet we also emphasize that Cree communities have never lost their capacity for healing. Through ceremony, land-based practices, ancestral teachings, and the resurgence of Cree governance and education systems, kinship relationships are actively being restored. This restoration is itself a therapeutic process, one that reconnects individuals to identity, land, history, and collective purpose.

Within Cree thought, wellness is never compartmentalized. One cannot address mental health without tending to emotional, physical, and spiritual well-being; nor can an individual heal in isolation from their family, community,

DOI: 10.4324/9781003670308-10

and land. The Medicine Wheel remains an essential framework for understanding this holistic process. It teaches that balance across the four aspects of the self is necessary for miyo pimâtisiwin—the good life. Each quadrant symbolizes interconnected teachings: the East as new beginnings and vision; the South as growth and relational learning; the West as introspection and transformation; and the North as wisdom, elderhood, and preparation for future generations. These directions are not abstract metaphors but active teachings that guide daily conduct, seasonal practices, and ceremonial responsibilities. Healing, in this worldview, unfolds in relation to the cycles of the land, the movement of the sun, and the laws of Creation.

Cree Customary Laws further ground this holistic wellness model. Teachings such as **kistêyihitamowin** (deep respect), **wâhkôhtowin** (kinship), **sôhkêyitamowin** (inner strength), and **wîcihtowin** (helping one another) are not academic concepts; they are lived principles that govern ethical behavior, community care, and spiritual alignment. They guide how we approach ceremony, how we honor Elders, how we build relationships, and how we maintain balance. These laws remind us that healing cannot occur without respect, humility, reciprocity, courage, and service to others.

Much of this knowledge is carried by our grandmothers and Elders, who remain the living libraries of our nations. Their stories, teachings, and ceremonial guidance hold therapeutic insight that exceeds the narrow definitions of wellness used in Western health systems. Elders help individuals understand their dreams, navigate grief, interpret spiritual experiences, and reconnect with ancestral responsibilities. Their leadership is quietly revolutionary, sustaining cultural continuity even in the face of longstanding colonial suppression.

This book honors the daily acts of leadership embodied by Cree women who continue to smudge their homes, cook for ceremony, tend fires, raise children in the language, and keep kinship systems alive. We uplift the strength of youth who reclaim nêhiyawêwin, participate in land-based education, and step into their roles as future leaders despite the intergenerational impacts of trauma. We honor fathers and uncles who return to their responsibilities through ceremony, and we honor the Elders whose visions anchor our collective healing.

Centering wâhkôhtowin throughout this book is both a pedagogical and ethical invitation. We call upon readers—not only Indigenous peoples but also all who engage with this work—to approach Cree knowledge relationally. Understanding our worldview is not an intellectual exercise; it requires being in relationship, participating in ceremony, respecting protocol, listening deeply, and allowing oneself to be transformed. Healing in Cree tradition is not an individual endeavor but a communal, intergenerational, and land-based process. Sweat lodges, moon ceremonies, pipe gatherings, talking circles, and seasonal land-based practices reconnect individuals to a larger circle of relations, reaffirming identity, balance, and belonging.

To reaffirm Cree ways of knowing and being is also a political act. It resists the fragmentation and assimilationist pressures imposed by colonial institutions that sought to erase Indigenous languages, governance systems, and spiritual practices. Reaffirmation is an assertion of intellectual sovereignty—it declares that Cree knowledge systems are legitimate, rigorous, and necessary for shaping our future. It insists that healing must be conducted in our language, on our land, and under our laws. In doing so, we create pathways for wellness that honor ancestral teachings and support the flourishing of generations yet to come.

Ultimately, to live wâhkôhtowin is to choose relationship over isolation, ceremony over disconnection, and balance over fragmentation. It is to walk toward miyo pimâtisiwin—a good life rooted in love, humility, kinship, and reciprocity with all of Creation (Figure 10.1).

FIGURE 10.1 The figure shows the Native Bafflos, and relationships with land.

Key Contributions

This book makes a significant and transformative contribution to the field of Indigenous mental health, decolonial healing studies, and community-led wellness programming. By reclaiming and centering Cree land-based knowledge systems, kinship philosophies, and ceremonial practices, it establishes that Indigenous healing frameworks are not simply cultural alternatives to Western psychology—they are complete, rigorous, and highly effective systems of wellness grounded in thousands of years of observation, ceremony, and relational ethics. The power of this book lies in its unapologetic articulation of a decolonial, community-anchored, and spiritually grounded model for mental health and healing. It simultaneously critiques the limitations and harms of Western mental health paradigms while illuminating the ancestral pathways that Cree societies have always relied upon for restoring balance, identity, and wellness.

A Decolonial Model of Indigenous Mental Health and Healing

One of this book's most significant contributions is its articulation of a decolonial, land-based model for Indigenous mental health—one that reframes healing not as an individualized clinical intervention, but as a lifelong relational responsibility embedded in kinship, ceremony, and land. Whereas Western mental health systems typically isolate mental illness from historical, cultural, relational, and ecological contexts, this book demonstrates that Cree understandings of wellness require addressing all dimensions of being: emotional, mental, spiritual, and physical. This holistic framework is grounded in foundational Cree teachings including **wâhkôhtowin** (kinship), **miyo pimâtisiwin** (living the good life), **kistêyihitamowin** (respect), and the Medicine Wheel teachings.

Rather than positioning ceremony as a supplemental cultural practice, this book reframes ceremony as the central therapeutic modality within Cree healing systems. Healing occurs in the Sweat Lodge, on the land while harvesting medicines, in the intergenerational conversations between grandmothers and youth, in the act of scraping a hide, cooking for a feast, paddling a canoe, or preparing tobacco for prayer. Healing emerges through relational accountability, kinship repair, ancestral memory, and ceremonial alignment—not isolated talk therapy sessions. The Land-Based Mental Health Healing Lodge proposed in the appendix operationalizes this worldview, offering a 12-week therapeutic program aligned with seasonal cycles, land-based responsibilities, and Cree spiritual law.

Traditional Ceremony as Scientific and Therapeutic Practice

Another groundbreaking contribution of this book is its assertion—supported through community narratives, Elder teachings, and land-based experience—that **ceremony is therapy**, and that traditional practices must be recognized as legitimate, evidence-based forms of mental health care. Sweat lodges, pipe ceremonies, moon ceremonies, rites of passage, and talking circles are not symbolic rituals; they are complex, embodied technologies for emotional release, identity formation, intergenerational healing, and spiritual realignment.

Through careful descriptions, this book explains how each ceremony supports specific aspects of healing. For example, sweat lodges create opportunities for emotional release, humility, purification, and community bonding; moon ceremonies restore teachings about women's roles, bodily sovereignty, and connection to water; puberty rites of passage teach responsibility, discipline, and personal purpose; and pipe ceremonies guide participants in reconnecting with spiritual law and ancestral guidance. A central argument woven through this book is that Canadian health systems—including the Non-Insured Health Benefits (NIHB) program—must formally recognize Indigenous ceremonial practitioners as health providers. When Elders and Knowledge Keepers deliver therapeutic ceremonies, they should be supported, respected, and compensated within health funding structures. This argument offers a crucial policy intervention that could shift the landscape of Indigenous mental health services across the country.

A Comprehensive Land-Based Healing Framework for Communities

The third major contribution of this book is its detailed articulation of a community-owned, land-based healing framework rooted in Cree epistemology, ceremonial practice, and kinship governance. Unlike many academic texts that offer theoretical insights without practical pathways, this book provides a comprehensive operational model for Indigenous mental health programming. The proposed Wapaniwiw Iskwew Land-Based Mental Health Healing Lodge (WILBMHHL) includes a multi-layered therapeutic system combining:

- Traditional healing ceremonies
- Indigenous clinical practices
- Inner Child Therapy
- Family Group Counseling
- Grief, loss, and anger therapies
- Art therapy and canine therapy
- Land-based skills such as hunting, fishing, snaring, tanning hides, wild harvesting, canoeing, and dogsledding

These interventions are woven together to reflect Cree pedagogy, intergenerational mentorship, and seasonal learning cycles. The healing lodge design demonstrates how programming can be culturally grounded, economically sustainable, and adaptable to the needs of diverse First Nations communities. This book provides a replicable blueprint for leaders, practitioners, and health organizations wishing to implement decolonial healing programs.

Narrative Inquiry as Healing Pedagogy and Research Method

The integration of narrative inquiry and Indigenous autoethnography is another significant contribution. Rather than distancing the researcher from the research, this book weaves personal stories, ceremonial experiences, and community memories throughout its chapters to model a Cree methodology

that values relational accountability and embodied knowledge. Story is not treated as anecdotal evidence—it is positioned as sacred pedagogy and therapeutic practice. Sharing our lived experience of intergenerational trauma, healing, and ceremonial transformation, the author demonstrates how storytelling can serve simultaneously as a healing tool, a research method, and a pedagogical process. This approach challenges Western academic norms that privilege objectivity, detachment, and abstraction. It instead affirms Indigenous research commitments grounded in reciprocity, humility, protocol, and ethical relationality.

Kinship as Theoretical, Ethical, and Healing Framework

One of this book's most profound intellectual contributions is its articulation of **wâhkôhtowin** as both a theoretical framework and a therapeutic model. By documenting Elder teachings from Ministikwan Lake Cree Nation, the text demonstrates how kinship is not only a familial structure but also a cosmological, ethical, and political system.

Within this framework, healing is not simply the restoration of an individual but the reconnection of relational systems: the ties between families, between youth and Elders, between people and land, and between communities and ancestral law. Interventions such as Family Group Counseling, land-based mentorship, and ceremonial rites of passage reflect this relational worldview.

Elders as Intellectual and Therapeutic Authorities

A further contribution is the centering of Elders as knowledge authorities, teachers, and therapeutic leaders. Rather than tokenizing Elders as cultural resources, this book positions them at the heart of Cree health governance. Their teachings are treated as theoretical frameworks, their ceremonial roles as clinical expertise, and their stories as intergenerational medicine. This corrective is vital in a field where Elders are often marginalized or excluded from professional health discourse.

Policy, Education, and Research Implications

This book offers significant implications for health policy, higher education, and research ethics. It calls for a paradigm shift in which Indigenous sovereignty guides all mental health programming, research design, and clinical practice. Key recommendations include:

- Funding Indigenous-led healing centers
- Recognizing ceremonial practitioners within health benefit programs

- Integrating Indigenous worldviews into mental health and social work education
- Applying relational accountability in research ethics
- Supporting language revitalization as a mental health intervention

This book is a bundle of teachings, a theoretical intervention, and a practical roadmap for Indigenous healing. Its contributions span mental health, decolonial research, policy transformation, and community resurgence. By grounding healing in Cree Natural Law, ceremony, and kinship, it offers a transformational model of care that responds directly to the harms of colonialism while building a future rooted in dignity, sovereignty, and relationship.

Breaking Cycles: Centering Indigenous Land-Based Health Justice

To meaningfully break the intergenerational and transgenerational cycles of trauma produced by colonialism, forced assimilation, and systemic violence, we must center Indigenous land-based health justice as both a theoretical framework and a lived, collective practice. This is not a symbolic gesture or a metaphorical aspiration; it is a political, cultural, and spiritual necessity grounded in Cree Natural Law, kinship systems, and ceremonial responsibilities. Across the personal narratives, scholarly analysis, Elder teachings, and community-rooted visions shared throughout this book, a central truth emerges: healing cannot be understood or enacted apart from land, language, ceremony, and relationships. Cree wellness is relationally and ecologically situated, and any meaningful shift toward Indigenous mental health justice must begin with this understanding.

Healing as a Return to Land, Kinship, and Ontological Sovereignty

Breaking cycles of trauma requires grappling with the reality that colonial harm was not inflicted solely upon individual bodies or minds—it systematically targeted Indigenous cosmologies, governance systems, gender roles, ecological relationships, and kinship laws. The separation of Indigenous peoples from land, language, and ceremony was intentional. Residential schools, the pass system, land dispossession, policing, and the outlawing of ceremony were deliberate strategies designed to fracture Indigenous identity and well-being.

Land-based health justice offers a path forward by insisting that healing is intrinsically tied to reclaiming Cree relationships with the land—relationships that embody spiritual, emotional, physical, and intellectual sovereignty. This reclamation is not about romanticizing a pre-contact era but about restoring the living teachings that continue to sustain Cree peoples today: wâhkôhtowin (kinship), miyo pimâtisiwin (the good life), kistêyihitamowin (respect), and sôhkêyihtamowin (strength of heart, body, spirit, and mind). Within this framework, land itself becomes a therapeutic force. Land is pedagogy, land is memory, land is ceremony. Healing emerges through practices such as snaring rabbits, harvesting medicines, canoeing, sweat lodge ceremonies, dog sledding, hide scraping, and preparing traditional foods. These activities are not simply cultural expressions; they are therapeutic interventions embedded in Cree law, identity, and relationship.

Ceremony as Central to Mental, Emotional, and Spiritual Healing

A powerful contribution of this book is its consistent demonstration that **ceremony is therapy**—not merely symbolically, but scientifically and spiritually. Ceremony facilitates emotional release, anchors identity, restores relational balance, and reconnects individuals to ancestors, community, and the land. Whether through sweat lodge, pipe ceremony, moon ceremony, rites of passage, naming ceremonies, or talking circles, Cree ceremony is a highly sophisticated healing methodology. These ceremonies create space for participants to cry, grieve, laugh, remember, release, and witness one another in deeply relational ways. Ceremony teaches emotional regulation, humility, and accountability. It provides structure, community oversight, and spiritual protection. It reconnects people to their gifts and their responsibilities—a process that many Western therapeutic models overlook. As Dr. Diana Steinhauer has emphasized, rites of passage are not simply cultural rituals; they are pedagogies of identity, responsibility, and spiritual development. Ceremony teaches individuals how to relate to themselves, others, and the spirit world. It teaches Natural Law and ensures that people are guided by ancestral principles throughout the lifespan. This book's discussion of ceremony reveals how Indigenous healing is both epistemic and embodied—how it exists not only as knowledge but also as practice and lived experience.

A Land-Based Mental Health Healing Lodge: Enacting Indigenous Health Sovereignty

Central to this manuscript is the proposal for a **Land-Based Mental Health Healing Lodge**, an Indigenous-governed therapeutic environment rooted in Cree cosmology, kinship principles, land-based pedagogy, and multilingual Cree immersion. This lodge represents a concrete, community-driven model for Indigenous mental health sovereignty.

Unlike Western clinical environments—often alienating, deficit-based, and disconnected from land—this healing lodge integrates ceremonies, seasonal cycles, traditional foods, cultural labor, and intergenerational mentorship. Therapeutic activities include:

- Inner Child Therapy indigenized through ceremony
- Land-based skill development (hunting, fishing, canoeing, hide scraping, harvesting)

- Grief and anger therapy
- Family Group Counseling rooted in wâhkôhtowin
- Art and canine therapy
- Cree language renewal
- Seasonal cultural camps and rites of passage

This model resists the fragmentation of Western mental health care. Healing in this context is relational, multi-generational, spiritually aligned, and grounded in Cree science and pedagogy.

Importantly, the healing lodge challenges structural inequities. It models a future where Indigenous communities govern their own health systems and where ceremony is recognized—not marginalized—as foundational to mental health.

Narrative as Medicine: Trauma, Testimony, and Community Healing

This book demonstrates that breaking cycles also requires validating Indigenous stories. Narrative is not simply descriptive; it is ceremonial and therapeutic. The author's personal testimony—alongside Elder narratives and community stories—functions as a decolonial research method and healing modality. Telling one's story disrupts colonial silencing and restores epistemic sovereignty. It allows others to witness pain, resilience, and transformation. Narrative medicine is deeply aligned with Cree oral traditions, where stories teach law, identity, ethics, and resilience. Through narrative, individuals and communities reclaim agency, reframe trauma, and strengthen relational bonds.

Story is ceremony. Story is pedagogy. Story is a form of justice.

Healing as Structural Transformation: Beyond the Clinic

Breaking cycles requires more than therapeutic interventions; it requires deep structural change. Indigenous health justice cannot be achieved within the same colonial conditions that produced illness. As scholars like Katz (2017) remind us, high rates of suicide, incarceration, addictions, and housing insecurity are not Indigenous failures—they are the direct outcomes of ongoing colonial violence and systemic inequity.

Thus, land-based health justice demands parallel movements toward:

- Health policy reform
- Recognition of traditional healing within NIHB and provincial systems

- Funding for Indigenous-led health infrastructure
- Indigenous authority over mental health governance
- Language revitalization as a health determinant
- Environmental protection and climate justice
- Culturally grounded education systems
- Economic sovereignty and food security

Healing cannot flourish under policies designed to constrain Indigenous self-determination. Land-based wellness requires material conditions that honor Indigenous rights, ecological relationships, and kinship responsibilities.

Relational Healing and the Rebuilding of Kinship Systems

This book continually emphasizes that trauma is not an individual phenomenon—it is relational and collective. Therefore, healing must also be relational and collective. Cree kinship systems, wâhkôhtowin, offer a foundational framework for rebuilding family systems, restoring child and youth well-being, and repairing intergenerational relationships broken by residential schools and the Sixties Scoop. Family Group Counseling and kinship-based therapeutic models reflect this worldview. Healing requires:

- Multi-generational engagement
- Elders' involvement in teaching Natural Law
- Youth leadership development
- Language immersion
- Community accountability
- Ceremonial participation as a family unit

Breaking cycles is a communal project, not an isolated clinical event.

Indigenous land-based health justice is not a static goal but a living, evolving practice grounded in collective memory, ancestral law, and self-determined futures. It requires consistent investment in Indigenous-led healing systems, Elder involvement, kinship networks, and land-based education. It requires restoring the right to practice ceremony, steward land, teach language, and govern health systems.

"Never forget who you are," the Elders remind us. Breaking cycles is ultimately about returning to that truth. It is a commitment to life—not only human life but also all life—and to the expansive kinship that Cree Natural Law teaches. To center Indigenous land-based health justice is to affirm that healing, when grounded in land, ceremony, and kinship, will lead future generations toward miyo pimâtisiwin: a good life rooted in balance, responsibility, and collective flourishing.

Political and Ethical Imperatives in Indigenous Land-Based Health Justice: A Conclusion

The political and ethical imperatives embedded within Indigenous land-based health justice extend far beyond the scope of reforming mental health services. They call for a profound reorientation of how health, healing, and humanity are conceptualized in this country. When we speak of Indigenous land-based health justice, we describe a framework grounded in Cree Natural Laws, kinship teachings (wâhkôhtowin), ceremony, and Indigenous ontologies. This framework insists on a departure from Western models that approach wellness through compartmentalized, biomedical, or deficit-based paradigms. Instead, it calls for systemic transformation that recognizes Indigenous sovereignty, relational ethics, and the profound healing power of land, language, and ancestral responsibilities. This manuscript makes clear that breaking cycles of trauma requires a paradigm shift—one that is political, ethical, spiritual, and ecological. Indigenous peoples have always known that healing emerges from the land, from relationships, from ceremony, and from collective responsibilities to past and future generations. Returning to these foundations is not nostalgic—it is a resurgence of Indigenous health governance, intellectual sovereignty, and nationhood.

Political Imperatives: From Recognition to Indigenous Governance

At the heart of Indigenous land-based health justice lies the political imperative of self-determination. Despite the Truth and Reconciliation Commission's Calls to Action and ongoing inquiries into systemic racism in health care, Canada's health policies remain deeply colonial. The state continues to determine which healing practices are legitimate, which knowledge systems are credible, and which bodies deserve culturally grounded care.

This is evident in federal programs such as NIHB, where Indigenous ceremonies—sweat lodge, rites of passage, moon lodge, talking circles—are still excluded from coverage. Meanwhile, Eurocentric psychiatry, Christian pastoral care, and Western therapeutic modalities receive institutional legitimacy, funding, and policy support. This disparity reflects the ongoing assumption that Western science is superior and Indigenous knowledge is supplementary, symbolic, or "alternative." Such policies enact what scholars term epistemic violence—a silencing of Indigenous worldviews and a denial of Indigenous healing sciences. True justice requires dismantling these colonial hierarchies and enabling Indigenous nations to design, fund, and govern their own healing systems. Indigenous jurisdiction over health is not optional—it is a political right. As thinkers like Coulthard (2014) remind us, decolonization is not achieved through state "recognition"; it is enacted through Indigenous resurgence. That resurgence includes the creation of land-based healing lodges, Cree-led teacher education programs, community-designed mental health models, and governance structures that reflect Indigenous law and philosophy.

Ethical Imperatives: Centering Indigenous Epistemologies and Protocols

The ethical foundations of Indigenous land-based health justice derive from Natural Law and relational responsibility. Cree principles such as:

- kistêyihitamowin (respect)
- wîcihitowin (helping one another)
- sôhkêyihtamowin (strength and courage)
- miyo pimâtisiwin (the good life)

are not abstract moral ideals—they are daily instructions about how to live, care, teach, and heal.

Western bioethics, grounded largely in individualism and informed consent models, cannot fully address the collective, spiritual, and relational dimensions of Indigenous wellness. Indigenous ethics demand more than technical guidelines—they require reciprocity, humility, relational accountability, and protocol-based engagement with communities, Elders, and the land.

Ethical Indigenous health practice includes:

- Offering tobacco and prayer before conducting research or therapy
- Recognizing Elders as intellectual authorities
- Observing ceremonial protocol
- Prioritizing community benefit over academic or institutional timelines
- Honoring local laws, teachings, and family systems

As scholars such as Wilson (2008) and Smith (2021) argue, Indigenous research methodologies must be relational, accountable, and grounded in Indigenous worldviews. Anything less perpetuates the very harms this work seeks to heal.

Colonialism as Ongoing Structural Violence

The study demonstrates that Indigenous health disparities cannot be understood as individual failings. They are the predictable outcomes of structural violence. Residential schools, forced relocation, land dispossession, the Sixties Scoop, the child welfare system, colonial policing, and environmental racism have produced generational wounds that manifest as mental health challenges, addictions, grief, and social inequity. As Katz (2017) and Reading and Wien (2009) show, the disproportionate rates of suicide, incarceration, child apprehension, and homelessness facing Indigenous peoples are not cultural deficiencies—they are symptoms of a state that continues to violate Indigenous rights and well-being.

Any health intervention that ignores this structural context is ethically inadequate.

Thus, Indigenous land-based health justice demands:

- **Policy reform** grounded in Indigenous sovereignty
- **Funding** for Indigenous-led healing lodges and programs
- **Recognition** of ceremony as legitimate therapeutic practice
- **Community governance** over mental health systems
- **Environmental protection** as part of health justice
- **Land return** as a determinant of wellness

Without these structural commitments, healing initiatives remain constrained by colonial systems.

Land as Ethical Foundation and Political Responsibility

In Cree knowledge systems, land is not an object or resource—it is a relation, a teacher, and an ancestor. Healing cannot occur without repairing relationships with the land. Land holds stories, memories, medicines, and teachings that Western clinical spaces cannot replicate.

As Dr. Kevin Lewis emphasizes, Indigenous peoples must be "in the driver's seat" when shaping health and research initiatives. Land-based healing is inseparable from land sovereignty; Indigenous health justice cannot be achieved on stolen, contaminated, or corporately controlled lands. Environmental degradation—through mining, pipelines, water pollution, forestry, and climate change—constitutes an assault on Indigenous health. Ethical mental health practice must therefore include ecological responsibility.

Protecting land is protecting life.

Accountability to Future Generations

Perhaps the most profound ethical and political imperative articulated throughout this manuscript is intergenerational responsibility. Cree knowledge systems always situate healing in relation to ancestors and future generations. The seven-generational prophecy calls upon us to make decisions not only for ourselves but also for those yet unborn. Programs like the WILBMHHL embody this responsibility. They create infrastructures of healing where language, ceremony, kinship, and land-based skills are passed forward in ways that strengthen community resilience.

Healing is therefore not simply recovery from trauma—it is the restoration of Indigenous futures.

A Ceremonial Offering: This Book as Bundle, Teacher, and Medicine

The closing of this manuscript is not an ending, but a ceremonial offering—a bundle of teachings carried with care and shared with humility. The stories, interviews, reflections, and visions presented here are not just academic contributions; they are sacred teachings held in trust for those who will one day walk these paths.

In Cree tradition, ceremony ends with gratitude, reflection, and reaffirmation of relationship. In that spirit, we honor:

- The Elders whose words guide every chapter
- The grandmothers who carried knowledge through eras of silence
- The youth reclaiming language and ceremony
- The land that continues to hold, heal, and teach
- The ancestors who dreamed us into being

This work is guided not by academic ambition but by spiritual responsibility. These teachings are not meant to be consumed—they are meant to be lived.

This book itself becomes ceremony:

- It begins with wâhkôhtowin—kinship, connection, and relation.
- It moves through personal story, community struggle, and collective healing.
- It pauses in sacred lodges and moonlit circles.
- It listens to the trembling voices of survivors reclaiming their identities.
- It honors the laughter, grief, strength, and hope of Indigenous communities.

Not every teaching could be shared; some remain in the lodge, some on the land, some in the quiet places of spirit. What is offered here is shared with integrity and given with love.

Returning to the Circle: A Closing Prayer

We end with the teachings that remind us:

> We are not alone.
>
> We are part of something older and more beautiful than the systems that tried to break us.
>
> Our healing is already in motion.
>
> The circle is not broken—it is waiting for us to return.

This book is a reminder that miyo pimâtisiwin—the good life—is a daily practice rooted in balance, humility, love, and responsibility. It is how we speak, how we help others, how we honor the land, and how we care for our communities.

To all who read this, may these teachings enter your life as medicine. May they remind you that:

- Healing is your birthright.
- Your ancestors walk with you.
- The land remembers your name.
- The circle welcomes you home.

As this written ceremony closes, we offer tobacco to the spirits, water to the land, and prayers to the sky. This is not an ending; it is a beginning—another step guided by spirit, held in the embrace of wâhkôhtowin.

Ekosani. Thank you. May your journey continue in beauty, responsible, and relation.

REFERENCES

Acoose, J., & Kelly, J. (1996). Iskwewak Kah'Ki Yaw Ni Wahkomakanak: neither indian princess nor easy squaws. Canadian Ethnic Studies, 28(2), 202. https://www.proquest.com/openview/fbdcd8c00769dc9181e64a0551053ce1/1?pq-origsite=gscholar&cbl=47027

Alfred, T. (2009). *Wasáse: Indigenous pathways of action and freedom*. ON, Canada: University of Toronto Press.

Anderson, K. (2016). *A recognition of being: Reconstructing native womanhood*. Canadian Scholars' Press.

Auger, D. (2020, Personal interview). Ministikwan Lake, SK.

Battiste, M. (2013). Decolonizing education: Nourishing the learning spirit. *Alberta Journal of Educational Research*, 60(3), 615–618.

Bombay, A., Matheson, K., & Anisman, H. (2014). The intergenerational effects of Indian Residential Schools: Implications for the concept of historical trauma. *Transcultural Psychiatry*, 51(3), 320–338.

Cardinal, H., & Hildebrand, W. (2000). *Treaty elders of Saskatchewan: Our dream is that our peoples will one day be clearly recognized as nations*. University of Calgary Press.

Chilisa, B. (2012). *Indigenous research methodologies*. Thousand Oaks, CA: SAGE Publications.

Clinebell, H. (2013). *Ecotherapy: Healing ourselves, healing the earth*. Routledge.

Coulthard, G. S. (2014). *Red Skin, White Masks: Rejecting the colonial politics of recognition*. Minneapolis: University of Minnesota Press.

Crookedneck, D. (2021, Personal interview). Ministikwan Lake Cree Nation, SK.

Czyżewski, M. (2011). Teorie dyskursu i dyskursy teorii. *Socjologicznym*. doi: 10.2478/kultura-2013-0011

Duran, E. (2006). *Healing the soul wound: Counseling with American Indians and other Native peoples*. New York: Teachers College Press.

Gone, J. P. (2013). Redressing First Nations historical trauma: Theorizing mechanisms for indigenous culture as mental health treatment. *Transcultural Psychiatry*, 50(5), 683–706.

Gone, J. P., & Kirmayer, L. J. (2010). On the wisdom of considering culture and context in psychopathology. In T. Millon, R. F. Krueger, & E. Simonsen (Eds.), *Contemporary directions in psychopathology: Scientific foundations of the DSM-V and ICD-11* (pp. 72–96). New York: Guilford Press.

Greenwood, M., de Leeuw, S., & Lindsay, N. M. (2018). *Determinants of Indigenous peoples' health in Canada: Beyond the social*. ON, Canada: Canadian Scholars' Press.

Hart, M. A. (2002). *Seeking Mino-Pimatisiwin: An Aboriginal approach to healing*. Winnipeg, MB, Canada: Fernwood Publishing.

Kingi, T. E. T. A. M. (2018). *Ko ngā pūtake o te mātānawe ki tā te rangatahi: An exploration of self-injury in rangatahi Māori* (Doctoral dissertation, Open Access Te Herenga Waka-Victoria University of Wellington).

Kirkness, V. J., & Barnhardt, R. (2001). First Nations and higher education: The four r's—respect, relevance, reciprocity, responsibility. In R. Hayoe & J. Pan (Eds.), *Knowledge across cultures: A contribution to dialogue among civilizations* (pp. 1–17). Hong Kong: The University of Hong Kong, Comparative Education Research Centre.

Kovach, M. (2009a). Conversation method in Indigenous research. *First Peoples Child & Family Review*, 5(1), 40–48.

Kovach, M. (2009b). *Indigenous methodologies: Characteristics, conversations, and contexts*. University of Toronto Press.

Lambert, L. (2014). *Research for Indigenous survival: Indigenous research methodologies in the behavioural sciences*. Pablo, MT: Salish Kootenai College Press.

Linklater, W. (2006). *Indian social work 350*. First Nations University of Canada, Saskatoon, SK.

Linklater, T. (2021). *Finding Community: The Story of Stolen Children* (Master's thesis, Trent University (Canada)). https://batadora.trentu.ca/_flysystem/fedora/2022-04/Finding_Community_the_Story_of_Stolen_Children.pdf

Mandelbaum, D. G. (1979). *The Plains Cree: An ethnographic, historical, and comparative study*. Winnipeg, MB: Canadian Plains Research Center.

McLeod, R. (2008). *Kinship wheel—Wahkotowin: Cree language "TH" dialect*. Trafford Publishing.

Michell, H. (2011a). *Land-based education: Embracing the rhythm of the earth*. BC, Canada: JCharlton Publishing.

Michell, H. (2011b). *Working with Elders and Indigenous knowledge systems*. Kanata, ON: JCharlton Publishing.

Michell, H. (2018). *Land-based education: Embracing the rhythms of the earth from an Indigenous perspective*. Vernon, BC: JCharlton Publishing.

Milburn, P. (2004). De la négociation dans la justice imposée. *Négociations*, 1(1), 27–38.

Night, J. (2018, Personal communication). First Nations University of Canada, Saskatoon, SK.

Partridge, A. (2021, Personal interview). Ministikwan Lake Cree Nation, SK.

Reading, C., & Wien, F. (2009). *Health inequalities and social determinants of Aboriginal peoples' health*. National Collaborating Centre for Aboriginal Health. Prince George, BC, Canada: National Collaborating Centre for Aboriginal Health.

Sarkar, K., Khajanchi, S., & Nieto, J. J. (2020). Modeling and forecasting the COVID-19 pandemic in India. *Chaos, Solitons & Fractals*, 139, 110049.

Simpson, L. (2014). Land as pedagogy: Nishnaabeg intelligence and rebellious transformation. *Decolonization: Indigeneity, Education & Society*, 3(3), 1–25.

Smith, L. T. (1999). *Decolonizing methodologies: Research and Indigenous peoples.* Dunedin, New Zealand: University of Otago Press.

Smith, L. T. (2012). *Decolonizing methodologies: Research and indigenous peoples.* Bloomsbury.

Smith, L. T. (2021). *Decolonizing methodologies: Research and Indigenous peoples* (3rd ed.). London, UK: Zed Books.

Sinclair, R., & Pooyak, S. (2007). *Aboriginal mentoring in Saskatoon: A cultural perspective.* Indigenous Peoples' Health Research Centre. https://cuisr.usask.ca/documents/publications/2005-2009/Aboriginal%20Mentoring%20in%20Saskatoon.pdf

Truth and Reconciliation Commission of Canada. (2015a). *Truth and reconciliation commission of Canada: Calls to action.* Canada: Truth and Reconciliation Commission of Canada.

Truth, and Reconciliation Commission of Canada. (2015b). *Final Report of the Truth and Reconciliation Commission of Canada, Volume One: Summary: Honouring the Truth, Reconciling for the Future.* James Lorimer & Company.

Tuck, E., & Yang, K. W. (2012). Decolonization is not a metaphor. *Decolonization: Indigeneity, Education & Society*, 1(1), 1–40.

Vizenor, G. (Ed.). (2008). *Survivance: Narratives of native presence.* U of Nebraska Press.

Vizina, Y. N. (2010). *Métis traditional environmental knowledge and science education* (Doctoral dissertation, University of Saskatchewan). https://harvest.usask.ca/server/api/core/bitstreams/e4e93b60-37a4-4169-b25a-be533ca514b2/content

Walter, E., & Linklater, M. (2006). Personal Communication.

Wesley-Esquimaux, C. C., & Smolewski, M. (2004). *Historic trauma and Aboriginal healing.* Ottawa: Aboriginal Healing Foundation, 3, pp. 1–99.

Weenie, A. (2010). *Self-study: The in-between space of an Aboriginal academic.* Regina, SK: University of Regina Press.

Wilson, S. (2008). *Research is ceremony: Indigenous research methods.* Black Point, NS: Fernwood Publishing.

Young, M. (2005). *Pimatisiwin: Walking in a good way.* Winnipeg, MB: Pemmican Publications Inc.

INDEX

Note: *Italic* page numbers refer to figures.

For Product Safety Concerns and Information please contact our EU representative GPSR@taylorandfrancis.com
Taylor & Francis Verlag GmbH, Kaufingerstraße 24, 80331 München, Germany

www.ingramcontent.com/pod-product-compliance
Ingram Content Group UK Ltd.
Pitfield, Milton Keynes, MK11 3LW, UK
UKHW022018180926
475701UK00005B/900

* 9 7 8 1 0 4 1 1 3 4 5 5 8 *